D1484104

OLD TESTAMENT THEOLOGY

OLD TESTAMENT THEOLOGY

by

Ludwig Köhler

Translated by A. S. Todd

THE WESTMINSTER PRESS

Philadelphia

© *Lutterworth Press, 1957*

This book originally appeared as *Theologie des Alten Testaments*, J. C. B. Mohr (Paul Siebeck), Tübingen, 1935. This translation has been made from the third revised edition, 1953.

Library of Congress Catalog Card No.: 58-7205

Typeset in Great Britain
Printed in the United States of America

Dedicated to
the Theological Faculty
of the University of Berne
as a token of gratitude·
for an honorary doctorate

FOREWORD

ONE may give a book the title "Old Testament Theology" if it manages to bring together and to relate those ideas and thoughts and concepts of the Old Testament which are or can be important. Before such a compilation is possible, however, a great deal of preliminary work has to be done. Exposition of the entire Old Testament must have reached a certain degree of adequacy and reliability. The literary and historical critics must have done their work. The students of comparative religion must have made their contribution—without it the Old Testament can be appreciated neither in its uniqueness nor in its dependence. All these various studies are a necessary presupposition of an Old Testament theology. It makes use of them as required, but it does not dabble in them itself; and one would do this present book less than justice were one to overlook the fact that it confines itself strictly within its proper limits.

The Old Testament itself does not offer any scheme for that compilation we call its theology. One must therefore borrow it from elsewhere and take good care that it does not distort the facts. No scheme could be borrowed either from the New Testament or from systematic theology if it were going to obtrude itself. A very simple scheme has therefore been chosen —theology, anthropology, soteriology, and it has proved possible, following this scheme, to put everything in its proper place and assign to it its proper importance. Only one chapter, that on the cult, was difficult to place. It does not belong to the realm of soteriology, for it is not part of the divine plan of salvation; nor yet does it belong to the realm of anthropology, being concerned with man's works, not with his nature. It is, however, the essential dialectic of the Old Testament cult that man tries to save himself by his works. We have therefore placed the cult at the end of the part on anthropology. For the rest, the book with its plan, its notes and indices must speak for itself. A foreword should not be a defence.

Perhaps it should be stated, however, that on account of space no attempt has been made to deal with the history of Old Testament theology and that intentionally not much space has been given to references to relevant literature. Those who know this literature will be able to read a great deal between the lines; they will also know that in the last decades the real theological merit of this literature was small. We welcome the new movement and wish it God speed! Those who know not merely the literature but also the young theologians of the day know that they all too often tend—and the fault is partly their teachers'—to settle questions of theology by invoking famous and not so famous names; but as teachers of Holy Scripture we must produce a theology which does not settle but decides; which does not enquire about names but about grounds, and judges accordingly. This book tries to serve that end, and how could it be otherwise in view of the famous date below? Reformed theology is always and can only be a theology based on clear grounds, not on names.

Zürich, on the anniversary of the publication of Luther's *Theses*, 1935.

LUDWIG KOHLER

FOREWORD TO THE THIRD REVISED EDITION

The book remains on the whole unaltered. The opportunity was taken to adjust the text in a number of places and anything of importance from the recent literature on the subject has been added.

L.K.

Advent, 1952.

TRANSLATOR'S NOTE

Biblical quotations follow the text of the Revised Version as far as is practicable, that is, except where the Hebrew text is emendated, or where a more exact rendering of the Hebrew is necessary to bring out the point in discussion.

A.S.T.

CONTENTS

Part One

GOD

Page

I. THE EXISTENCE OF GOD

II. THE NATURE OF GOD

III. THE NAMES AND DESIGNATIONS OF GOD

Part Two

MAN

Part Three

JUDGMENT AND SALVATION

Part One

GOD

I. THE EXISTENCE OF GOD

1. GOD'S EXISTENCE

THE assumption that God exists is the Old Testament's greatest gift to mankind. In the Old Testament God's existence is entirely a foregone conclusion, always presupposed; reference is continually being made to it; it is never denied or questioned. The fool says in his heart "there is no God", Ps. 14: 1, Ps. 53: 1, and the foolish women may speak like that (Job 2: 10); or man may deny Him and say "this is not He", לא הוא, Jer. 5: 12. But these are the words of people who are lacking in understanding, so lacking that they can be described in the same breath as corrupt[1] and having done abominable works. They speak like that not in order to deny God but in order to evade His judgment and His claims upon them. They call in question His action as it affects their lives, but they do not call in question His existence. It is practical atheism, as the sinner practises it; not theoretical atheism. The latter is unknown to the Old Testament.

More than that: according to the Old Testament the whole world knows God. The man of faith seeks Him to have his requests answered by Him; Ps. 34: 5. All peoples praise Him; Ps. 117: 1. Fire and hail, snow and vapour and stormy wind, mountains and hills, fruitful trees and cedars, beasts and cattle, creeping things and flying fowl declare His honour—Ps. 148: 8-10. The trees of the field clap their hands at the coming of His people; Isa. 55: 12. The morning stars sang together when He laid the foundations of the earth; Job 38: 7. Heaven and earth, the seas and everything that moveth therein are commanded to laud Him—Ps. 69: 34—and from the rising of the sun to the going down of the same His name is great among the Gentiles, Mal. 1: 11. As the literature of the Old Testament expanded with the centuries, so the voice of praise to God became ever louder from its pages; but even on the most ancient that voice is never lacking and every outburst is a confession of the ever-present belief that God *is*.

Even sin[2] and apostasy and godlessness must in their way bear witness to the fact that God is, since they exist only if

God does. The sinner is the man who fails to turn to God,
Isa. 9: 13, and does not seek Him. The sinner forgets Him,
Isa. 17: 10; forsakes Him, Isa. 1: 4; rejects Him, Num. 11: 20;
despises Him, Deut. 31: 20; revolts against Him,[3] 1 Kings 8: 50,
Isa. 1: 2; deals treacherously with Him, Jer. 3: 20; hearkens
not to Him nor inclines his ear, Jer. 7: 24, and goes after other
gods. But for all the abundance of these expressions, though
they are all of them *Noes* to God, none of them amounts to a
not; even apostasy argues for the existence of God. The existence of God is no problem for the Old Testament. And even if
in Esther His name does not appear and is only timidly hinted
at in the paraphrase "from another place", 4: 14—a restraint
which the book paid for by almost being excluded from the
Canon—nevertheless this writing is clearly grounded in faith
in the existence of God. For the Old Testament the existence of
God is unquestionable. The questions are how God is and who
He is.

II. THE NATURE OF GOD

THE New Testament has three statements which look like definitions of God's nature: "God is a Spirit", John 4: 24, "God is light", 1 John 1: 5; and "God is love", 1 John 4: 8. The Old Testament has no statement to compare with these. Isaiah is the only one who even comes near to giving a definition, and that only once—"The Egyptians are men, and not God, and their horses flesh, and not spirit", 31: 3; but the emphasis here is on the distinction between the spiritual reliable world and the fleshly and therefore perishable world; it is not an attempt to define the nature of God. Two other sentences: "God is not a man that he should lie; neither the son of man,[4] that he should repent", Num. 23: 19, and "For I the Lord change not", Mal. 3: 6, have the same meaning and are again concerned with God's constancy and trustworthiness.

If however there is no pronouncement in the Old Testament on God's nature as such, the silence is nevertheless eloquent of at least one negative definition which must be set forth before the positive statements about God can be properly appreciated. The God of the Old Testament has no sexual characteristic; and that distinguishes Him immediately from all the other gods of the ancient world.[5] For all of them practically without exception have that characteristic, have their goddess at their side, and between god and goddess there is played the human game of love even to the extent of adultery in Homer. The God of the Old Testament is One, is Person, is Man, is taken for a man (Gen. 18) and acts like a man, but the man has no wife at his side. God has no goddess.

Nor can it be objected that God is portrayed as the husband of the people of Israel. "And it shall be at that day, saith the Lord, that thou (the people of Israel) shalt call me Ishi (my husband) and shalt call me no more Baali (my master)"; Hos. 2: 16. This idea of the marriage of God with His people runs through prophetic thought from Hosea's time onwards: Jer. 2: 2, Isa. 50: 1, 54: 1-6, 62: 5. In Ezekiel the situation becomes grotesque—God is the husband of two unchaste sisters, the people of Israel and the people of Judah—chapter 23. But this is only imagery and metaphor and never really belongs to the number of those anthropomorphic descriptions of God which we must shortly study. The entire language of wedlock as applied to God remains metaphor and only metaphor. The wife Israel and the wife Judah are no goddesses. God has no goddess. Sex is not relevant to Him. He is spoken of as man so that we should understand Him not as thing, power, or impersonal Being, but as one set over against us in a personal relationship. Again, however, this manner of speaking is only a concession to our human insufficiency of understanding and is not a true and adequate representation of an actual state of affairs. God is no man. God is simply God.

The question can therefore be posed whether it is right to translate בְּנֵי אֱלֹהִים, Gen. 6: 2, Job 1: 6, "sons of God" as is always done. Certainly the dictionary and the grammar books do not support it. The word for "men, mankind" is אָדָם and for "cattle" (as whole) is בָּקָר and when one wants to say "a man" or "an ox" one says בֶּן־אָדָם and בֶּן־בָּקָר. Similarly by בְּנֵי אֱלֹהִים one means "god-like beings, divine beings".[6] The idea that God had begotten sons,[7] an idea which would involve a mother goddess, is quite foreign to the Old Testament.

3. ANTHROPOMORPHISMS AND THEIR MEANING

1. The language which ascribes to God the attributes of man is neither restrained nor incidental; indeed, anthropomorphism is to be found on every page of the Old Testament in a wealth of detail, unashamed and even drastic. God speaks, Gen. 1: 3; converses, Lev. 4: 1; calls, Lev. 1: 1; He hears, Ex. 16: 12; sees, Gen. 1: 4; smells, 1 Sam. 26: 19; laughs, Ps. 2: 4; and hisses, Isa. 7: 18. He has eyes, Amos 9: 4, which He sets on sinners; hands, with which He grasps them, Amos 9: 2; a hand, that is against the prophets that see vanity, Ezek. 13: 9; fingers, with which He writes the tables of the Law, Deut. 9: 10; an arm, which He stretches out with might, Jer. 27: 5, and which He lays bare before all nations to separate them, Isa. 52: 10; ears, Num. 11: 18, 14: 28, Ezek. 8: 18, 2 Kings 19: 28; feet, under which He whirls the clouds like dust, Nah. 1: 3, and for which there is even a footstool, Isa. 66: 1; a mouth, with which He instructs the peoples, Jer. 9: 12; lips that are full of indignation and a tongue that is as a devouring fire, Isa. 30: 27; a head, that has a defence, Ps. 60: 7; a face which He maketh to shine upon His saints, Num. 6: 25, and which He hides to the terror of the creature, Ps. 104: 29; and a back which Moses was permitted to see, Ex. 33: 23. His heart turns within Him and His emotions are kindled, Hos. 11: 8.[8]

Not only is God represented as possessing parts of the human body; He also has feelings and passions like those of a man. Alongside anthropomorphisms in the strict sense there are anthropopathisms. He feels delight, Jer. 9: 24; shows favour, Isa. 60: 10; He rejoices with joy and exultation, Zeph. 3: 17. But he also rebukes, Isa. 17: 13; He hates, Deut. 12: 31; He rejects, Jer. 14: 19; He abhors, Ps. 106: 40; He feels disgust, Lev. 20: 23. He is provoked to anger, Jer. 7: 18, and can be jealous; indeed this is an outstanding trait of His character. While the gods of a Pantheon need to be tolerant and permit their worshippers to invoke other gods, the God of the Old Testament never ceases to insist upon His exclusiveness. "I am a jealous God", Ex. 20: 5, Deut. 5: 9. The position of this text is noteworthy—it is in the Decalogue—a significant place and one that was always immediately relevant to everyone under the Old Covenant. While His outward jealousy is unchanged (see pp. 52, 66) His inward reactions are variable. He can repent of what He has undertaken; Gen. 6: 6, Jonah 3: 10. He can be moved to intense anger: it is kindled against Israel's insubordination, 2 Sam. 24: 1, and His anger and His jealousy smoke against the impenitent, Deut. 29: 20. Things can be a trouble to Him, so that He is weary to bear them; Isa. 1: 14.

Likewise God's works and ways are described in bold anthropomorphisms. He treads down the peoples as in a winepress, so that His garments are sprinkled with their lifeblood, Isa. 63: 1-6. He rideth upon the heaven; Deut. 33: 26. He goes forth out of Seir and marches out of the field of Edom; Judg. 5: 4. He bursts forth from His temple and treads upon the high places of the earth, Mic. 1: 3. He comes down to see the Tower of Babel, Gen. 11: 5. He walks in His garden in the cool of the day, Gen. 3: 8. Like a Homeric hero He scoffs at His enemies, Ps. 2: 4, 59: 8. He bends Judah as a bow and places Ephraim thereon as the arrow, Zech. 9: 13. For He is a man of war, Ex. 15: 3, and mighty in battle, Ps. 24: 8. When Hosea compares Him to a moth and rottenness, 5: 12, to a lion and a young lion, 5: 14, to a lion that roars, 11: 10, to a panther that watches by the way, to the dew that brings growth, 14: 6, he is probably making his own spontaneous similes; but that is not true of the great majority of anthropomorphisms, to which we have made only scant reference. They are not creations of the moment, but of long usage and therefore of real significance.

2. A history of the anthropomorphism of the Old Testament has not yet been written. It would be of no great value even theologically. For we find very little variation in the anthropomorphisms from one part of the Old Testament to another or from one period of time to another. Probably the most important variation is that while the Jahwist speaks of actual visible appearances of God (Gen. 2: 7, 8, 21, 22; 3: 8; 11: 5, 7; 18: 1 f.) the Elohist speaks of appearances in the night and in a dream. This concerns passages where the attitude of the Elohist is more refined and theologically more profound; it does not hold for anthropomorphisms pertaining to anger and passion. There are certainly a great number of anthropomorphisms in the Psalter, which as a whole and in its final form is late, and in the later Prophets: this may be due in part to the fact that the later writers simply make full use of the forms of expression they have taken over from their predecessors; it shows also however that they had no objection to these forms. Anthropomorphisms remain relevant in the Old Testament; they suffer no "spiritualization".

It is also to be noted that they show no evidence of classification. The Old Testament does not know a wise God in one place and a warlike or inventive or ill-humoured or friendly or formidable God in another place. The character of God varies according to what is appropriate at any one moment. God is not presented as belonging to a strict or carefully distinguished type; He is presented as changeable and therefore very much alive, but always the same God. The result is a great richness in the conception of God.[9]

3. One realizes at this point the function of the anthropomorphisms. Their intention is not in the least to reduce God to a rank similar to that of man. To describe God in terms of human characteristics is not to humanize Him. That has never happened except in unreasonable polemic. Rather the purpose of anthropomorphisms is to make God accessible to man. They hold open the door for encounter and controversy between God's will and man's will. They represent God as person. They avoid the error of presenting God as a careless and soulless abstract Idea or a fixed Principle standing over against man

like a strong silent battlement. God is personal. He has a will, He exists in controversy ready to communicate Himself, offended at men's sins yet with a ready ear for their supplication and compassion for their confessions of guilt: in a word, God is a living God. Through the anthropomorphisms of the Old Testament God stands before man as the personal and living God, who meets him with will and with works, who directs His will and His words towards men and draws near to men. God is the living God (Jer. 10: 10).

4. TYPES OF GOD

1. Though the anthropomorphisms do not lend themselves to classification in clearly defined groups, there are nevertheless other features from which attempts have justifiably been made to establish a type. The theology of the ancient world knows an abundance of such types among the gods: the god of war, the god of the weather, the god of fertility, the god of invention and of art, the god of the different spheres of nature. As soon as the God of the Old Testament is viewed from the angle of the theology of the ancient world He is subjected to the process of classification in types, and the Persians call Him "the God of heaven" (2 Chron. 36: 23, Ezra 1: 2). This represents the adaptation by the monotheistic Jews of the polytheistic expression of their overlords,[10] an expression moreover which is wide and ambiguous enough to preserve for the Jews their monotheism. A limitation to heaven is not intended by them; therefore the title does not really present us with a type.

2. We have to consider other types, however. But first one must try to form a picture from the given material. Then one is in a position to decide whether it is really a matter of particular and individual types, and whether the Old Testament conception of God has been produced through the conjunction of several types or through the emergence of one type preferred above its rivals, or whether an originally unified divine form has been subsequently split up into several types through the stressing of certain characteristics and activities; or whether yet another explanation of the phenomena is to be sought.

3. The war God. When the Hebrew goes to war, he sanctifies it; קַדְּשׁוּ, Jer. 6: 4, Micah 3: 5. He abstains from sexual intercourse; 1 Sam. 21: 5, 2 Sam. 11: 11. The men of war are the consecrated of the Lord; Isa. 13: 3. God is their banner in the

field; Ex. 17: 15. God is in the camp when His people are
defeated; Num. 14: 42-45. He is the shield and sword of Israel;
Deut. 33: 29. The spoils of war are devoted to God; Josh. 6: 17.
What is not burned is put into the treasury of the house of the
Lord; Josh. 6: 24. In war and through war Israel executes the
fierce wrath of God; 1 Sam. 28: 18. Thanks to God, Israel
overcomes her enemies; Ps. 44: 6. When the king of Israel lets
go out of his hand the king whom he has defeated, then he is
taking from God a man devoted to God and must compensate
for it with his own life; 1 Kings 20: 42. Therefore David too
sanctifies and dedicates the booty taken from defeated peoples
to God; 2 Sam. 8: 11. There can be no doubt that war in Israel
and for Israel is a holy affair,[11] though it has to be said that this
manner of speaking becomes less common in later times and the
last wars before the Exile are described in almost entirely
worldly terms.

If from the foregoing one could still say these represent
merely the way Israel thought about war, the Old Testament
goes further and rules such an explanation out of court. God is
a warrior, Ex. 15: 3, and mighty in battle, Ps. 24: 8. Wars are
the wars of Jahweh; Num. 21: 14, 1 Sam. 18: 17, 25: 28. God
has war with Amalek from generation to generation, Ex. 17: 16.
He musters the hosts for battle,[12] Isa. 13: 4. He is the enemy
of the enemies of Israel and the adversary of her adversaries,
Ex. 23: 22. He sends His terror before Israel and discomfits[13]
the foe, Ex. 23: 27 f., Deut. 7: 20, Josh. 24: 12. He walks in the
midst of the camp of Israel to deliver up her enemies before
her, Deut. 23: 14. He discomfits the five kings of the Amorites,
inflicts a crushing defeat on them and causes stones from heaven
to fall on them, Josh. 10: 10 f. He fights for Israel, Josh. 10: 14.
Israel's enemies are Jahweh's enemies, Judg. 5: 31. He is the
god of the armies of Israel, 1 Sam. 17: 45. The spoil is the spoil
of the enemies of Jahweh, 1 Sam. 30: 26. He breaks the enemies
of David, 2 Sam. 5: 20, and when the sound of marching is
heard in the tops of the mulberry trees, then He is going out
before David, to smite the host of the Philistines, 2 Sam. 5: 24.
He takes the field with our hosts, Ps. 44: 9. Without doubt the
God of the Old Testament is a war God (§ 5, 3 f.).

4. The weather God. The theophanies show clearly that God is
also a weather God. When the rain clouds seem to threaten
another flood, then His bow will be seen in the sky; Gen. 9: 13.
The Lord goes before redeemed Israel in a pillar of cloud by

day, in a pillar of fire by night; Ex. 13: 21. He comes in a thick cloud to speak to Moses; Ex. 19: 9. There are thunders and lightnings and Mount Sinai is altogether on smoke because God descends on it in fire. Smoke ascends before Him and the whole mountain quakes greatly; Ex. 19: 16-18. In the flame of fire, which does not consume the bush, God appears to Moses, Ex. 3: 2 and in thunder He gives him instruction, 19: 19. When He comes to Israel's aid from afar the earth trembles and the heavens drop water, Judg. 5: 4. His tread shakes the mountains and causes the valleys to be reft asunder, Mic. 1: 3 f. He has His way in the whirlwind and in the storm, and is enveloped in clouds: the sea is dried up, and the rivers likewise, the trees of the forests on the mountain slopes shrivel up, the earth resounds and the rocks are set on fire by Him; Nah. 1: 3-6. His revelation of Himself occurs amidst storm wind and clouds and brightness and fire and lightning; Ezek. 1. All these—and we could add to their number—are forms in which the weather God makes His appearance. The question is, however, whether these characteristics alone are sufficient to supply a complete picture of the God of the Old Testament or whether, since patently they are not, the Old Testament conception of God has taken shape and developed from an original form which can be associated with the characteristics of the weather god.

5. *The God of fertility.* The fertility with which man is concerned and which, as the general history of religion shows, has given rise to such a variety of images of god—this fertility is threefold. There is the fertility of the human family, the increase of the herd and the growth of the plants. But when one examines the Old Testament material on this subject, and particularly the material which is most closely related to God, one does not find a connected line of thought but only isolated traces. Are these perhaps the broken remains of a world that has disappeared from view?

In the foreground there stand two stories whose purpose cannot be mistaken—the story of the sacrifice of Isaac and the story of the golden calf; Gen. 22: 1-14, Ex. 32: 1-35. God commands Abraham to sacrifice his beloved and only son. When Abraham proceeds to do it in utter obedience, God commands him to stop, and instead of his son Abraham sacrifices a ram. To this context belongs the commandment "The first born of thy sons shalt thou give unto me", Ex. 22: 29. The remainder of the commandment, which states that this

shall be done "likewise" with oxen and with sheep, and with
goats, i.e. that they shall be kept for seven days and be offered
to God on the eighth day, permits no other interpretation than
that here is a law of human sacrifices, sacrifice of the first born.
The story of the forbidden sacrifice of Isaac represents the fight
against this practice. When subsequently the original purpose
of the sacrifice was irrelevant, since the first born of the family
was no longer sacrificed, a new and loftier interpretation was
put on the story (God's testing of Abraham's faith) but that in
no way disproves the earlier meaning; rather it confirms it, as
does also the fact that even in the latest periods the practice
continued of redeeming[14] the first born of the family with the
sacrifice of an animal; Ex. 13: 12-15, 13: 2, 34: 19-20. God is
the one who shuts up a mother's womb so that she has no
children, 1 Sam. 1: 5; He is the one also who opens it that she
may have them, Gen. 29: 31, when He remembers her, 1 Sam.
1: 19; the fruit of the womb is His reward, Ps. 127: 3. God is a
God of human fertility.

He is also a *God of animal fertility.* When Moses departs to the
top of the mountain Aaron makes a golden bull for the people.
"That is thy god". They build an altar before it and celebrate
the next day a feast to the Lord and make merry. But Moses
judges them severely and grinds the image of the bull to
powder. This is no way to worship God. Yet in Dan and in
Bethel there stand golden bulls, 1 Kings 12: 26-32, and even
Hos. 10: 5 knows of the worship of the bull. The bull is the
father, the begetter of the herd. The story of the bull-idol that
Aaron makes and of the punishment that is exacted shows the
violent rejection of this whole idea; it also shows however that
such rejection was necessary. It was all the more necessary
since it is God who is the originator of all animal fruitfulness.
God blesses the fruit of cattle, the increase of kine and the young
of flocks, Deut. 28: 4. But it is curious that this thought emerges
only very seldom and insignificantly. It is often said that God
gives sheep and kine, cattle and herds but very seldom that He
causes their increase.

Finally God is a *God of plant fertility.* And in this connexion
the important thing is not that He created them. God the
creator is different from God the begetter. "He causeth the
grass to grow for the cattle and herb for the service of man:
that he may bring forth food out of the earth and wine that
maketh glad the heart of man, and oil to make his face to

shine. . . . The trees of the Lord are satisfied", Ps. 104: 14-16. But these thoughts are new to Israel. When God first declared Himself to the people of Israel they were entering a wilderness with little or no vegetation. Even Hosea still has to tell them that it is God, not a Baal, that gives the corn and the wine, the oil and the flax; 2: 5-9. When Israel seeks God under every green tree she exchanges God for a Baal and practises idolatry. Plant fertility is to be traced back to God, therefore, but it is hardly the sphere where He manifests Himself most clearly: it is not particularly typical of God.

6. *The God of discovery*. Other peoples tell of a god teaching men agriculture and cattle breeding, building and forging, the use of fire and of knowledge. In the Old Testament Abel is a shepherd, Cain a tiller of the ground and Noah a husbandman, Gen. 4: 2, 9: 20; though we are never told how they became such. Enoch is a builder of a city, Jubal discovers music, Tubalcain is the father of metal-workers (Gen. 4: 17, 21, 22) but there is not a word about what led to all this. Isaiah is the only one who understands that God has instructed, הוֹרָה, the farmer (28: 26) how he should sow his field. Otherwise God's instruction, תּוֹרָה, always concerns religion and morals and worship.

7. *Conclusion*. The above paragraphs represent more or less all that the Old Testament has to offer concerning particular rôles in which God appears. Now the question must be posed whether from any one of them the whole Old Testament teaching on God could arise; and the answer is in the negative. The subsequent question, how the four illustrated types are related to the high level of the Old Testament conception of God—and it will be our next task (§ 5) to examine this—cannot be answered uniformly but must be treated case by case. The Old Testament has obviously only a very slight and incidental interest in God as the inventor and teacher of practical matters. The thought of God as the God of fertility is, as will be further illustrated (§ 23) a result of the conflict between Jahweh and the Baals. The idea of God as the God of the weather is part of the Old Testament's own original wisdom, and has its ground in God's own particular revelation of Himself in history (§ 29). The same holds for the concept of God as God of war (§ 5, 3 f.).

None of the four types, however, presents God to us in that

character which constitutes the Old Testament's special
contribution. What is this special contribution?

5. GOD THE LORD

1. The divine name Jahweh occurs more than 6,700 times
in the Old Testament. In speech Judaism uses instead the word
אֲדֹנָי, the *pluralis excellentiae*, and this expression has become
such a fixed usage that it is best and most correctly translated
"the Lord". This is the κύριος of the Septuagint. God is called
in the Old Testament "Lord".

The etymology of אָדֹון is obscure but the usage shows
without any shadow of doubt that אָדֹון with its forms means
the Lord as the ruler,[15] as בַּעַל means the Lord as the possessor
and owner. *God is the ruling Lord: that is the one fundamental
statement in the theology of the Old Testament.* אָדֹון מֹשֵׁל הָאֱלֹהִים
would be the Hebrew of that sentence. Everything else derives
from it. Everything else leans upon it. Everything else can be
understood with reference to it and only to it. Everything else
subordinates itself to it.

The way in which God rules as Lord, the extent of His rule in
terms of space and time, the effects of His rule, both the direct
and the not so obvious but indirect—these matters may be the
subject of controversy; but the basic fact is always one and
the same and inviolable, "God is the Lord".

Whatever and whoever comes face to face with God is
servant, subordinate, follower or executor. To God belongs as
His part the will, the decision, the arrangement, the setting of
the aim. To the others who are not God there falls the part of
obedience, submission, receiving and carrying out. *Religion in
the Old Testament is the relation between command and obedience.*
It is a relationship of wills: the subjection of the ruled to the
will of the ruler. Therefore to be a man of religion, to believe,
is in Old Testament language עָבַד, to serve God. That explains
why the book of Proverbs can say that the fear of the Lord is
the beginning of knowledge, 1: 7—it is the fear of the servant
before his ruling Lord. Only when one sees that clearly can one
understand the Old Testament. This is the cardinal point for
all its assertions; all its conceptions and opinions are to be
understood with reference to it. This is the axis about which
the whole Old Testament revolves: at one end the ruling Lord,
at the other end the obedient servant.

2. Alongside the concept of Lord there stand others less common and less fundamental, which amount to the same thing and so are to be regarded as supporting cast. Buber[16] wanted to understand the whole of the book of Judges, and more, in that way on the basis of 8: 23. He has rightly recognized however that the sentence: "Jahweh (alone) shall rule over you", 8: 23 is axiomatic. God is the ruler, but He is ruler because He is Lord and not vice versa. The rule of God in the Old Testament is merely a corollary of His lordship.

The kingship of God[17] is a further corollary from His lordship, and a very significant one. God is king, and the rejection of earthly kingship (1 Sam. 8: 6-7, Hos. 7: 3; 10: 3; 13: 10-11; 8: 4), together with the fact that Ezekiel, that greatest of all champions of God's honour, has no thought of a king in Israel at the day of salvation, but sets נָשִׂיא—"an almighty one"[18] in his place, gives the clue to the right understanding of the kingship of God. "Jahweh, your God, is your king", 1 Sam. 12: 12; "Jahweh is our king", Isa. 33: 22; "I, Jahweh, am your king", Isa. 43: 15; "the king Jahweh", Ps. 98: 6; "I will be king over you", Ezek. 20: 33; there are fifty such utterances.

3. What is meant when we say God is Lord and when we say God is king? The duties of the king are clearly set out and defined in 1 Sam. 8: 20: he gives judgment to his people in all disputes, he goes out before them and he fights their battles. One can see here clearly the limitations and the divergences from the normal idea of kingship as we know it. The king in the Old Testament is, according to the clear interpretation of the passage, not a constant phenomenon who, by his actions and commands, commissions and claims, directs the course of his subjects' lives. Rather the position of king is an extraordinary one, foreign to the normal ordered life, to which one turns for help and salvation in time of need, in disputes and in war. The king is always there but he is not always exercising his kingship. His power is constant, but it is only called for in crises. It is unconditional, but it is exercised only as help when one cries for it, not as the source of initiative necessary for the ordinary course of life. Only when these limitations have been noted can we begin to understand what is meant by saying that God is both Lord and King.

a) Since God is Lord and King, He imposes His will on His people (on the extent of His authority see § 22, 3). He controls their behaviour through instructions and commands, חֻקִּים and מִצְוֹת, which He gives.

b) To inform His people of His will, He sends messengers to them. "Whom shall I send?"—"Send me!" Isa. 6: 8. Those we call prophets are God's messengers, שְׁלוּחִים, Mal. 3: 1. It is for this reason that so many of their utterances begin in the message form of the ancient world—"Thus saith the Lord": they are messages.[19]

c) Since God is Lord and King, He is "judge", שֹׁפֵט, in His people's disputes: first of all in disputes amongst themselves. There the word does not have the present-day meaning of one who guards a body of enacted law, who tests the defendant's guilt or innocence by law, in order to give his verdict; rather the judge is primarily the one who, by his pronouncement, מִשְׁפָּט, settles the quarrel for the disputants. He is *arbiter*, not *judex*. He does not so much say what is right, rather he helps to make things right; God is the great champion of justice,[20] arbitrator and peacemaker. And peace, here and elsewhere in the Old Testament, means above all the situation where everything can follow its own proper undisturbed course to success.[21] Because he is God, this arbitrator however makes pronouncements whose reference extends beyond the particular dispute and claims man's attention and directs his thinking for future occasions. מִשְׁפָּט from being arbitrary pronouncements become directives in justice.

d) Since God is a champion of justice He takes the part of the just against the unjust as witness:[22] "God is witness between you and me—if you do this and this injury to me". Gen. 31: 50 does not mean merely that God can witness to this injury having been done, it means rather that God helps me to obtain justice against this injustice. Therefore עֵדוּת means not simply evidence but it means protective and authoritative "orders" (i.e. of an arbitrator witnessing to the rights of a party).

e) All that accounts for the great variety in the groupings of God's pronouncements as Lord and Judge: God's "testimonies, statutes and judgments", Deut. 4: 45; His "commandments, statutes and judgments", Deut. 5: 31; 6: 1; His "statutes, his commandments, his judgments and his testimonies", 1 Kings 2: 3, etc. In whatever arrangement the words appear, they all say that God is the Lord.

f) Since God is king, He fights Israel's battles, 1 Sam. 8: 20; battles are the settlements of the disputes which Israel has with other peoples and in which the right is involved. The whole book of Judges is built round the idea that to judge Israel is to fight her battles. "Othniel judged Israel, and (=that means) he went out to war" and crushed the oppressor; Judg. 3: 10. The definition of this word "judged" occurs in the previous verse—he saved Israel. To judge and to go to war and to help to obtain what is right are all the same, when God does it or when He grants His spirit to the action or to the persons commissioned by Him; Judg. 3: 10. The battles of Jahweh are the instruments of His help in securing rights. We observe here that what we called the war god character (§ 4) is not an independent character but a particular and certainly necessary aspect of the fact that God is the Lord. The actions of God for His people in war are called צִדְקוֹת יַהְוֶה, Judg. 5: 11, 1 Sam. 12: 7, Isa. 45: 24, Mic. 6: 5, Ps. 103: 6, Dan. 9: 16. Should that be translated acts of salvation or blessings or victories or acts of righteousness? It makes no difference. The best translation is still "help to secure rights". God is the helper against injustice, for He is the Lord. He is Lord who on His own initiative provides for prosperity of life for those in His care by testimony, assistance, arbitration and, when necessary, by intervention with power.

g) When a person is Lord, those who belong to him and are subject to him are called by his name. So in that day seven women who have lost their husbands shall take hold of one man and shall say "let us be called by thy name", Isa. 4: 1. For man must belong or he cannot exist; the Old Testament knows nothing of an "autonomous" man who stands alone. Thus those who belong to God as Lord are called by God's name: "We are as they that were not called by thy name", Isa. 63: 19. Israel is the people that is called by the name of the Lord (Deut. 28: 10; Jer. 14: 9; Dan. 9: 19; 2 Chron. 7: 14). There are many nations that are called by His name, Amos 9: 12, and many individuals, Isa. 43: 7. They are His called, Isa. 48: 12.

h) The lordship of God finds expression in numerous designations that are given to Him. Thus He is called father of the nation, Jer. 3: 4, 19, as the obedient wife calls her husband father, Jer. 3: 4; He is a father to Israel, Jer. 31: 9, to whom one should pay regard and respect as to the master, Mal. 1: 6.

He is called the Lord of all the earth (Josh. 3: 11, 13; Mic. 4: 13; Zech. 4: 14; 6: 5, Ps. 97: 5) and the Lord of lords (Deut. 10: 17; Ps. 136: 3). The most significant of all these titles however are those which demonstrate that God is not a violent and powerful but a gracious and long-suffering lord. He is a God of forgiveness, Neh. 9. 17. To Him belong mercies and forgivenesses, Dan. 9: 9, and His forgiveness is not a mark of weakness, so that one should treat Him lightly; on the contrary, its effect like its purpose is that one fears before Him because He forgives, Ps. 130: 4.[23] "He does not afflict willingly or grieve the children of men", Lam. 3: 33. He is slow to anger, אֶרֶךְ אַפַּיִם therefore long-suffering. He is full of love, רחם, and full of favour, חֵן,[24] and He lives on terms of fellowship with His own, חֶסֶד.[25] But none of these characteristics is quite so distinctive as this—that He is just, צַדִּיק.

4. What does it mean when the Old Testament says God is צַדִּיק just? Stade once with a certain sourness headed a paragraph: "Jahweh protector of justice and morality but not just".[26] The original sense of the assertion that God is just persists in later contexts: Jahweh is "a just God and a saviour", and there is none else, Isa. 45: 21. It can be seen that this is an expression of ancient usage from the fact that later it is transferred to the messianic king; he too is "just and having salvation", Zech. 9: 9.[27] God's justness lies in the fact that He saves His own. It is a concept that is related to fellowship; not as Stade, in order to discredit it, wrongly presupposes—one that hangs in mid-air.[28] God saves because He is just and He is just because He saves. If this connexion is correct—and it must be because it is explicit in the very text of the Old Testament—then what is the sense of the word we translate "just"? Obviously that person is just, who offers fellowship with himself and intervenes for fellowship. Man is צַדִּיק when he offers fellowship; he is then righteous and "blameless, upright", two meanings which the word always possesses ("righteous" Ezek. 18: 5-9, Gen. 6: 9, 18: 24; "blameless" Gen. 20: 4; "upright" Ps. 5: 12, 34: 15, 55: 22 and frequently). God is צַדִּיק when He acknowledges His fellowship with His worshipper in saving him, and in afflicting His enemies, Ex. 9: 27, when every morning He brings forth His judgment to light, Zeph. 3: 5 when He cuts asunder the cords of the wicked, Ps. 129: 4, when He permits

Israel's sinful countrymen to perish but leaves a remnant that is escaped, Ezra 9: 15. Therefore one can say appropriately "Jahweh is kind and just". The same God who defends and maintains His fellowship with men exercises judgment on those who are disloyal to the relationship and those who oppose it. His justness is bound up with fellowship.

It was long incomprehensible to us how the "juristic" conception of God's justness, which is widely accepted and very important, could have any tolerable relationship with the idea of Lord, which is the Old Testament's fundamental insight into and greatest description of the nature of God. It is clear to us now, however, that justness in the Old Testament is not a juristic concept but one having reference to relationships. There lies the solution to the problem; it explains also why the two ideas, the Lordship of God and His justice, are so closely intertwined. The Lord cannot exist without fellowship with those He rules. He can rule over them in this context of fellowship only in such a way as to help them and to protect them against whatever would destroy them either without or within. Therefore He is called just.

We have come to the end of our section on the nature of God as we find it in the Old Testament, and it is clear that we have really said very little. The task remains of establishing who belong to the fellowship over which God is Lord, how He acts towards them, and what His plan and purpose for them is. Before we can speak of these, however, there are two preliminary matters which must be cleared up. The first concerns the divine name, and why God has a name; and the second concerns God's history, that is to say, how from being recognized by a small flock He has become ruler of the whole earth that should fear Him (Ps. 33: 8). But everything that remains to be said about the revelation of God in the Old Testament, however rich in content and significance it may be, is but a corollary of the statement, "God is the Lord". *This statement is the backbone of Old Testament theology.*

III. THE NAMES AND DESIGNATIONS OF GOD

6. אֱלֹהִים: GOD, THE GOD, (THE) GODS. GOD'S RELATEDNESS

1. GOD is called in Hebrew אֱלֹהִים but אֱלֹהִים means not only God, it means also a God, the God, Gods and the Gods.[29] Whoever sets about showing how and why this is possible uncovers one of the many theological difficulties which are encountered in the Old Testament.

2. אֱלֹהִים is plural in form and can also be plural in meaning. "Thou shalt have none other gods אֱלֹהִים אֲחֵרִים before me", Ex. 20: 3. These "other gods" are mentioned 63 times (Deut. 18, Jer. 18. 1 and 2 Kings 11). "But where are thy gods that thou hast made thee? Let them arise, if they can save thee in the time of thy trouble; for according to the number of thy cities are thy gods, O Judah" (Jer. 2: 28, 11: 13). "Other gods of the gods of the people which are round about you", Deut. 6: 14, Judg. 2: 12. "The Lord your God, he is God of gods", Deut. 10: 17, Ps. 136: 2. There can be no doubt that אֱלֹהִים means gods and that (originally) both in form and in context it is plural.

3. We find also that the word can retain its plural form and impose the plural on those parts of the sentence that are grammatically related to it, and can yet be singular in meaning. "God caused me to wander" is what Abraham is saying, but if it were not that this is so certainly his meaning, it could also be translated "Gods caused me to wander". In Deut. 5: 26, 1 Sam. 17: 26, Jer. 10: 10, 23: 36 the reading is "living gods", the sense is "the living God". "The Lord, for he is (singular) an holy God" Josh. 24: 19; but the text says אֱלֹהִים קְדֹשִׁים. The same grammatical phenomenon appears in 1 Sam. 2: 25, 2 Sam. 7: 23, Ps. 58: 11, Gen. 35: 7, 1 Sam. 4: 8. These plurals with singular meaning, and for some reason there are only eleven of them out of a possible 2,000 or so, constitute a real philological enigma. They cannot be a later introduction, since the singular usage is in firm and obvious agreement with later theological thinking. Are they then the last remains of a lost mode of expression? This is certainly a more reasonable explanation than that which says it is a linguistic whim.

4. As a rule and in the overwhelming majority of cases אֱלֹהִים means a God, the God or God. Which of the three it happens to be depends on the context, but always the singular is meant, as the grammar confirms in the sentence where it occurs: "In the beginning God created the heaven and the earth", Gen. 1: 1. Here the meaning is simply God, the one and only, a proper name like "God" in English. Sometimes the article is there[30] הָאֱלֹהִים "the Lord, he is God, there is none else beside him", Deut. 4: 35, "Am I (a) God?" 2 Kings 5: 7, "the everlasting God, the Lord", Isa. 40: 28, "This holy God", 1 Sam. 6: 20, "Call upon thy God, if so be that (the) God will think upon us that we perish not", Jonah 1: 6. Here "thy God" is equivalent to the God whom thou dost worship and "(the) God" is equivalent to the God concerned.

5. When one arranges these various meanings of אֱלֹהִים in logical order one makes the following (logical) series: 1. אֱלֹהִים means (the) divine beings, deities, gods. 2. When worshippers (whether an individual or a group) know only one deity or direct their attention to only one of the several they know or worship, it means the deity, the God or a God. 3. Where only one deity is recognized it means simply God. All three meanings occur in the Old Testament and they contribute to the problem of revelation (§§ 34-40). But before we turn to deal with that another task confronts us. God figures in the Old Testament mostly in connexion with his worshippers. God is somebody's God. We must first make a survey of this relatedness.

6. God's Relatedness.

a) *The God of a people.* Jahweh is the God of Israel, Ex. 5: 1; that is to say, of the people of Israel.[31] This expression occurs frequently, but the expression "the God of the Israelites" or the other "the God of the house of Israel" never does. One finds of course the term "the God of Jacob", 2 Sam. 23: 1, Isa. 2: 3, Ps. 20: 1, 75: 9, 81: 1, 146: 5, etc. The God of Israel is the common domestic term, so to speak, the God of Jacob the more solemn term used only on certain occasions: both stand for the God of the people of Israel just as one speaks of the gods of Egypt, Ex. 12: 12, of the Amorites, Josh. 24: 15, of Aram, of Moab, of the Ammonities, of the Philistines, Judg. 10: 6, of the children of Seir, 2 Chron. 25: 14, of Edom, 2 Chron.

25: 20. For all nations have their gods, Deut. 12: 2, 13: 8; every
nation made gods of their own, 2 Kings 17: 29. They are most
easily distinguished by the addition of the name of the worshippers. The Philistines in Ashdod speak of "our god Dagon",
1 Sam. 5: 7; there shall be no one left in Moab that burneth
incense to "his god", Jer. 48: 35; the Israelites in Egypt tell
Pharaoh of their God, "the God of the Hebrews", Ex. 3: 18,
and "the Lord, the God of the Hebrews", Ex. 9: 1. God is called
after His people, for no people is without its God.

b) *The God of a land.* Other gods in the Old Testament are
called "strange gods", "gods of a foreign land", Gen. 35: 2, 4,
Deut. 31: 16, Jer. 5: 19, Dan. 11: 39. "Like as ye have forsaken
me and served strange gods (gods of a foreign land) in your
land", Jer. 5: 19. Thus the Assyrians call Jahweh the God of
the land, 2 Kings 17: 26, 27 in the same way as they speak of the
god of the land of Samaria and of all the gods of the countries,
2 Kings 18: 34, 35. *The God of the Old Testament however is not
called the God of a land.* Once He is called "God in Israel",
1 Kings 18: 36, but clearly the idea is "among the people", not
"in the land of Israel", since at the beginning of the same sentence He is referred to as the God of the patriarchs. On the other
hand the land of Israel bears the name "the inheritance of the
Lord" from which to be expelled means for David the hated
worship of other gods; and this expression is very important.
But though the land may be called after Jahweh, Jahweh is
not called after the land.

c) *The God of a place.* Where a city has power over the region
round about it, the god is called after the city: the god of
Ekron, 2 Kings 1: 2; the god of Hamath, of Arpad and Sepha,
2 Kings 18: 34; of Sidon, Judg. 10: 6, and of Damascus, 2
Chron. 28: 23. Similarly Jahweh is the God of Jerusalem, 2
Chron. 32: 19, but this is the expression used by the Assyrians
and it is not an acceptable expression. The text says "They
spake of the God of Jerusalem, as of the gods of the peoples of
the earth, which are the work of men's hands".

The God of the Old Testament is recognized even by the sort
of name one does not use for Him.

d) *The God of individuals.* When a god is the god of a nation,
each person belonging to that nation is conscious of his or her
relationship to this god, and can speak of him in purely personal
terms as "my" god; or, if the person should choose to link
himself with the other members of the nation, as "our God",

"thy god", "your god", etc. That is the standard usage above all of the Psalms and it requires no comment. But are there individuals mentioned by name as having God as their god? Can one say for example: the God of Noah, of Gad, of Simeon, of Baruch? The fact is that this mode of expression does occur, but within certain particular limits. God is the God of Abraham, Gen. 26: 24; of Abraham and Isaac, Gen. 28: 13, 32: 10; of Israel, Gen. 33: 20; of Abraham, Isaac and Jacob, Ex. 3: 6; of Abraham, Isaac and Israel! 1 Kings 18: 36; of Elijah, 2 Kings 2: 14; of David, 2 Kings 20: 5; of Hezekiah, 2 Chron. 32: 17. Elisha the prophet speaks of the God of Elijah his master. Isaiah calls him the God of David before David's successor, and in a legend the King of Assyria calls Him the God of Hezekiah. One should also mention that Moses speaks of the "God of my father", Ex. 18: 4 (it is not clear who is meant; is it his ancestor Jacob=Israel?)

Nisroch is called the god of Sennacherib, 2 Kings 19: 37, and we hear of the god of Nahor[32] alongside the God of Abraham, Gen. 31: 53. Similarly we read of the gods of the Kings of Aram, 2 Chron. 28: 23, but these are all foreign gods to whose names are appended the name of their respective worshippers in order to identify them more clearly. To-day one would quite naturally speak of the God of Moses, Moses being the "founder" of Old Testament religion. *It is very significant that the Old Testament does not do this.* On the contrary, with the few exceptions we have noted no name is attached to God other than that of the patriarchs. He is not even the God of a prophet, even of Isaiah or Amos or the like. He is the God of the patriarchs to whom He appeared before the nation was in being, to whom He revealed Himself, and it is the patriarchs who are meant when He is called, as He often is, the God of your fathers.[33]

e) *The God of the whole world.* Jahweh is the God of the heaven and the earth, Gen. 24: 3; heaven and earth is an expression for the whole world. That is also the meaning of the phrases the God of all flesh, Jer. 32: 27; the God of the spirits of all flesh, Num. 27: 16, and the God of all the kingdoms of the earth, Isa. 37: 16. Only the extent of the concept's reference varies: not the concept itself.

f) *God Absolute.* The implication of the phrase "God of the whole world" is again expressed quite simply in the innumerable instances of the word God by itself; God who has no additional name, no limiting relatedness to persons, no attribute whatsoever by which one would have to distinguish Him from others of His class, since there is none like Him. In the beginning God created the heaven and the earth, Gen. 1: 1. "I am God and there is none else; I am God and there is none like me", Isa. 46: 9.

7. אֱלוֹהַּ

The form אֱלוֹהַּ is comparatively rare; it occurs forty times in Job (3: 4—40: 2)[34] and fifteen times elsewhere.[35] In Ps. 18: 31 the reading אֱלוֹהַּ occurs instead of אֵל, the reading in the same text in 2 Sam. 22: 32, and Prov. 30: 5 has it instead of Jahweh in the same text in Ps. 18: 30. Apart from its linguistic difficulty this name has no other noteworthy feature.

8. JAHWEH

1. The true Old Testament divine name, to which all the others are secondary, is Jahweh. The word brings with it, however, a host of problems. What does it mean? What is the extent of its usage? What is its origin? What is its particular theological significance?—and there are as many difficulties as there are questions.

When one asks the philological question about the meaning of the name Jahweh it is important to recognize first of all— and this holds for all divine names in the Old Testament—that this philological question is not directly a theological question; indeed it is very indirectly that. The meaning of the majority of divine names was a dark mystery to their respective worshippers and a matter of indifference. The important thing theologically in the matter of a divine name is not what its essential and original meaning is, but only what realm of ideas and confession and revelation the worshippers associate with their god's name. In fact, the history of religion can supply a whole series of instances where there is a great divergence between the significance of the god for the worshipper and the significance of the god's name for the linguist. The gods too have their history and their divinity has its changes of form, and even in those cases where originally the name of the god accurately and clearly describes his nature, the name can fall into utter insignificance. Yet the nature of the god can develop and even grow into something quite different. Philological theology is faulty theology. Such discrepancy between the significance of the name and that of the nature of the god is, however, always a phenomenon with a historical reason. Only gods whose nature and significance have undergone a change forsake their name's original context, and this naturally always constitutes a theological problem, admittedly of a secondary order but not unimportant. This is exactly what happened in the case of Jahweh.

2. Currency, Form and Meaning of the Name Jahweh

a) More than 6,700 times God is called Jahweh in the Old Testament. It is lacking only in Ecclesiastes and Esther. The number is seen in its true proportions, however, when one compares it with the number of instances of the name אֱלֹהִים which in its three meanings God, a god, Gods, appears only 2,500 times. In addition it has to be remembered that the divine name Jahweh is disguised in a great number of proper names like Nethaniah, Nethaniahu (=Jahwehgiver), Johanan, Jehohanan (=Jahweh is the gracious one), Joab, Joah (= Jahweh is he who is a Father or a Brother). The number of these proper names compounded with Jahweh, all of which are intended as a conscious confession of Jahweh, reaches far into the hundreds.

b) It is indisputable[36] that Jahweh is the correct pronunciation and that the form Jehovah, though well established in all modern languages, is a quite foolish monstrosity. The word Jahweh is formed from the root הוה with the consonantal prefix י; it is therefore a normal substantive. This too is indisputable. Jahweh again is not both designation and name as Baal and Adon are. Baal can mean a possessor and Adon can mean a lord or master as well as being divine names. But Jahweh is only a name. All names, or certainly the vast majority, are originally not sounds only; they are intelligible sounds. The Semites had always known that Baal meant possessor, for they used it in that way as well as for the name of a god. There is not the slightest trace, however, of the word Jahweh being a term for something. Jahweh occurs only as a name. "I am Jahweh", Ex. 6: 2. There God introduces Himself. He continues "By my name Jahweh I was not known to them (the patriarchs)", Ex. 6: 3. Jahweh is a name and nothing else. And to confirm it there is the fact that one finds the most varied selection of appendages to the name: "Jahweh the God of Israel, Jahweh our God, Jahweh Sabaoth", etc., but never Jahweh with a genitive.[37] Jahweh is nothing but a name.

c) What is the meaning of the name Jahweh? There are scores of names in the Old Testament whose meaning was at once evident to the person who spoke Hebrew and remained so. "And it came to pass . . . that she called his name Benoni (the son of my sorrow)", Gen. 35: 18, but his father called him Benjamin ("the son of the right hand" or of fortune). "Call me not Naomi (the pleasant one) call me Mara (the bitter one), for the Almighty hath dealt very bitterly with me", הֵמַר Ruth 1: 20. Jahweh occurs more than 6,700 times and on only one solitary occasion is there any attempt made to give the name an intelligible meaning. Moses wants to know by what name he should call God when he comes to the children of Israel and speaks to them of the God of their fathers and they ask him "What is his name?" Then he is to answer אֲשֶׁר אֶהְיֶה אֶהְיֶה, "I am that I am," and אֶהְיֶה, "I am hath sent me unto you" (Ex. 3: 13-14). Anyone who is familiar with the Old Testament knows that there are in it countless other names with popular and inexact interpretations where verification is impossible and an approximation which makes good sense must suffice. Perhaps the name Jahweh belongs to this category.

In the first place it is striking that the name Jahweh is explained in two ways, not in one; for "I am that I am" and "I am" are not the same thing. And then what do the explanations mean? Is "I am" equivalent to the Ultimate Reality? Is "I am that I am" equivalent to the Unchangeable One, the Eternal One (the explanation Judaism has adopted) or to "who I am my works will demonstrate", or to the Unnameable One? All these interpretations are possible: none proves itself more probable than another: each wears an air of philosophy that is foreign to the Old Testament and whichever is the right interpretation it occurs only once, for the Old Testament never repeats this "I am that I am" or "I am". The interpretation of Jahweh remains therefore solitary and singular, and no one ventures to work on it further.[38]

d) What does Jahweh mean? The attempts that have been made to answer this question without reference to Ex. 3: 13-14 are legion. One has only to work through the semitic roots that have the three consonants *h w h* with their possible usages and one may arrive at any of the following equally probable solutions:—"the Falling One" (the holy meteorite), or "the Felling One" (by lightning, therefore a storm god), or "the

Blowing One" (the wind-and-weather God), or many another. But however much these suggestions may deserve notice linguistically, they are of little consequence theologically, for none of them can be decisively accepted instead of the others and none of them leads to the Jahweh of the Old Testament. It is possible, however, with strict adherence to rules of philology and by comparison with other clear and well known Hebraic formations to derive the name from the root *hwh*. Its meaning is then Existence, Being, Life, or—since such abstracts were distasteful to the Hebrews—the Existing One, the Living One.* In that case the explanation found in Ex. 3: 13 is on the right track.

3. Origin of Jahweh

a) The question of Jahweh's origin is partly a question for theology, partly a question for the history of religion. Where does the name Jahweh come from? Why is God called by the name Jahweh and not by another name? If the name had a meaning, if it meant "the Real One, the Only One, the Eternal One" or something of that sort and this meaning fulfilled the purpose of differentiating God unmistakably from all others, so that God was revealed a God by the mere name, then the theological situation would be different. But this is not so. The Old Testament knows Jahweh only as a name, which in itself says absolutely nothing about God, and from which no conclusions can ever be drawn about the nature of God, simply because the name as a mere name affords no information whatsoever. The question then arises: why this name? and where did it come from? Everything that exists, even though its content cannot be explained, at least has a history.

b) In Ex. 6: 2-3 we find a statement of historical character: "I am Jahweh, and I appeared unto Abraham, unto Isaac and unto Jacob as El Shaddai, but by my name Jahweh I was not known to them". Gen. 17: 1 expresses the same idea: "Jahweh appeared to Abram, and said unto him, I am El Shaddai". What we have here is progressive revelation. At the first and preparatory stage, God makes Himself known to Abraham, from whom stems not only Israel but also Ishmael, as El Shaddai. At the second and final stage where Moses plays the chief rôle, Moses, who through the Exodus founded the people of the Old Covenant, the same God makes Himself known as Jahweh; and this name remains for all time.

* See Koehler, *Die Welt des Orients*, 1950, 404 f.

If these were the only statements we possessed, there could be but one conclusion; but there are other statements. One of them, speaking of the time of Enosh, the grandson of the first man, says "Then began men to call upon the name Jahweh", Gen. 4: 26. How this name came to be known or what meaning was associated with it we are not told; we are only told that the name Jahweh was known and reverenced in the very earliest times. This of course does not agree with Ex. 6: 2-3. The third statement, Ex. 3: 13-14, with which we have already dealt is not clear in all its details. Two things are clear, however: that God designates himself to Moses as the God who was worshipped by the fathers of Israel, and that God brings to light for Moses the name Jahweh as a name hitherto unknown.

c) We have in fact two quite contradictory statements: the one that the name Jahweh was always known, i.e. from the time of Enosh, the other that the name Jahweh was first learned in the days of Moses. We are bound to ask which of the two statements is correct. This much is certain—that, if we assume that the name Jahweh really was always known, then we are faced with three very difficult questions: *1*. How could the assertion be made that the name first became current in the days of Moses? *2*. How did it happen that Jahweh became the God only of Israel? *3*. Why is it that no traces remain of the knowledge of this name before Moses' day? To these questions there is just no answer. If on the other hand we treat the other statement as historically accurate, that in Israel the name Jahweh first became known in the time of Moses, then the three questions disappear automatically. It is in Moses' time too that the names compounded with Jahweh begin to appear; there are none before that time.[39] If the time of Moses is really the time when the name Jahweh became known, then we can understand why Jahweh became the divine name for the people of Israel.[40] The assertion that the worship of Jahweh begins with Moses is in accordance with the general view of the Old Testament. The divergence from this in Gen. 4: 26 is to be explained as a naïve application of a later usage to earliest times by an author who is not concerned with questions of history and theology. Since in his own day God is always called Jahweh, when he is telling about early man's[41] calling on God he says inaccurately that Enosh began to use the name Jahweh.

d) The following points are therefore established: *1*. Jahweh is a proper name. *2*. The Old Testament does not know what this proper name means. *3*. This not knowing is a no longer knowing, since the name Jahweh cannot be meaningless. *4*. It follows that the name Jahweh as a name with a meaning that is known belongs outside the Old Testament and before it in time. *5*. Since it was through Moses that Israel came to knowledge of the name Jahweh, it must be Moses who learned the name outside Israel. Then in all probability Moses learned it either from the Egyptians or from the Midianites, and the Egyptians are immediately ruled out because the word Jahweh is not Egyptian but Semitic. The most probable account of the matter is therefore that the name was borrowed from the Midianites.

One might object that Moses did not learn the name Jahweh from men but by direct revelation, but the objection cannot be sustained because the text runs "I am Jahweh" and not "You should call me Jahweh, should use the word Jahweh as my name". The meaning of the name would not in that case be included in the revelation; the name would be merely a sound serving as a name. That clearly contradicts Ex. 6: 2, however, and from the days of the Masorah and the Septuagint until the present day the attempt has been made to understand the word Jahweh not as a sound but as a meaningful name. The sentence "I am Jahweh" is meaningful only when it can be interpreted "I am the God whose name, Jahweh, you have already heard". The question is, then, where had Moses heard the name Jahweh?

We offer here then the Kenite hypothesis. It can be briefly outlined historically, not theologically, as follows. When Moses comes to the holy place where God reveals Himself, Ex. 3: 5, he is on Midianite territory.[42] Who regard the place as a holy place? Obviously the Midianites are the people who so regard it, and it is therefore the Midianites who knew and worshipped God as Jahweh before Moses. This is confirmed by the fact that Jethro, the priest of Midian (Ex. 3: 1) when he visits Moses immediately offers a sacrifice for Jahweh, Ex. 18: 12. One section of the Midianites is the Kenites. There was an occasion when Saul treated them with consideration because they had allied themselves with Israel at the Exodus from Egypt, 1 Sam. 15: 5-6. David also treats them as friends, 1 Sam. 30: 29. In the battle under Deborah it is a Kenite woman, Jael, who kills Sisera and who is celebrated for it, Judg. 5: 24 ff. The Kenites stand therefore in close relationship to Israel. Moreover the Rechabites, of whom we are twice told that they worshipped

God with especial zeal, 2 Kings 10: 15 ff., Jer. 35, are in fact Kenites, 1 Chron. 2: 55. One tradition asserts that Moses' father-in-law, usually named Jethro or Reuel, was called Hobab (Judg. 4: 11) and Hobab was a Kenite, 4: 11. This Kenite at the Exodus journeys through the wilderness with Israel, Num. 10: 29-32. Moses' close connexion with the Kenites stands out very clearly here. Finally the mark of Cain, which is a mark of protection, is evidence that the sons of Cain, the Kenites, though fugitives and wanderers are nevertheless under Jahweh's care, Gen. 4: 13-15. There is therefore strong support for the theory that Moses took over the divine name Jahweh from the Kenites. The theory explains the origin of the name Jahweh; it is not however to be imagined that the Israelites under Moses simply took over the religion of the Kenites.[42]

9. EL AND EL SHADDAI

The designations שַׁדַּי and אֵל שַׁדַּי have but limited currency. The word אֵל on the other hand is a common and indeed the earliest appellation for God.[43] It occurs both alone and in compounds (§ 10). But what does שַׁדַּי mean and why is it used when it is used? In Job God is called שַׁדַּי thirty-one times, and besides these there are six other certain instances. שַׁדַּי occurs eight times. The derivation of the word is not clear[44] and its age is uncertain, since Gen. 43: 14 and 49: 25 may indeed be old but are also rather odd. All the other contexts are of late date. One could therefore pass it over quickly if it were not for Gen. 17: 1 and Ex. 6: 3. These two passages are related. Ex. 6: 3 runs: "I appeared unto Abraham, unto Isaac, and unto Jacob as אֵל שַׁדַּי" and Gen. 17: 1: "The Lord appeared to Abram, and said unto him, I am אֵל שַׁדַּי; walk before me and be thou perfect." According to the writer of the priestly material, to which both of these passages belong, אֵל שַׁדַּי is therefore the solemn revealed name in which God made Himself known to the Patriarchs, who had not yet heard His name Jahweh. But is this historically accurate? And what is the meaning of the revealed name אֵל שַׁדַּי?

To the latter question certainly there is no answer, not merely because we to-day can no longer explain its meaning, but, and this is of considerably greater importance, because the Old Testament does not reckon seriously with this form. It carries no weight in the Old Testament and has no effect. No particular sense is applicable. Nowhere is it claimed that any one special item of revelation is connected with אֵל שַׁדַּי. שַׁדַּי and אֵל שַׁדַּי when they occur are distinct names but only names. The theory is probably correct therefore which suggests that the choice of name in Gen. 17: 1 and Ex. 6: 3 is purely arbitrary. The priestly writer, when he wants to keep apart the three stages of revelation to mankind (Adam and Noah) to Israel's ancestors (Abraham) and to the true Israel (Moses), and when he wants to claim a knowledge of God for mankind in general and at the same time to reserve the knowledge of the divine name for the revelation to Moses—the priestly writer in these circumstances uses for the revelation to Abraham a particular divine name, and he chooses שַׁדַּי. He make this choice, not because there is historical justification for it, but merely because this name is available, i.e. not on purpose but merely by chance. Whatever the truth of the matter is, the names שַׁדַּי and אֵל שַׁדַּי occur, but only occasionally, and with no substantial bearing on Old Testament revelation.

10. EL IN COMPOUNDS

God is called in the Old Testament both אֱלֹהִים and אֵל.[45] The first word occurs far more frequently, the second is obviously obsolescent but retained in all manner of compounds—proper names like Samuel or Jezreel and combinations with attributes like אֵל עֶלְיוֹן, "God most high"—because it was more convenient. The difference between the two words then is not a difference in sense, for both mean a God, the God or God; but only of usage. A multitude of expressions are formed with אֵל: "God Most High", Gen. 14: 18; "God in the heavens" Lam. 3: 41; "God that seeth" (?), Gen. 16: 13; "God Shaddai", (§ 9); "the Everlasting God", Gen. 21: 33; "The God who appeared unto you", Gen. 35: 1; "the God who answered me in the day of my distress", Gen. 35: 3; "the God of thy father", Gen. 49: 25; "the jealous God", Ex. 20: 5, Josh. 24: 19; "a God full of compassion and gracious", Ex. 34: 6; "the gracious God", Jonah 4: 2; "an other God", Ex. 34: 14; "the faithful God", Deut. 7: 9; "the great and terrible God", Deut. 7: 21; "the God of faithfulness", Deut. 32: 4; "the living God", Josh. 3: 10; "the God of the covenant", Judg. 9: 46; "the God of knowledge", 1 Sam. 2: 3; "a just God and a saviour", Isa. 45: 21; "the God of recompenses", Jer. 51: 56; "the God of glory (of brightness)", Ps. 29: 3. These expressions are intentionally set down here almost entirely in a random series. They could be separated into two groups, one where the expression clearly refers to Jahweh, another where it might refer to a particular god; but that has nothing to do with the use of the word אֵל. Such classification is for other reasons. אֵל is merely another word for אֱלֹהִים which is used in old expressions or for reasons of choice of vocabulary, not of meaning.[46]

The question does of course remain what the individual expressions cited above signify, and in so far as it is really a matter of theology it will demand an answer. It will have to come when God's work is described: it is independent of the word אֵל.

II. THE GOD OF THE FATHERS

In Deuteronomy it is in keeping with the theological style to describe Jahweh as the God of our, or your, fathers, just as in the same book there is a marked predilection for thy (231 times) or your (44 times) or our God (22 times). The theological import of it is clear: God is from generation to generation the God of Israel. Therefore He is called the God of the Fathers and the revelation to Isaac is "I am the God of Abraham thy father", Gen. 26: 24, to Jacob "I am the God of Abraham[47] thy father and (the God) of Isaac", Gen. 28: 13, and to Moses "I am the God of thy father, the God of Abraham, the God of Isaac and the God of Jacob", Ex. 3: 6. The point is that God is the same with whatever generation of men He is dealing and both before one knows His name and after.

Albrecht Alt[48] in his study on this subject follows a quite different track. For him the God of Abraham means the God who revealed Himself to Abraham, and to support this interpretation Alt produces impressive parallels. According to Alt, in the Old Testament the phrase "the God of Jacob" is found in the form "the Strong One of Jacob", the phrase "the God of Isaac" as "the Fear of Isaac" and (a clever conjecture on Alt's part)[49] the "God of Abraham" as "the Shield of Abraham". This would mean that according to the tradition God had made Himself known to Abraham as the Shield, to Isaac as the Mighty One, and to Jacob as the Fearful One. Theologically this is of little consequence, since these names have little or no after history but appear only here and there, and since they contain no elements which would not come to notice in other ways also. For if God is called a Shield it means that He protects and shelters; if He is called the Mighty One it means that He is active and able; if He is called the Fearful One it means that one should fear His holiness (see § 13).

12. JAHWEH SABAOTH

The word Sabaoth occurs 279 times in all in the Old Testament, and on account of its frequency alone it deserves special attention. Moreover the distribution of the expression throughout the Old Testament documents is striking, for it is not found from Genesis to Judges[50] nor in Isaiah 56-66, Ezekiel, Ezra, and Nehemiah; and that can hardly be accidental. The fact that it is also not found in Joel, Obadiah, Jonah, Proverbs, Job, Song of Solomon, Ruth, Lamentations, Ecclesiastes, Esther, Daniel and 2 Chronicles may on the other hand have no significance. Even more striking however is the frequency of the expression in Jeremiah (77 times) Haggai (14 times) Zechariah 1-8 (44 times, while in Zech. 9-14 it occurs only 9 times) and Malachi (24 times). In these books there is a distinct liking for the expression, and Jeremiah (with his distinctive style), Zech. 1-8, Haggai and Malachi certainly belong together in respect of time. The strange thing is that though Ezekiel also belongs to this group he avoids what they obviously like. This problem has never yet been solved; indeed it has scarcely been attempted. The remaining instances (1 Samuel 5 times, 2 Samuel 6 times, 1 Kings 3 times, 2 Kings 5 times, Isaiah 1-39 54 times, 40-45 6 times, Amos 10 times, Hosea, Micah, Habakkuk once each, Nahum and Zephaniah twice each, Psalms 15 times, 1 Chronicles 3 times) are not unduly remarkable. But why has the author of Isa. 40-55, the contemporary of Ezekiel, used it only 6 times when Jahweh Sabaoth would have suited his rhetorical style so eminently? On the whole it is clear that the distribution of the expression is far from being accidental and that therefore the phrase must have not merely a meaning but also a particular point.

Sabaoth occurs in combinations of titles in the following frequency: יְהוָה צְבָאוֹת 206, י׳צ׳ שְׁמוֹ 36, י׳צ׳ אֱלֹהֵי יִשְׂרָאֵל י׳ אֱלֹהַי 11, צְבָאוֹת 9, י׳ אֱלֹהִים (!) 5, י׳ אֱלֹהֵי יִשְׂרָאֵל צ׳ י׳ אֱלֹהֵי צ׳ 3 (only Jer.), י׳ אֱלֹהֵיהֶם י׳צ׳ 2, אֱלֹהֵי הַצְּבָאוֹת י׳ 3, שְׁמוֹ י׳ אֱלֹהֵי צ׳ 2 (only Amos),

אֱלֹהִים צ׳ 2, and יַהְוֶה הַצְּבָאוֹת 1 (Amos 9: 5). The oldest instances of the expression in any form are in Amos and Hosea.

It is difficult to decide, however, in what order the various usages are to be put. There can be no doubt that either יַהְוֶה צְבָאוֹת or יַהְוֶה אֱלֹהֵי צְבָאוֹת is the original usage on which all the others have been built. If יַהְוֶה צְבָאוֹת is the original then it must mean (the God whose name is) Jahweh who is (also) called צְבָאוֹת and the question remains what is the meaning of צְבָאוֹת. Is it a divine name? There remains also the question how the expression י׳ אֱלֹהֵי צְבָאוֹת arose, which can only mean: Jahweh the God of צְבָאוֹת. But how can the divine name צְבָאוֹת become that of which there is a God? Conversely if י׳ אֱלֹהֵי צ׳ is the original expression, then it has to be interpreted: (the God whose name is) Jahweh, who is the God of the צְבָאוֹת, and we still have to ask what the צְבָאוֹת are. But before we concern ourselves with that question, let it be said that the other expression י׳ צ׳ easily permits of being understood as an abbreviation of the longer expression. Jahweh, the God of Sabaoth, becomes Jahweh (the God of) Sabaoth, and this shorter form is the commonest. All these things would seem to confirm that אֱלֹהֵי צ׳ is the original title.

Now concerning the meaning of צְבָאוֹת three suggestions have been made: a) the earthly hosts of Israel, b) the heavenly hosts, c) the stars as the heavenly hosts. All three are possible. A decision about them can only be reached by considering which is most probable in view of the distribution of the expression. The suggestion then that the earthly hosts are intended and that Jahweh is the war God of Israel immediately breaks down, for the expression is never found in the period when Israel was fighting "the battles of the Lord", and it is much in evidence in those times when Israel was at peace and was preaching that salvation was "not by might, nor by power, but by my spirit", Zech. 4: 6. So also the suggestion that the hosts are the angels is groundless, for there is little systematic angelology in the Old Testament and what there is is late, and certainly it is completely lacking in the period when the expression is most used.

We are left therefore with the third suggestion that the צְבָאוֹת are the stars, and this interpretation is certainly very significant. It contains within it the repudiation of the heathen belief that the stars are gods. We shall learn more of the struggle against this belief later (p. 153) how it was in the Babylonian period, to which the books of Jeremiah, Haggai, Zechariah and Malachi belong (which together use the phrase 159 times out of a possible 279)—it was in this period that the controversy was in prominence. The reason for Ezekiel's not having the expression will be the same one which accounts for his refraining from saying anything unfriendly about Babylon. The name Jahweh Sabaoth implies that the stars in the heavens are not beings with wills but things created by Jahweh to be His instruments. It is a phrase that is the fruit of Israel's growing appreciation of the fact that their God is the God of the whole world and therefore also the God of the Cosmos. The same truth is implicit in the common and expressive statements, that Jahweh set the sun in the heavens, that He hath made a tabernacle for it, Ps. 19: 4, that sunset and sunrise are His work, Ps. 104: 19-24, that He can cause it to go down when He pleases, Amos 8: 9. God is Lord even of the sun, and the sun is no god.

An impressive and well-grounded explanation of the word Sabaoth has recently been put forward by V. Maag,[51] according to which the Sabaoth are the whole body of the numinous powers of Canaan which are integrated into the nature of God. When Israel became involved with Babylonian star divinities then presumably these would be integrated also.

13. THE HOLY ONE OF ISRAEL, THE HOLY GOD

1. The concept of holiness permits of several interpretations in the Old Testament. Had holiness signified from the beginning something quite independent, a thing in itself, having no connexion with other things, then it would be difficult to understand how the meaning "holy unto someone" or "something holy in relation to something else" could have arisen. Consequently the meaning must have developed in the reverse order. At the first stage in the growth of the idea a thing would be holy unto another thing, later it would become holy in itself. Both stages are represented in examples, indeed the first still occurs in later times, and the examples show very clearly what "holy" means in the Old Testament.

Num. 6: 8, all the days that one binds oneself with a vow of separation one is holy unto the Lord; Neh. 8: 9, the day on

which the law is read before the people that they should understand it is holy unto Jahweh; Lev. 21: 6, the priests are holy
unto their God; Num. 15: 40, the Israelites are holy unto their
God; Deut. 7: 6, Israel is a people holy unto Jahweh, Israel's
God. In all of these "holy" means kept in reserve and set aside
for somebody. It will be noticed that in all the passages mentioned holiness has as its consequence a limitation, a restriction
on habits and practices and celebrations which otherwise
would be quite permissible. The fact that Israel is holy unto
Jahweh means they must do nothing which will displease Jahweh, and in this holiness are the roots of the jealousy of the Lord
that only He should be worshipped and not other gods also.[52]

2. One can well understand from the nature of this original
meaning that it was only slowly and comparatively late that
the idea of holiness was transferred to God Himself. The first
in the Old Testament to make a point of calling God the Holy
One is Isaiah: God the Holy One, 5: 16; the Holy One of Israel,
1: 4, 5: 19, 24, 10: 20, 30: 11, 12, 15, 31: 1 (12: 6, 17: 7, 29: 19,
37: 23 are by a later writer); holy, holy, holy is the Lord of
hosts, 6: 3. The only texts earlier than these Isaiah ones are
1 Sam. 6: 20, "Who is able to stand before the Lord, this Holy
God?", and Hos. 11: 9 "I am God and not man; the Holy One
in the midst of thee". Later too the expression is infrequent.

3. What does it mean when God is called the Holy One?
The content of the idea has changed. The people of Bethshe-
mesh acknowledge Jahweh as the Holy One because they fear
Him as the Terrible and Incalculable One. In Hosea God calls
Himself the Holy One because He is Lord of His own will, who
does not execute the fierceness of His anger and does not return
to destroy Ephraim. That God is holy means here that in His
decision He is independent and free. Holy means superior,
almighty. Therefore men must fear Him. For that reason also
He can accept the sacrifice of Abel and reject that of Cain,
Gen. 4: 4-5. For that reason "Jacob hath he loved but Esau
hath he hated", Mal. 1: 2-3. God is free of considerations and
conditions, absolutely free master of His own will, of His
feelings, even of His wrath; mighty, not having any responsibility or requiring any justification, exalted over all, Lord
absolutely of His resolutions and decisions and therefore to be
feared absolutely. *Holy is at once exalted, supreme and fearful.*

4. This sort of divine holiness continues in prominence, but
in the revelation as a result of which Isaiah is made a messenger

of God to His people, 6: 1-13, a new deeper sort of holiness is made known to man. Isaiah sees the majesty of God and perceives His holiness, and then what he is aware of is not his own perishableness and the vanity and nothingness of his being, but his sinfulness. "Woe is me! for I am undone; because I am a man of unclean lips and I dwell in the midst of a people of unclean lips". Then the prophet's iniquity is taken away, and because it is taken away he can stand before the throne of God and undertake God's commission. Here holiness is the opposite of sinfulness. God is holy because He does not tolerate sin, He uncovers it, He rebukes it, refuses to connive at it, punishes it or atoning for it forgives it. Sin separates a person from the holy God. Where it is forgiven man has "access" (Romans 5: 2) to God. Holiness is here goodness, the *summum bonum*. For Isaiah God is the Holy One of Israel, because God holds the fate of Israel firmly in His hands where nothing can alter it, and demands of Israel the avoidance of all sin.

A later generation in the Old Testament carried this twofold concept of the holiness of God further and tried in laws of ritual (see § 52) to achieve a division of life into a holy part and a profane part in order to create within the people of Israel the holy context necessary for the holiness of God. The priesthood which did this, did not see that it was thereby depriving God of a part of life, the profane part, and really seeking to impair His complete lordship.

14. THE LIVING GOD

The assertion that God is a living God is found only occasionally in the Old Testament; it is found late and intended to combat the idea that God has no life and no power. Thus Jeremiah receives the revelation which he must pass on to his people, that God is not asleep and idle but watches over His word, to perform it, 1: 12; and in the legends David says to the Philistine and Hezekiah to the Assyrian that for their impudence revenge will be taken on them, for these strangers reproach with their words the living God; 1 Sam. 17: 26, 36, 2 Kings 19: 4, 16, Isa. 37: 4, 17. Not a dead God but the living God spoke out of the midst of the fire at Sinai, Deut. 5: 26, and the living God is in the midst of Israel and will drive the Canaanites before Him, Josh. 3: 10. The Israelites will be called the sons of the living God, Hosea 1: 10; the Lord, the true God, He is the living God, Jer. 10: 10, but the prophet must mention no more the burden of the Lord to the people, for they would pervert the words of the living God; Jer. 23: 36.[53] Concerning the living Jahweh a descendant of David learned that God gave him strength in war and victory over his enemies—no other god is a living God as Jahweh is; 2 Sam. 22: 47, Ps. 18: 46.[54] The soul of the Psalmist thirsteth after God, who is the living God; Ps. 42: 2, 84: 2. Both passages show that the idea is a current one, but it is wrong to credit it with any particular contribution to theology.

15. THE TERRIBLE GOD

1. The word terrible here permits of not the slightest mollification but means really terror-inspiring. God lops the boughs from the trees with a strength that strikes terror, מַעֲרָצָה, into men, Isa. 10: 33. He is with the prophet as a mighty one and a terrible גִּבּוֹר עָרִיץ, Jer. 20. 11. He shows Himself to be a terrible God, אֵל נַעֲרָץ, Ps. 89: 8, and is mighty and formidable, נוֹרָא, above all them that are round about Him. God is fearful, because He is capable of doing amazing deeds, deeds that display might and great power and therefore inspire fear. It is the ability to do such deeds that is hoped for in the earthly king, that his enemies may fall under him, Ps. 45: 5-6. God has that ability. He does great and terrible things for His people Israel, 2 Sam. 7: 23. He did terrible things by the Red Sea, Ps. 106: 22. It is a terrible thing that He does before Israel, Ex. 34: 10, Ps. 66: 3; He Himself is terrible in His doing toward the children of men, 66: 5. That refers to His actions in history, when He brought Israel out of Egypt and led them safe and dry over Jordan. Would that there were some clarity in the text of Ps. 139: 14 that we might know whether the wonderful making of man is really also called fearful—the θαυμαστόν a φοβερόν! Jahweh Himself is terrible, Ps. 47: 2; He is the great and dreadful God, Dan. 9: 4, Neh. 1: 5, 9: 32.

One thing more deserves to be noted about these quotations. They are not very old, and they increase in later literature. They are not associated with any great author; they come to us in complete anonymity. They set side by side the Terrible One and the Great One, the Terrible One and the Wonderful One, and the context of the thoughts involved in such combinations is the controversy over belief in other gods. Since Jahweh is the Great and Terrible One, He is superior to all other gods. The

most remarkable thing of all, however, is this, that the idea of
the fearfulness of God is not one single idea alongside others but
gathers others within itself.

2. God grants forgiveness: if God should mark a person's
iniquities that person cannot stand. God has an incontestable
right to mark men's iniquities, but it is not a right that He
chooses to exercise unconditionally; He administers forgiveness
instead, Ps. 130: 4. In this way He gains recognition, for the
man whose sin is pardoned must observe and follow the will of
God; such a man lives in fear before God. This fear of the Lord
is in a context of grace. Because God forgives man, man stands
before Him in the fear that is His due. This fear is the result,
it is the operation, the intended operation of grace. God forgives
man *in order that* man may fear God. Fear of God is fear of
forgiveness. It is not a freely determined human emotion; it is
determined by grace.

3. One might wonder whether the brief passage in the Psalms
could really support so much theology,[55] if it were not that
other passages come to the rescue to prove that the teaching
concerning the fearful God and fear of God is not a chance
notion but an essential part of Old Testament theology. Thus
in the sermon in Deuteronomy Jahweh is Israel's God: He has
done great and fearful things for His people before their eyes,
things capable of arousing fear in the hearts of those who see
Jahweh do them, Deut. 10: 21. Because God has done these
fearful things He is God of gods and Lord of lords, the great
God, the mighty, and the terrible, Deut. 10: 17. For a god's
nature is as his works. God is great and mighty and terrible,
therefore He is not a respecter of persons and He takes no
bribes. He does not need to do so; He is independent of these
things. He executes the judgment of the fatherless and the
widow, however, and loves the stranger in giving him food
and raiment, Deut. 10: 17-18. This fearful God, Jahweh, Israel
His people must fear, Deut. 10: 12, 20; and since the term
נוֹרָא, "fearful", which is used of God, can contain the idea
that one must always observe before Him a certain circum-
spection because one does not know the moment the terror may
break out, the meaning of "fearing God" deepens. For Israel to
fear God is to walk in all His ways, to love Him and serve Him
with heart and soul, Deut. 10: 12, to keep His commandments
and His statutes, 10: 13, to cleave unto Him and swear by His

name, 10: 20. Fear of Jahweh, His glorious and fearful name (*sic!*) involves Israel's observing to do all the words of the law, Deut. 28: 58. "Fear God, and keep his commandments" is really the end of the matter and the whole duty of man; Eccles. 12: 13.

It will be observed then that the idea of the terrible God and its kindred ideas undergo within the Old Testament a clear and radical change. God is terrible because at times He does things which terrify the whole world. These deeds He does for the sake of His people; He is able and willing to do them for them at any time. The attitude of man before this might is an attitude of fear, for man is unequal to the revelation of it; the mere sight of it is dreadful. But then God's might is not merely a threat directed against those who want to oppose the will of this Mighty One or frustrate it; God's might becomes at once a claim. The Superior One demands from His people a constant attitude. Israel fears God in being obedient to Him. *Fear of God is obedience*. It is no longer the constant expectation that God of His great superiority could do fearful deeds; rather it is the constant recognition of His greatness in complying with His will. It is to be noted nevertheless that though the second type of fear of God takes precedence over the first it does not supplant it. The terrible God remains terrible.

16. THE MOST HIGH GOD

When one calls a god the Most High God one sees Him as one god among others who are also high but who are excelled by Him in highness. The expression "the Most High" is a polytheistic appellation. For monotheists it is meaningless, a light without a shadow. The polytheistic thinking involved in the superlative "Highest" is also present in the Old Testament. Jahweh is most high above all the earth; He is exalted far above all gods, Ps. 97: 9. But there are nowhere more than traces of these comparisons and one can never say that they really are the last traces of a formerly important concept. Israel never had a polytheistic Pantheon, in which such an expression would be appropriate: rather the expression occurs incidentally in flights of poetic fancy such as Ps. 97 represents, which has merely fallen into the language of the polytheistic Pantheon— Hebrew rustics wearing for a moment Babylonian court-dress. It is from there they take the expression the "Most High God", without noting that in their religion it is irrelevant. They only consider that it sounds well. It has absolutely no theological content. It occurs in no ancient texts of theological importance; it is a favourite word in the Psalms (22 of the 33 instances; in addition it occurs in these Psalm-like passages—1 Sam. 2: 10, Num. 24: 16, Deut. 32: 8, 2 Sam. 22: 14; Isa. 14: 14, Lam. 3: 35, 38. Verses 18, 19, 20, 22 of Gen. 14 have more theological content but they are, like the whole chapter, in a realm of their own; a realm that has never really been explained).

17. OTHER NAMES FOR GOD

The Old Testament revelation is alive, its context is human history, and it is in keeping with this that it does not confine its selection of divine names to a limited few of fixed content but goes on producing new ones. Of these we can distinguish three groups.

1. The names which form the first group are inventions of the moment. According to the particular situation in which an individual or a group of people find themselves they give God a descriptive form of address, which can be extraordinarily rich in content and association, but never succeeds in gaining entrance to the relatively limited group of recognized divine names. Since these inventions of the moment come and go it is difficult to estimate their theological importance in spite of their richness of content. In general one should not rate them too highly.

The following are examples of these names of the moment: He that is strong in power, Isaiah 40: 26; my strength, Ps. 18: 2; the stone(?) of Israel, Gen. 49: 24; my Maker, Job 36: 3; God that performeth all things for me, Ps. 57: 2; He that loveth the stranger, Deut. 10: 18; the true God, 2 Chron. 15: 3; thou God of truth, Ps. 31: 6; who prepareth rain for the earth, Ps. 147: 8; thy teacher, Isa. 30: 20; the Holy One of Jacob (like the Holy One of Israel), Isa. 29: 23; the high God, Mic. 6: 6; God of my life, Ps. 42: 8; a strong tower, Ps. 61: 3. We have intentionally chosen isolated examples in order to distinguish this group from the second group, which often it very closely resembles.

2. The second group contains those forms which may likewise have arisen from certain particular circumstances of the moment but which because of the frequency of their occurrence appear as recognized divine names and whose meaning is still immediately apparent. This last point, so important in distinguishing the second group from the third, does not mean that the names in question have necessarily preserved the full significance of their content. Indeed, because of their currency they have not. In a great variety of appellations it is the protection which God gives His own that is expressed: He is their Protector, their Help, their Refuge, their Fortress, their Rock, their Strength. The form of expression varies. Isa. 45: 24 is quite objective: "Only in the Lord is righteousness and strength". In Ps. 18: 2, on the other hand, there is a much more personal and possessive usage. "The Lord is my rock, and my fortress and my deliverer: my God, my strong rock, in him will I trust, my shield and the horn of my salvation, my high tower". And since one can say—instead of my—thy, his, our, your, their, it is but a small step to the expression the Rock, the Tower, the Shield, etc., which then become divine names. Forms like the rock of my refuge, Ps. 94: 22, or the rock of our salvation, Ps. 95: 1, help the transition, and צוּר certainly became in this way a name: the Rock, his work is perfect, Deut. 32: 4; there is no rock like our God, 1 Sam. 2: 2; is there a God beside me? yea there is no Rock; I know not any, Isa. 44: 8, Hab. 1: 12. In a name formed in such a way there is no particular theological significance.

3. The third group, finally, is made up of names which are interesting from the point of view of the history of religion but theologically are of no consequence. In this group are names like God, who rides (upon) the heaven, Deut. 33:26; the Lord who rideth upon a swift cloud, Isa. 19: 1; that rideth through the deserts, Ps. 68: 4; that rideth upon the heavens of heavens, which are of old, Ps. 68: 33; He sitteth upon the Cherubim, Ps. 99: 1. The student of comparative religion is in his element here (there is no doubt that such a usage is the last hem into which anyone who is knowledgeable by comparisons and transpositions can put enough material for a whole garment). These usages are not simply free poetic inventions; they are too incomprehensible for that. Rather they are the last echoes of lost myths, which earlier or elsewhere were once current and meaningful. The theologian however can and must take up a different attitude to these usages. He must treat them as gay-coloured tinsel, just as the clergyman makes nothing of the fact that a chorale is sung like a folk song. It is not a folk song just because he makes no fuss. In the same way these scraps of myth are no longer myths but only marks of origin, evidence that the Old Testament revelation also once existed in the midst of the religions, but existed as a guest whom the national costume could not rob of the identity of its particular mission.

IV. THE SCOPE (THE HISTORY) OF GOD'S ACTIVITY

18. INTRODUCTION

DIVINE revelation in the Old Testament is not a single revelation of a harmonious system of lines of thought, but a long gradual movement gathering momentum in the context of history. Therefore it is appropriately presented not as systematic theology but as history. The God of the Old Testament has a history. It is the history of a slow development from a narrow sphere and limited influence to far-reaching and indeed all-inclusive government. If one overlooks this aspect of Old Testament revelation and thinks only in terms of the latest ways in which God had made Himself known, then such disregard of history renders most of the Old Testament meaningless. Conversely every individual part of the Old Testament revelation is reduced to an unconnected fragment when one forgets that it is part of a great connected whole. One avoids both dangers only when one writes *the history* of the God of the Old Testament, in order to see His government stretching ever further and more comprehensively, and at the same time treats the individual aspects of this government in their historical contexts in order to see them from that perspective and to see the meaning which they then had or did not have, and the meaning which finally, in conjunction with others, they acquired.

19. THE FACT OF REVELATION

The fact that God reveals Himself is fundamental. He appears to Abraham, Gen. 12: 7; He makes known His name and therefore His nature, Ex. 6: 3; He does not belong to the number of the dumb gods, Hab. 2: 18. The initiative is not with men, with their seeking or imagining; the initiative is solely with God. The fact that God has fellowship with man is due to His free and groundless will and is His first and fundamental deed. One must be careful to distinguish between His functions: God answers, when He wills it, the cry of every man that calls upon His name, Ps. 3: 5; that is the function of the God that is known in dealing with individual members of the people to which His worship is entrusted. But the unknown God does not make Himself known indiscriminately to any individuals He likes; He is no private God. Rather He makes himself known only to the chosen leaders of His people, and not for their own personal sakes but for the sake of the whole people. God is concerned only with the people as a whole. The leaders (historically only Moses, and Abraham merely as a precursor, a proleptic figure in the view of the priestly writer) are simply mediators of the revelation, but mediators without special position. God can reveal Himself, He wills to reveal Himself; He has revealed Himself, and to Israel. Why and for what purpose He has done so is not disclosed. All that is said is that the revelation is an act of God's free will, and therefore sheer grace; and that is in no way due to any excellence which Israel possessed and other nations did not possess—Amos 9: 7, Mal. 1: 1-3. The idea of a special "religiousness" in Israel has no place in the Old Testament. *God willed to make Himself known to Israel at the time of Moses and through him*—that is the first sentence of the history of God.

20. THE COVENANT OR THE AGREEMENT AS THE FORM OF THE RELATIONSHIP BETWEEN JAHWEH AND ISRAEL

Introductory

1. God's saying to Israel through Moses "I am Jahweh" and Israel's consequent knowledge "Our God is called Jahweh" and "we are the people of Jahweh", Ex. 6: 2-7, constitutes the foundation of revelation. The practical import of this will be discussed in § 22. Here let it be noted that this revelation stands theoretically in a context of polytheism. Jahweh is a proper name and proper names serve to distinguish beings of the same kind from one another according to their individuality.

2. When we find that God's imparting His name to Israel produces a lasting relationship between Jahweh and Israel, so that Israel from now on is Jahweh's people and Jahweh Israel's God, the question immediately arises concerning the form of this relationship. For a relationship cannot exist without assuming a clear form. The form is the covenant or agreement, the בְּרִית. What does that mean?

3. Following a well-tested rule, one always proceeds in the elucidation of a theological concept from the sense which the concept has in untheological and not yet theological usage; and the more important the concept is, the more strictly this rule applies. This is based on the fact that when God reveals Himself, He uses the speech and the ideas and concepts of men, since only so can His revelation be received by men. When the concept is taken untheologically the theological meaning is disclosed, even when the theological and the untheological meaning are not absolutely identical. If the two differ it will then become evident in one of two ways; either the expression is gradually dislocated or it is emptied of all theological content.

4. In accordance with this proved rule we will now discuss in detail, because of its great importance, the concept בְּרִית; covenant or agreement. The word occurs 285 times and in the Septuagint is rendered 257 times for certain διαθήκη. It has a rich phraseology which offers few real difficulties. Its meaning is sufficiently clear from its usage, so that the difficult question of its derivation does not need to be introduced to help in its explanation, but without prejudice can be left aside.

5. The untheological usage of the word Covenant. Abraham and Abimelech have a difference, they therefore make a covenant, come to an agreement or arrangement with one another כָּרְתוּ בְרִית, Gen. 21: 27. Laban and his son-in-law Jacob come to an agreement about Laban's daughters who have become Jacob's wives, Gen. 31: 44. Jonathan and David come to an agreement about what their mutual attitude will be after the death of Saul, 1 Sam. 23: 18. Solomon and Hiram make a league together—this is the appropriate rendering of בְּרִית here concerning their mutual relations, 1 Kings 5: 12. The word בְּרִית, nearly always translated covenant by older theologians, in the passages quoted, is equivalent to agreement or arrangement or league. Neither the context of the agreement nor its form is essential to the concept but only the fact that two parties, voluntarily and of their own free will, make an agreement which binds the one to the other in respect of the content of the agreement, while in other respects they remain perfectly free. בְּרִית is an agreement of two independent parties about something fixed and defined.

6. It should be stated here that בְּרִית does not ever occur in the above-mentioned sense when used for the arrangement into which Jahweh enters with Israel. The only possible exception[56] is Ps. 50: 5, but בְּרִיתִי reads properly not "a covenant with me" but "my (established by me) covenant".

The idea that the בְּרִית between Jahweh and Israel rests
on the free resolution of both partners is entirely foreign to
the Old Testament. The one responsible for this agreement
is always God alone. It is always said that God makes a
covenant with somebody, never that God and somebody make
a covenant.

J. Begrich* has worked it out ingeniously that *Berith*
originally meant "an arrangement between two unequal
partners", in which the more powerful partner binds himself
to a certain attitude towards the less powerful if certain conditions are fulfilled by the less powerful. This meaning agrees
well with the derivation of the word which I have given in my
Lexicon, p. 152a (table-fellowship, which a healthy person
offers to a sick person, one therefore who because of his sickness
is socially and religiously suspect). The concept becomes then
"thought of more and more as being an agreement" (p. 4).

7. Even in untheological contexts the phenomenon of the
two partners making an agreement is rare. Usually someone
comes to terms with someone else, that is to say the impulse
and resolve come from one of the two partners, not from both.
But it is essential to the nature of the affair, that this one-sided
initiative does not prejudice the free decision of the other
person. In so far as the two sides are parties to the agreement,
however different their position and power may be, they regard
one another as being free and with equal rights. בְּרִית is
always (on both sides) a voluntary bond. It is never a one-sided
decision. Israel, small and oppressed, makes a covenant with
Assyria in order to receive help, Hos. 12: 1. Only because the
Gibeonites succeed in their pretence that they are from a far
country, not from the surrounding country, and therefore free
to act, does Joshua concede to their request and make a
covenant with them; Josh. 9: 1-16. One can also come to an
agreement involving mutual rights and obligations with
peoples whom one has in one's power and could annihilate,
Deut. 7: 2, Ex. 34: 12-15. The besieged men of Jabesh propose
a covenant to Nahash: they will be subservient to him, but the
agreement will also protect them from his caprice, 1 Sam. 11: 1.
When Benhadad of Aram is a prisoner of war he proposes a
covenant to his captor Ahab: he makes many concessions but

* In his valuable study, *Berit. Ein Beitrag zur Erfassung einer alttestamentlichen Denkform (Z.A.W.* 60, 1944, 1-10).

through the covenant he obtains his freedom, I Kings 20: 34.

8. בְּרִית is therefore in its untheological meaning an arrangement, *entente*, agreement, bargain or covenant. The translation chosen depends on the importance, the duration and public or private character of the understanding reached. It is always a question of rights and a relationship based on rights between two partners concerning a definite matter. The partners are free to enter into the arrangement or to reject it (and to suffer the consequences of such rejection). They are bound by fixed arrangement to abide by the agreement for the agreed time or until it is otherwise terminated. They stand in a relationship determined by rights and obligations as far as the content of the agreement is concerned. The agreement always has a fixed and carefully defined content. There is no such thing as an agreement without definite content.

21. THE THEOLOGICAL USE OF THE WORD COVENANT

1. We have already said that the summons to make a covenant always comes from Jahweh as the one partner. God is the one who concludes it. Israel can choose whether she will accept it or not. She is not compelled to enter into a covenant; it is a matter of free decision. God makes the covenant with Israel כָּרַת בְּרִית אֶת־ (mostly) or כָּרַת בְּרִית עִם (often). Later this phraseology was found no longer appropriate, since it did not express the constraint of God's will. Thus we find הֵקִים בְּרִית אֶת־ God "establishes, institutes" a covenant with (Gen. 6: 18 and seven other passages) or הֵקִים בְּרִית בֵּינוֹ וּבֵין . . . God "establishes, institutes" a covenant between Himself and Israel, Gen. 9: 17, 17: 7. In these the authoritative, constraining, initiating will of God receives still clearer expression. Indeed one finds נָתַן בְּרִיתוֹ בֵּינוֹ וּבֵין, God "gives, grants" His covenant between Himself and Israel, Gen. 17: 2. In all these instances the other partner is still mentioned, although his part in the conclusion of the covenant is considerably reduced. In Num. 25: 12, הִנְנִי נֹתֵן לוֹ אֶת־בְּרִיתִי, "Behold I give unto him my covenant, put my covenant at his disposal", the second partner has become the mere recipient and usufructuary.

2. One should not overlook this change in usage, the sequence of which we have noted and which corresponds to the course of history, for this change indicates that the covenant or agreement form was more and more found *unsuited* to represent the relationship between Jahweh and Israel. When Israel is brought into a covenant with Jahweh, the one aspect of the connexion is clearly expressed, namely that of the mutual obligations; but the other aspect—the fact that it is an *entente* between two partners, who enter into it of their own free will and decision, detracts from the exclusive action and dominion of God and is therefore questionable. This questioning produces the change in usage. The idea of בְּרִית is preserved, but the change in usage is really such as to destroy the essential character of the בְּרִית altogether. It is not unparalleled for theological usage to retain old and traditional ideas and forms of a word even where it has long since destroyed their meaning. Theology is always conservative in its vocabulary.

3. The change in usage did not however achieve its purpose of giving expression to the exclusive action and lordship of God. The simple sentence that Israel is Jahweh's peculiar treasure, "if ye will obey my voice and keep my covenant" (it is significant that it does not read "the covenant with me") "then ye shall be a peculiar treasure unto me from among all peoples: for all the earth is mine", Ex. 19: 5—that sentence achieves at one stroke what could never be said using the בְּרִית-idea, no matter how flexible it might be.

22. THE ESSENTIAL CONTENT OF THE COVENANT OR AGREEMENT CONCEPT

1. What does it mean when we say that Jahweh entered into an agreement with the people of Israel? For the answer to this question three points are important and in this order: 1. the correct defining of the limits of the concept, so that it is understood what the covenant does not mean; 2. the ways in which the covenant clearly demonstrates its operation; 3. the context within which it has its being. It should also be remembered that Old Testament revelation, although it is true revelation, that is to say of universal validity, nevertheless represents a historical quantity; that is to say, it is adapted to the understanding of its day and to the confessional standards and confessional forms then prevailing. For the child, two times two equals four is the beginning and end of arithmetic. The mathematician sees far beyond that, but two times two is four for him also with the same unconditional validity as for the child.

2. The definitions of the covenant. The covenant is a relationship with the people and not with individuals. Jahweʾ is concerned with the people and deals with the people, not with the
individual. The individual stands within the covenant, which
Jahweh has made, but he stands within this covenant not
because he is an individual personality in his own right, for that
means nothing for the Old Testament, but because he is a
member of the people. The people is not the sum of its members,
it is not a mathematical quantity. On the contrary, it is represented in any group of members you like, even in individuals;
but the individual is never alone where the covenant is concerned. Always, whether by himself or in a number, he is *pars
pro toto*. It is an axiom of the Old Testament revelation that
God deals with society, with the people, or—to put it more
accurately—with the community. *The individual can live before
God only as a member of the community.*

3. The people is not a limited community; its size is variable
and it grows. The number of the Hebrews who gathered round
Moses and the number of the tribes to which they belonged
may have been ever so small, it was nevertheless an unrestricted
open number. That means they might annex as many more
later, in the wilderness, at the occupation of the Promised Land
or in the Palestinian period, and they could do it without
prejudice. Among the people of Israel there is no distinction
between first and later, between originals and newcomers.
A city which became Hebrew in the time of David—one thinks
of Jerusalem and the position of equality the inhabitants of
Jerusalem enjoy in Isaiah with the men of Judah—belongs as
much to the people of Israel as the descendants of the original
company under Moses. The covenant with Jahweh is valid for
them in exactly the same way, and indeed it is valid not
merely from the time of their entry into it, but from the
beginning it was meant also for them. The idea of the people of
Israel, as far as the covenant concept is concerned, is taken out
of the category of time altogether; it is supra-temporal, or
a-temporal. The people of Israel with whom Jahweh makes the
covenant is no empirical quantity but a spiritual quantity, for
which numerical increase and historical waxing or waning (with
the fall of Samaria Judah became the people of Israel) is of no
consequence. That wonderful word in Galatians 4: 26, 28, "the
Jerusalem above . . . is our mother. Now ye brethren" (Galatians!) "are children of promise"—belongs to a context of

ETT

revelation. The historian must enquire how many Hebrews were present when the covenant was given at Sinai and who they were, but for the theologian the question does not arise. The people of Israel is an unrestricted quantity. Any of its members can at any time and of any incident of earlier times say: "we". *The earlier is always the living present to all who come after.*

4. It is understandable that God's revelation of Himself to Israel contains nothing that was entirely unintelligible to Moses' contemporaries. Revelation always presupposes a certain measure of mental capacity in men and to that measure it is adapted. At the same time it transcends all human capacity of comprehension. It is like the tree, of which the earth knows only the roots underneath, but which without roots would swing absurdly in the air.

5. Features of the covenant. From the time of the giving of the covenant onwards Israel belongs to Jahweh. He is Israel's only God. The other gods are not denied, they are ignored. As far as Israel is concerned they do not exist; even if they do exist, Israel (and this includes the individual Israelite) may on no account bow down to them and serve them, לֹא תָעָבְדֵם Ex. 20: 5.[57] And corresponding to this negative there is a positive. When the children of Israel call on a god, they must call on Jahweh. When in giving a name to a child they make confession of a god, they must by means of a name containing Jahweh confess Jahweh. When they swear or curse they must swear or curse by Jahweh. When they pray to a god, they must pray to Jahweh and by naming Jahweh declare that Jahweh is their God. When a sacrifice, a consecration, a vow, an atonement or any other holy ordinance that was customary or necessary took place, it did not take place without the name Jahweh being invoked. Everything was done "in the name of Jahweh", that is to say, with an invocation of the name Jahweh. We cannot deal here with the actual matters involved; only the theology of it is our concern and this theology is summarized and fully expressed in the formula "in the name of Jahweh". When one names a god, one names always Jahweh. One can name no other, for it is fully intended, and no explanations should be allowed to cloud the truth of it, when it is said that Jahweh "is a jealous God". Israel's obligation under the covenant is to have only Jahweh as its God. And Jahweh guards jealously against any neglect or violation of this obligation. It remains only to say that all important matters of a single day or an entire life stand within this theology, for they take place within the invocation of Jahweh.[58] Nothing is secularized any more, little is rationalized. One does always and undergoes only what can take place "in the name of Jahweh". The relationship to Jahweh as the only true God is everlasting, ever relevant, constantly taking shape afresh, presenting itself to the mind, alive.

6. Historically speaking, Israel, whatever the extent of its experience at the time of Moses may have been, even before the revelation of Jahweh, was not without God and did not live without religion. But the Old Testament revelation does not begin by sweeping aside all former customs, regulations, practices and celebrations and replacing them with a completely new system; rather—as far as we can judge—they are left undisturbed. They are given a new relationship, a new direction. They are related to Jahweh. Only for Jahweh can one sacrifice, dedicate, make a vow, swear, celebrate a festival and so on. The ethnic form becomes Jahwistic. From this point of view it is determined, for all practical purposes, what can be left as it was and what can be disposed of. That is a matter for the future and of course belongs to the sphere of the history of religion; it is not of importance theologically. What is of importance theologically—and it is profoundly so—is that now everything is tied up with Jahweh.

7. This exclusive relationship with Jahweh is obedience to Jahweh. *Israel is Jahweh's people because Israel is obedient to Jahweh,* and only to Jahweh. Israelites obey Jahweh in that they sacrifice to Him, name their children after Him, keep oaths and vows for Him, offer their prayers to Him and call upon His name. To these we have to add another important department of life—the life of the community with its rules, arrangements, obligations, commands and restrictions, the whole province that we call ethics. Even in the time of Moses all matters pertaining to community life were worked out according to rules of some kind. But these regulations, probably connected formerly with local gods, are now connected with Jahweh. Right is what is right before Jahweh: wrong is what is wrong before Jahweh. If a man honours his father he is obedient to Jahweh. If a man commits adultery he is disobedient to Jahweh. Propriety and morality come under the care of Jahweh.

Jahweh watches over them, orders them, demands them, punishes their violation, makes decisions when there is a lack of clarity or lack of unity. The entire life of the community goes on under His attentive supervision; it has its source in His will and finds its reward or its punishment in His pleasure or wrath. Again it is not a question of new statutes and ordinances. The Old Testament knows nothing of these, and, if there had been any, some clear trace of their introduction would certainly have come down to us. The old customs and the traditional morality remain, but brought into a new context—they have been related to the will of Jahweh. Their observation is therefore, from now on, obedience to the will of Jahweh.

8. The covenant revealed through Moses, the so called Sinai Covenant between Jahweh and Israel, is therefore characterized by the fact that *Jahweh protects Israel as His people*—that is Jahweh's obligation and Israel's right—and that *Israel worships Jahweh and obeys Him*; that is Israel's obligation and Jahweh's right. None of these constituent parts can be neglected without detriment to the covenant. For it is a covenant made by both partners of their own free will. Jahweh's free will, which is the source of the initiative, is taken so much for granted that it is not mentioned. The fact that Israel enters the covenant of its own free will is however repeatedly and emphatically declared, perhaps most clearly of all in Joshua 24: 15, 21-22: "And if it seem evil unto you to serve (to worship) the Lord, choose you this day whom ye will serve (worship)". And Joshua said unto the people, "Ye are witnesses against yourselves that ye have chosen you the Lord, to serve (worship) him". Election in the Old Testament is a reciprocal relationship: Jahweh chooses Israel, Israel chooses Jahweh; both do it in complete independence.

9. The obligations which arise for Israel from this covenant and the rights and privileges which accrue to Jahweh from it are defined above. What really are Jahweh's obligations, however, and Israel's rights? The simplest formula is found in Jahweh's promise: "I will be your God", Ex. 6: 7. What does that mean? Obviously it means that Jahweh espouses His people's cause when they are in need. Jahweh is Israel's helper. "The Lord hath helped us", I Sam. 7: 12. At the beginning of His revelation there stands the statement: "I am Jahweh, thy God, who brought thee out of the land of Egypt, out of the house of bondage". To help Israel is Jahweh's business and duty. He helps the people whenever their position is endangered; that is why the writer of Deuteronomy can always say that the decision for or against Jahweh is a decision for life or death; 4: 1, 9, 15; 5: 33; 6: 2; etc. Israel is kept alive by adhering faithfully to the covenant with Jahweh.

10. Scope of the covenant. For the understanding of the Old Testament revelation it is of supreme importance that the scope within which Jahweh's covenant with Israel operates and is defined should be correctly established. This can best be achieved by removing all false ideas.

a) The covenant does not apply to individuals, but to the people as a whole. The fate and also the attitude of the individual is of importance for the covenant only in so far as the individual is part of the whole people. The personal fate of the individual is not affected by the covenant: his position is the same as that of men who do not stand within the covenant because they do not belong to the people of Israel. Therefore there is a complete absence of all individual piety, and until the time of David, or even Jeremiah, religion has nothing to do with individual character.

Also the whole important sphere of sickness, healing, death and life after death is not a sphere where Jahweh operates, simply because the people in its entirety and inviolability continues, no matter how many individuals die. This limitation accounts for the fact that the Israelites were so inclined to borrow meaning and assistance from the worship of other gods and from heathen magic when faced with sickness or death.

b) Jahweh's covenant with Israel is a covenant with those competent to enter into such a thing; that is to say, with the men: they represent the people. The children, the women, the slaves and the non-Israelites are not the people, but the possessions of the people. Woman has no place in this revelation, therefore she is a constant danger to the worship of Jahweh. The Decalogue addresses the man only; Hannah and Peninnah do not take part in the sacrifice with Elkanah, 1 Sam. 1: 4-5; the wife of a man's bosom entices him to serve other gods, Deut. 13: 7 ff. The male is man, Gen. 2: 7, and the people of Israel consists of men. It was only with the greatest difficulty that the Old Testament overcame this limitation.

c) Jahweh is not bound up with any land, neither with Egypt, nor with the wilderness, nor with Canaan, least of all with the whole earth. For that reason He has nothing to do with nature, with weather or light or water, with plants and their growth, with animals and their increase, or with the birth of men. Nature is not Jahweh's sphere. When the time comes, however, that the fruitfulness of their lands and their herds and their marriages is a problem, Israel has great difficulty in knowing how to relate the problem to Jahweh. The revelation to Moses leaves this an open question and it is left for the prophets to give the necessary answer. Until that day comes, however, the oracle is empty and silent.

d) Jahweh is not a god of the peoples and much less a world-god. What the attitude of other peoples is to Him who protects them and guides their history, in whose hands the shaping of their history rests—all these questions lie outside the Old Testament revelation of Moses' time, for they lie outside the scope of Israel's vision and concern. What history is, Israel has still to experience, and who guides the course of history is a question she has still to learn to ask; but only centuries after Moses is the time ripe for revelation of these points.

e) Finally, it is obvious that there is no connexion between Jahweh and Creation included in the Sinai covenant. Jahweh exists, Israel exists, the world as the locus of both exists. But how all this has come about, how it began and who created it, these are all thoughts which as yet have no real meaning. The revelation which Moses mediates operates therefore in a very limited area, it covers only a small range of thought and it is quite elementary in its confession: a God here, a community there, both come together of free choice and offer one another assistance and obedience respectively; what more is needed? Even to say that this occurs in the context of history is for Israel in Moses' time too much. The relationship grows, however, and fills all things: history, Nature, the ethos of nations, the Cosmos, until there is nothing that this revelation does not give into the hands of God.

Jahweh's covenant with Israel, bound to which Moses' Israelites march out into the wilderness and into the future, is a relationship founded on the narrow scope of that which is necessary for the time being. It is a centre, from the point of view of theology, from which there do not yet radiate any lines of thought answering the question of the systematic theologian. The later history of the covenant must first create the opportunity for such thought. Similarly the covenant is a relationship in a human context. Of their own free will, as the Bible expressly says, Jahweh and Israel have come together as equal partners, though the one partner is God who guarantees protection, and the other is man who gives obedience. Jahweh and Israel come together as friends, and their relationship is one of trust and reliance. Will it last?

23. ALTERATIONS TO THE COVENANT IDEA
AS A RESULT OF THE OCCUPATION

1. The whole course of events which stretches from Joshua to David, and in which other tribes join Moses' Hebrews in order to bring themselves within the covenant between Jahweh and Israel and therefore also within the name Israel, in which they then immigrate into Canaan and gradually take possession of the whole land—this course of events we call the *Landnahme*[59] —the occupation. It brings with it great transformations; one does not always know when one should call them setbacks and when one should call them developments.

2. The roving Bedouin whose only home is the group to which he belongs becomes a peasant whose home is the land which, almost as a native of that soil,[60] he occupies. The idea of a homeland arises and with it the question, what homeland means from God's point of view. This homeland is not without history and not without "religion". At its springs, under its towering trees and on its high places live gods, and these gods are worshipped. What connexion have these gods with Jahweh? Are they to be placed alongside Him, under Him or above Him? Are they like Him? Is their history Jahweh's history?

3. The new homeland cannot be without these gods, for they offer what Jahweh does not offer, at least up till then has not offered. Jahweh offers protection, has done so since the exodus from Egypt and still did so at the entrance into Canaan. He has now a history which later shall be gratefully related in story and in many a Psalm. But for the peasant the necessity of protection is not nearly so obvious. He leads a settled existence, and being settled is a safeguard in itself, safeguard both against hunger and against an enemy. The fixed possession which the Bedouin finds a burden and cannot use secures a man against hunger; and peace, undisturbed prosperity, secures him against foes. Does Jahweh give also a fixed possession and prosperity? There is one thing more and it is important. Protection is not a service that is being rendered constantly. Jahweh does not protect Israel with unbroken attention like someone set to guard a child, but rather as occasion arises, in hours of need, as one summoned by his friend to assist. Protection is an occasional service. But property and above all growth and prosperity require a constant influence, they need uninterrupted bless-sing.[61] In place of protection, which is always available but not always being invoked because it is not always necessary, comes blessing that is operative all the time.

That is an exceptionally important change; and another equally important change accompanies it. Corresponding to Jahweh's protection was Israel's obedience. Was it in service? It certainly was when circumstances demanded it. But more and more it was also something else. It was primarily an attitude and disposition towards Jahweh, a silent recognition of His lordship within the covenant. Israelites were always ready to render their obedience to Jahweh, in order to be worthy of His protection. When Israel becomes a nation of peasants, that changes. Because they need the blessing of Jahweh continually, daily, with an urgency which was never present in anything like the same degree when only Jahweh's protection was involved, they must now also observe their obedience continually and daily, not just as an attitude; they must also make it a service to be rendered in actual and visible practice. Out of obedience grows worship: the real cult comes into being. It is henceforth not merely regular; it is constant. For the cult preserves the blessing.

This cult is however no new thing and not of Israel's crea-tion; less still is it a revelation from Jahweh. It is an annexation of the traditional cult of the conquered land. At its holy places, on its altars and as far as possible with its forms it is practised. But now every cult carries its own defined theology within itself. Will the theology of the traditional Canaanite cult simply combine with the revelation of God, which Israel possessed, to underline, to operate as a relevant form of expression perhaps even complementary, or will it dim, distort, corrupt and obstruct? And if blessing is the new catchword now governing the whole relationship between Jahweh and Israel, what does that mean?

Blessing means for Israel now settled in Palestine what it had meant for the indigenous folk of Canaan—abundance of wheat and olives and the fruit of the vine, increase of herds, large families of children; in a word, fertility. The God of blessing is a god of fertility. He forsakes the almost human sphere of history and makes His dwelling in the almost animal sphere of nature. God rules nature. He is not yet in nature as its creator. This line of thought does not necessarily lead to that and certainly does not yet do so. The world as a whole does not yet come within the scope of Israel's vision. She lives still in the limited area of her own small corner, and only when Israel knows what the world really is will God reveal to her what He Himself means for the world. But God rules nature at the moment as it is, as the producer and begetter. From Him comes growth and fertility. Can that be viewed in terms of the covenant, or will God Himself now become a part, the motive part of nature and almost a power?

These briefly are the changes which the settlement in Canaan brings with it. They are considerable and extensive. Everything has become different, and, when Israel's whole way of thinking has changed, can she still have in proper perspective the revelation of her God? That is the question.

4. We come now to the theological results of the alteration of the covenant idea caused by the settlement. The whole covenant was contained in the saying: "I will take you to me for a people and I will be to you a God", Ex. 6: 7. That saying has no historical perspective, and that means also no territorial perspective. For there is no such thing as history without a locus. Now Canaan has become the land of Israel, however, and since Israel is the people of Jahweh, Canaan is consequently the land of Jahweh. He always wanted to give it to the people of Israel; He promised Abraham in that regard that a people should grow from his seed and that this seed should inherit the land. The last part of the promise is still lacking in Gen. 12: 2 but it is there in 15: 18. The promise, however, requires to be supplemented. Since Canaan belongs to the Canaanites the promise is not fulfilled unless Canaan is taken from them. Commentators on Gen. 9: 18-27 are agreed that in this passage originally not Ham but Canaan is the offender, for Canaan is the accursed one. Ham has come in as a gloss. We are dealing here with the nemesis of history, if you like with the philosophy of history, but not with theology and revelation. So it is in all passages which speak of Jahweh giving Canaan to Israel.

If the land belongs to Jahweh, who gives it to Israel, then all that the land possesses belongs to Jahweh also: its powers and especially its holy places at which, in spring and tree and vegetation, powers of divinity are apparent. The lord and possessor of the land is the Baal of the land, and still to-day in Arabic they speak of cultivated land as distinct from wilderness as "possessed" by men. For the Hebrew nomad turned peasant Jahweh is therefore the Baal of Palestine, even though the expression cannot be found in these words in the Old Testament. Often it is just that which is taken for granted that is not declared. But if Jahweh has become a Baal, then the God who up till now has ruled the free and (so to speak) spiritual sphere of historical relationship is henceforth taken over into the quite different sphere of nature. From now on He is responsible for growth and barrenness; he shuts up a woman's womb, 1 Sam. 1: 5, and He opens it that she may bear children, Gen. 29: 31. Fertility is brought into connexion with Him; all fertility, of the field and of the herd and of marriage. It is not a far cry from that point to the picture of Jahweh as the husband (that is also בַּעַל in the Hebrew, Deut. 22: 22) and Israel his wife forming a not merely figurative but, in the collective thinking of the ancient world, a unit actually imagined real, the people of Israel; Hos. 2: 18.

A whole series of ways of speaking of the connexion between Jahweh and Israel presents itself here; and they are not only metaphor, they are thought of as in some way or other realities.[62] Israel commits adultery, Jer. 3: 8; they go a whoring from under their God, Hos. 4: 12; after other gods, Judg. 8: 33; she is a whorish woman, Ezek. 16: 30; it is her nature, Jer. 3: 2. All this, and much that could be added, is more than metaphor; it is really meant and indicates that, far more than we can prove, the worship of Jahweh too and the celebration of His festivals stand in the context of the ideas and usages connected with fertility. If Jahweh becomes lord and owner of the land, then the holy places also fall to Him. It is Jahweh who is worshipped there, but this worship does not grow up in place of another that is put aside; the Old Testament knows nothing of that; rather the old worship is applied to Jahweh. It is Jahweh who once revealed Himself at these holy places and founded them. All Old Testament theophany stories which tell of the establishment of holy places and their cult, and there are many (e.g. Gen. 28: 10-22, 32: 22-32,[63] 35: 1-7, Josh. 5: 13-15, Judg. 13: 9-21), are taken over from other gods and referred to Jahweh. He is decked out in motley and multifarious garments utterly unsuited to His character, and it is important to recognize this in order to distinguish clearly between what is revelation and what is tradition and disguise. With the cult places and their claims there are transferred also their practices, their rites and sacrifices. If Jahweh gives the peasant of Israel His blessing, he for his part offers his sacrifices as thanks and supplication and atonement. We shall say more about this later (§ 52). Here it is important to notice that the bleeding sacrifice, זֶבַח, with its emphasis on fellowship, is supplanted by the offering or burnt offering which brings down a blessing, עֹלָה: it is not fellowship with Jahweh but Jahweh's blessing that now is the primary concern.

5. This sketch, which can easily be made a picture with a wealth of detail, must suffice in this present situation where the interest is in theology. The point is clear. The occupation and the assumption by Israel of a peasant culture influences, obscures, confuses, blunts and gravely prejudices the original Old Testament revelation. One cannot yet say that Israel deserts Jahweh. But certainly one must say that Israel is pushed away from Him. When and how does the reaction come?

24. STATE RELIGION

1. Moses, executing Jahweh's commission, had founded the people. David by his gifts as a man of action and even more by his gifts of personality had given them a consciousness of unity. Solomon makes the people into a state, which is a state based not merely on the fact that they have a common land and destiny but also on a thorough organization. Solomon rules as king over a kingdom. However small and insignificant the subsequently divided Israel and Judah are, from the time of Solomon they retain the consciousness that they are not merely peoples but states and kingdoms. A people knows itself a unity; a state is by its rulers, here its king, constituted a unity. In this case that has two important consequences.

2. One is the placing of the Temple in Jerusalem, and its theology. In itself the Temple which Solomon builds in Jerusalem is merely the chapel royal, and is lightly esteemed as such for centuries by the ancient sanctuaries with their long and venerable histories.[64] Because it is the King's Temple, however, and the Temple of the Kingdom, it assumes a certain preeminence and more and more takes the lead.[65] In a way it embodies the state and becomes its symbol. In terms of the

covenant between Jahweh and Israel as Moses mediated it, that should not have been possible, for there was no place in it for a building. But Jahweh has now long since ceased to be merely Israel's covenant partner; He is also the God of the land of Palestine. To this thought the Temple in Jerusalem gives expression in stone. Every building has its spiritual foundations, and reveals a certain outlook. The building in Jerusalem represents not merely the thought that here the kingdom and state of Israel comes before its God—a thought which the other sanctuaries vehemently contested and the emergence of which must have been greatly slowed down until 721 B.C. by the fact of two kingdoms[66]—but in its particular architecture it represents a particular theology. The Temple is Jahweh's house. Jahweh has a dwelling place, and this dwelling place, a long lightless cubicle, encloses Jahweh and holds Him fast. In addition, this dwelling is separated from His people by halls and courts. Jahweh's dwelling is secure and remote. These are the thoughts to which the Temple buildings gives visible and tangible form: and besides all this we have to remember that these edifice ideas did not emanate from the people and from their realms of thought; they are borrowed from abroad, they are foreign[67] and new. The Temple represents the transference to Jahweh of a foreign ethnic theology.

3. The question where, according to the ancient utterances of the Old Testament, Jahweh dwells, is hard to answer. When He hastens to Israel's succour in Palestine, it is from the far south He comes, Judg. 5: 4, Mic. 1: 3, in a mighty theophany. The mountain of the Lord is called the place of His abode sometimes under the name Sinai, sometimes Horeb. As the people wander in the desert He is present as a sort of shade. If and when He wills it He reveals Himself at holy places. But he is not in heaven as a fixed place above the earth, nor does He remain at one place in any fixed area. He lives in a sort of naïve undescribed limited omnipresence within call of His people: where exactly is never specified. Now, however, He occupies His fixed abode "in the thick darkness" (1 Kings 8: 12) of the rear chamber[68] of the Temple.

4. Even more significant than this specification of Jahweh's habitat is His being separated from the people by hall and court. At the old sanctuaries this is quite unknown. Their central point is the altar to which any Israelite duly sanctified, 1 Sam. 16: 5, and with bare feet, Ex. 3: 5, may come. Here

amongst His fellow-countrymen Jahweh is present. In the
Temple at Jerusalem this does not happen. He sits in that
forbidden rear chamber separated from his cult-companions by
a wide dusky hall.[69] He has become superior and unapproach-
able like the gods of Egypt and Babylon. His Temple owes its
pattern to theirs. If the Temple succeeds in its claim to be the
only valid sanctuary, the theology of this edifice-thinking must
succeed also. Will it do so?

5. The other consequence of the fact that Israel—thanks to
Solomon—becomes a power, a state organized as a unity under
the king, is still more important. Israel as a state ranges itself
alongside other states; it appears, so to speak, on the stage of
world history. Peoples do not live an isolated life in a vacuum;
they too have mutual relationships, they think in terms of
neighbourhood and distance, war and peace, goodwill and
contempt. But these things find only occasional expression as
the situation arises. They recede before the real matter of
living; they are insignificant and dull. A state is a people that
has become conscious of itself. It sees other peoples as states
and lives over against them, taking it for granted that they too
are states, conscious unities, and acts in this assumption for
and against them. When Israel becomes a state, Jahweh becomes a state divinity. Thereupon He comes into relationship
with the other gods; and relationship here means necessarily
competition. Israel had long realized that the people of Israel
had Jahweh for their god just as the people of Moab had
Kamos and the people of Amman had Melek, but that was a
realization without much consequence. For the people live
alongside one another. The sentence "Jahweh is our God" had
only an internal relevance, a relevance for Israel itself. When
Israel became a state and thought of itself as a state the relevance altered. It has now also an outward direction. The states
stand alongside one another in order and amongst themselves
they compare their position, their power, their prosperity and
—this is the point—their gods. Jahweh comes alongside the
other gods. Is He one of them? Is He nothing in comparison to
them? Is He greater than they?

When Jezebel becomes the wife of the king of Israel her
husband builds a temple of Baal in Samaria and sets up an
altar in it for Baal, not for Jahweh; 1 Kings 16: 32. This is no
longer Baal, the god of the land of Palestine with whom Jahweh
is identified; this is Baal, the Tyrian state-god to whom Jahweh

is and remains opposed. The fact that this Baal cult quickly disappeared does not matter: the fact remains that Jahweh henceforth is subject to comparison with the other gods, and soon to the company of the small gods of neighbouring states are added the world gods of the great powers, especially of Babylon. The problem of polytheism is arising. There are only three possible solutions: either a polytheistic Pantheon with clearly defined hierarchy, in which Jahweh would be allocated one of the lowest places, or atheism in which all gods would simply disappear, or monotheism, and then how will Jahweh fare? And what will lead to the right solution? *The answer is history.*

25. JAHWEH THE GOD OF HISTORY

1. In Amos we find a series of seven similar prophecies of doom of which the last, the severest, the most detailed and the most urgent is addressed to Israel; 1: 3—2: 3, 6-16. They refer to six neighbouring peoples and, as we have said, conclude with Israel. What is the point of intimating doom to neighbouring peoples before Israel at Bethel? No prophet speaks into the air. The only reasonable explanation is that there were representatives of these neighbouring peoples there present at the festival of Jahweh in Bethel. From the standpoint of polytheism that is quite understandable and legitimate. At home the Moabite worships Kamos, the Ammonite Melek and the Aramaean Rimmon, but why should he not go to Bethel to worship Jahweh in the land of Jahweh? Now suddenly Jahweh through His messenger Amos addresses the people of Moab and Ammon and of Aram and tells them that their fates also are decreed by His will. Jahweh makes Himself master of the sphere of history. He is not only the God of Israel. "Are ye better than these kingdoms? Is your border greater than their border?" 6: 2. "Have not I brought up Israel out of the land of Egypt and the Philistines from Kaphtor and the Aramaeans from Kir?" 9: 7. *Jahweh is Lord of the peoples and of their fates.*

2. Here one must pause a little longer, for this confession that Jahweh is master of the destinies of the peoples and occupies the field of history as His own, when one thinks of it carefully, dismisses all earlier, lesser and inadequate confessions as sun melts snow and makes way for a whole crop of new applications and consequences. That is what happens in the free unrestrained world of logical thinking. In the light of this confession all gods disappear and even the name Jahweh pales. Only God exists: and God is God to whom all kingdoms and all men owe their existence, their prosperity and their future, who stands over against all men indiscriminately, in power, goodness and intimacy: one God and one body of mankind. History, shackled as it is to tradition, knows nothing of such pure imperturbable logic in the consequences of the confession. History is held back by what has been handed down, restricted to easy stages, fulfilled out of the struggles of the new with the old, characterized by the dull confused conflict of imperfect insights.

3. It is worth finding out, by a study of the message of Amos as the earliest literary prophet, just how laboriously and timidly the revelation that Jahweh is the God of history—which logically would lead immediately to belief in the one God and to a doctrine of this one God as the Creator of the universe, lord of nature and ruler of the world—how laboriously that revelation seeks to assert itself.

a) Throughout Amos the situation is still that Israel stands in a particular relationship to Jahweh. "You only have I known of all the families of the earth, therefore I will visit upon you all your iniquities", 3: 2. On the one side stands Jahweh, on the other the earth (soil, arable land, אֲדָמָה). The earth has different peoples on it, related to one another and therefore called families (מִשְׁפָּחָה), v. I. Here two things are striking: the designation arable land for the earth and the designation (related) families for the peoples. Are the roaming tribes of the wilderness excepted and is the reckoning confined to a small number of peoples which, like Moab, Ammon, Aram, and Edom, are, because of the tradition of the patriarchs (Gen. 19: 30-38, 25: 25 would be examples while others have not been preserved) considered to be related? And what of the Philistines and Phoenicians mentioned in the series of prophecies of doom? Have they been added not because of relatedness but because of neighbourhood? However that may be, the point is that here the earth and its complement of peoples is still not considered in its entirety, not even according to the dimensions that were known in Amos' time. Jahweh is concerned with a group of peoples only, not with all. Among these peoples, however, He wills to know only Israel and to have to do only with Israel. It is significant that it does not say, as modern scholars have assumed, "only Israel has He chosen". It is further significant that the dealings which Jahweh wills to have with Israel take shape in judgment, in punishment for Israel's iniquities. The context of the historical connexion is an ethical context: in it the concern is with right and wrong behaviour.

b) The situation therefore is this; Jahweh is concerned with several peoples. His sphere of influence stretches beyond Israel. But this sphere is neither boundless and absolute, nor is it defined by any actual marks other than the contingencies of history. The sphere of Jahweh is not fixed but growing, and this growth depends entirely on historical circumstances. Jahweh the tribal God is on the way to becoming the God of mankind; but in the interim He remains the God of a group of peoples (those that matter to Israel). Prophets are not systematic theologians with thoughts coming in clear logical sequence, they are men with imperfect confessions limited and conditioned by history.

c) One thing above all is important. Jahweh, who is the God of the peoples, emerges from imprisonment in the context of nature and its gifts into the sphere of history and its judgment. Not blessing but justice is here the watchword. As once the men of Israel were a community before Jahweh bound by obligation to friendly—that is to say, just and brotherly[70]—behaviour among themselves, so also the peoples round about Israel, be they small or great, are all bound by obligation to reciprocate friendly—that is to say, just and brotherly—conduct before the judgment seat of Jahweh. The Tyrians have "remembered not the brotherly covenant", 1: 9, but have acted with savage cruelty; therefore they deserve punishment. The Edomites "have pursued their brother with the sword", 1: 11, and did cast off all pity, 1: 11; therefore they deserve punishment. The Israelites "sell the righteous for gold" and "turn aside the rights of the poor", 2: 6, 7; that is to Jahweh no less a fault; therefore they deserve punishment.

4. All of this is a return in a new context and with greater depth to the old covenant-revelation of Moses. The idea of a nature god is abolished. Jahweh is the God of the peoples. He is the God of history. He is the God of justice, social justice among individuals and political justice amongst the peoples. *Jahweh, God of history and of justice, is the God of punishment.*

26. GOD AND ELECTION

1. If Jahweh is the God of Israel and at the same time the God of other peoples, in what relation does Israel stand to the peoples? "What advantage then hath the Jew?" Rom. 3: 1. In Amos we read "You only have I known of all the families of the earth". One feels the matter is not covered by this expression. It is too incidental and arbitrary. In its place comes the other more fitting statement: Jahweh has chosen Israel.

2. Election occurs in the Old Testament in a double sense. There is election by Israel, for which Joshua 24: 14-24 is the classic passage: "therefore we also will serve (worship) the Lord; for—he is our God", v. 18. One should not minimize the value of this Joshua passage because it happens to be the only one. For it is as important as it is unique. It is a synopsis of the Elohist's theology and of his conception of history. Israel's fathers served other gods, 24: 2. Then Jahweh fetched Abraham, caused Israel to spring from him, freed them from bondage in Egypt and led them to Canaan: and now Israel decides for Jahweh and chooses (24: 15, 22) Him for their God.

3. Occasionally election is made by Jahweh and Israel together or by Jahweh: Jahweh and Israel together choose Israel's king, 2 Sam. 16: 18; Jahweh chooses Abraham, Neh. 9: 7; Aaron, Ps. 105: 26; David, Ps. 78: 70; Solomon, 1 Chron. 28: 5, 10; 29: 1; Zerubbabel, Hagg. 2: 23; people who may burn incense before Him, Num. 16: 7; men who may dwell in His courts, Ps. 65: 4; priests, 1 Sam. 2: 28; the king at any time, Deut. 17: 15; the priestly tribe, Deut. 18: 5; 21: 5; His holy city, 1 Kings 8: 16; His cult places (19 times in Deuteronomy and 10 times elsewhere). Jahweh chooses Jacob and Israel for His peculiar treasure, Ps. 135: 4; He has chosen not the tribe of Ephraim but chosen the tribe of Judah, Ps. 78: 67-68; He chooses what Israel mocks, that which will make them shudder, Isa. 66: 4. Because of the diversity of the objects of Jahweh's choice the concept is for long in a state of flux. Theological words which have hardened into fundamental principles are never altered so freely. The last two examples in particular illustrate that. It is only after 721 B.C. that it is possible to say that Ephraim was not chosen but rejected (מָאַס). If the election of Israel had been a basic idea, one would hardly have found this incidental remark in a Psalm.

4. Israel's Election by Jahweh. While Deuteronomy is very fond of the word choose (30 of the 153 instances are found there and other instances are to be assigned to the deuteronomist) and the prophets from Amos to Jeremiah are quite ignorant of its theological usage, with the beginning of the Exile it really comes into prominence: "The two families which the Lord did choose and did cast off", Jer. 33: 24; "in the day when (in Egypt) I chose Israel", Ezek. 20: 5. But the chief exponent of Jahweh's election of Israel is Deutero-Isaiah: "Jacob whom I have chosen", 41: 8; "I choose thee, I do not cast thee away", 41: 9; "Israel, whom I have chosen", 44: 1; "Jeshurun whom I have chosen", 44: 2; "the Holy One of Israel who hath chosen thee", 49: 7. When the children of Israel were inclined to believe they had been cast off, when in fact the people were saying they were cast off, Jer. 33: 24, then they are assured of the fact that Jahweh has chosen them. Belief in election may be older (though there is no good evidence); certainly now it becomes important and it is now emphasized. It is emphasized particularly because (and this is noteworthy) in Old Testament proclamation election is not something indestructible. Election stands side by side with rejection, Isa. 41: 9. There is to be found even the self-contradictory idea of a second election after the first has broken down and been replaced by rejection: "The Lord has compassion on Jacob and chooses Israel again", Isa. 14: 1; "Jahweh chooses again Jerusalem", Zech. 1: 17.

5. Jahweh's choosing of Israel is a phrase which in the Old Testament does not play as great a part as is often supposed. Its place is where the God of Israel becomes God of the peoples and the question of Israel's privilege arises.

27. GOD OF THE PEOPLES AND GOD OF THE WORLD

1. The disappearance of the northern Kingdom means for Judah that there falls to her and to her tiny people the whole inheritance of tradition and obligation and expectation and promise connected with the name Israel. From now on, Judah is the people of Israel. But does Judah in exile remain the people of Israel? Judah as a people ceases to be; Judah as a community, as the community of Jewry, begins, and this community is now the people of Israel. All the promises of Jahweh to His covenant partner Israel pass now to this community. But though these promises remain the same, the community itself is not the same as the old people of Israel nor is Jahweh the old

God. *Now, since the Exile, the God of Israel is—God*. This must be briefly demonstrated.

2. The changed conditions created for Israel by the Exile are obvious. The people are in a strange and unclean land, Ps. 137: 4; they can no longer perform the sacrifices and rites which belong to the altar; they are in a land where strange and mighty gods hold sway and where theirs is the cult; they are no longer held together by ties of homeland and kinship but each man can choose for himself to which cult he will attach himself. This last point is the crucial one, for it means the transformation of Jewry. Israel ceases to be a people, to which and to the religion of which one belongs without being questioned about it, and becomes a community which owes its existence to the fact that individually men declare that they want to belong to it and to its God. In place of membership by birth and residential qualifications comes membership by free and responsible resolve. That man is a Jew who wants to be a Jew, though he could just as well attach himself to the Babylonian community and its impressive cult. And whoever connects himself with the Jewish community, takes on a whole series of duties—circumcision, prayer, fasting, the observation of laws pertaining to food and of the Sabbath, the payment of the cult tax, and disdain of others. This community is centred not on a new Temple somewhere in Babylon, however, but on the synagogue, on many synagogues. The one community of those exiles faithful to Jahweh consists of many small local communities: and each local community has its own synagogue: each synagogue has its meetings, its rolls of Scripture, its expositions, its instructors and its pupils. The Temple is replaced by the School, sacrifice by Scripture, priest by Rabbi, pilgrimage by Sabbath and Sabbath walk to the Synagogue.

3. This type of worship is quite unlike that which was offered at the Temple, it is more regular, more instructive, more spiritual; above all it is something quite different from the Temple offices. For that reason it can remain undisturbed even when in Jerusalem the Temple and the Temple cult are again operating. The synagogue was meant to be a substitute for the Temple. But when the Temple is rebuilt the synagogue does not simply disappear, it remains. Temple and synagogue, priest and scribe, sacrifice and exposition go on side by side. The Temple serves only the Jews in Jerusalem; the synagogue serves Jewry throughout the world. The synagogue internationalized the Jews. It does not matter where the Jew lives. He can build a synagogue anywhere and set its face towards Jerusalem, Dan 6: 10. God hears his prayers and marks his piety anywhere, since God is the God of the whole world.

4. At the very time that Judah is homeless and the glory of Jahweh departs from Jerusalem and no one knows where it goes, Ezek. 8: 4, 9: 3, 10: 4, 18-22, 11: 22-23, and when the power of the mighty Babylonian gods has to all appearances proved itself far superior to the power of Jahweh—in that day when Jahweh's cause seems utterly lost, the community of Jahweh, in a strange land and in the hands of strange gods, recognizes that all other gods are nothing; Isa. 41: 24. It becomes clear that Jahweh is the Creator, 40: 12-14; Lord of nature, 41: 17-20; master of the stars, 40: 26; director of the course of history, 40: 21-25; announcer of the future and fulfiller of what is promised, 41: 21-24, 44: 6-8;—in short, the only God. He is God *simpliciter,* "that ye may know and believe me and understand that I am he; before me there was no God formed, neither shall there be after me", 43: 10. No one would speak of Jahweh any longer were it not that in all living theology ancient tradition is strong. *But wherever the name Jahweh occurs now it is God who is meant, the one and only God, or simply God.*

These paragraphs briefly outline the historical course of the Old Testament revelation in so far as it is theology in the strictest sense—that is to say, revelation concerning God Himself. We pass now to speak of God's works.

V. GOD IN HIS WORKS

28. GOD CREATES THE WORLD

THE world is a created world. It has not always been there, neither did it come into being of its own accord; it has been created. God has created it: "In the beginning God created the heaven and the earth" (that is to say the "world", Gen. 1: 1).

The thought that God created the world is of late date, however. It is not a promise but a deduction from the Old Testament revelation. For that reason we find it in three forms of varying degrees of clarity.

1. Jahweh makes, עָשָׂה, earth and heaven and as a potter fashions man and breathes into his nostrils. That is an ancient piece of myth, borrowed from an earlier day (without qualms) since only the fact is important.

2. God makes, קָנָה, the heaven and the earth, Gen. 14: 19, 22; the people of Israel, Ex. 15: 16, Deut. 32: 6; his congregation, Ps. 74: 2; the mountain land of Palestine, Ps. 78: 54; the reins of the faithful, Ps. 139: 13; wisdom, Prov. 8: 22; the earth is full of the creatures, קִנְיָן, of God, which He has made, Ps. 104: 24. In all these passages the making or forming is still a work on which He has expended care and trouble, and through which He makes Himself the possessor of things. These things are reckoned more as individual things than in terms of a complete scheme of creation.[71]

3. The correct and theologically sound word for create is first found in the word בָּרָא. Only when we reach Gen. 1: 1—2: 4 do we have a careful theological and to any extent satisfactory account of the matter. God creates here no longer with His hand or with industrious carefulness. He says "let be" and it is so. Creation then is by the word, but one may not simply assume here the theological doctrine of the Word of God. That is not yet there; only the verbal form "God said" is there and this limitation must be faithfully observed. Nevertheless the passage is really and truly speaking about the creation of the world. It is not an individual thing that is created; it is everything. Step by step creation proceeds and always the prior is necessary to make possible the existence of the later. Creation is once and for all, since plants and animals and men are given by the Creator the gift of fertility in order that the species may remain even when the first representatives die. Whatever owes its existence to God's creative word is well created and as a whole everything is very good. And it is for our time, for man's time and as the beginning of the life of this earth of ours that the whole is created; God's creation is our world. Creation, in sun, moon and stars, serves for the fixing of times of worship; the Sabbath has its origin in cosmogony, the true cult is in fact the object of creation. It is no enigmatical impenetrable affair: the Creator works according to a purpose and pattern; there is no more rational page in the Bible than that which contains the account of creation.

The all-important factor remains this:—God stands there wholly transcendent, in self-evident omnipotence. The greatness of His might in bringing this creation into being is neither wondered at (as it is in Psalm 8) nor even declared. That did not require to be put into words; and when one compares the countless passages in the Old Testament where God's acts of creation are objects of wonder and marvel, נוֹרָאוֹת and נִפְלָאוֹת, then one realizes that the first account of creation is in fact a "last" account.

To this must be added two things. First, creation is set here in conscious and clear connexion with the whole course of revelation and lawgiving to the people of God. The myths of Paradise and the Fall are put aside: there is no gulf between Gen. 2: 4a and 5: 1: indeed, were it not that the starting point, the creation, is a universal and the goal, the holy people of the holy God (Lev. 19: 2) a particular, even the flood myth would be set aside. As it is, however, it serves a good purpose in making the transition from the context of mankind to the context of a people. In creation everything is good; peace reigns, man and beast feed only on plants. How the trouble comes we are not told, but the flood brings to an end the glory of creation. Fear and dread is upon all creatures, Gen. 9: 2; the taking of flesh is permitted (though it is not stated, it must be assumed that from now on beasts of prey feed on the others); mankind as such remains bound to God by only one vague obligation. "At the hand of man" (the word here means almost but not quite non-Jew) "even at the hand of every man's brother will I

require the life of man", Gen. 9: 5. For the rest, God, though He
is the creator of the whole world, is only concerned as yet with
the Jews. From Noah the story of the race passes quickly over
Shem to Abraham, and of his children, Ishmael and Isaac, only
Isaac is of importance and even he only with a view to Jacob.
Noah, Abraham and Moses represent the threefold narrowing of
the covenant together with the threefold unfolding of the law
until in the Holy Land a holy people knows how it should serve
its holy God. This is the one important perspective in the
understanding of the creation. The creation of the world by
God in the Old Testament is no independent fact; creation is
intended to be the opening of history. The Old Testament
history of creation does not answer the question "How did the
world come into being?" with the answer: "God created it",
but answers the question "From where does the history of God's
people derive its meaning?" with the answer: "God has given
the history of His people its meaning through creation." In
other words, *the Creation in the Old Testament does not belong
to the sphere of natural science but to the history of man.*

The second perspective which is necessary for the understanding of the creation story may be expressed in this way:
the account of creation in Gen. 1: 1—2: 4a is not a final declara-
tion; it is an announcement. God rests on the seventh day.
Will this rest last for ever, and if not, what will God do when
it comes to an end? In six days the world was created and then
there was a day of rest. That is symbolic of man's week of six
working days and then the Sabbath. And are man's week and
man's Sabbath an end and purpose in themselves or are they
in turn symbols? And if so, of what are they symbols? The
answer can only be—a "world-week" with six normal periods
and then the world's Sabbath. Will this be six periods of a
thousand years and then will the thousand years' Sabbath be
the thousand years' kingdom of Revelation 20: 1-6?

The account of creation is part of a history which is characterized by figures and dates. A purely chronological concern, so
that one would know for instance what year one had to write
as a date, is hardly probable. Another question is far more
important and therefore much earlier—the motive of this
arithmetic: how long will the world last? The exodus from
Egypt, that great act of redemption, took place in the year
2666[72] from the creation of the world. That is approximately
two-thirds of a world era of four thousand years. At almost the

year four thousand one is in the time of the book of Daniel, which clearly announces the end of the world.[73] There are completed by then four periods of a thousand years. Is this coincidence or intention? As there is a division of the duration of the world into seven periods, so also there is a division into four, and this seems to underlie the dates of the priestly material. In other words, the creation is not the beginning of an incalculable time sequence about which nobody knows and about the length of which nobody even asks: creation is the first in a series of events which together make up a definite world age, so that at any point in the process one can ask when the end and the fulfilment will come. To the beginning there corresponds an end, to creation there corresponds a consummation, to the "very good" here a "perfectly glorious" there: they belong together. *Creation in Old Testament theology is an eschatological concept.* The fact that God is the creator of the world means that He compasses the complete time process, ruling, determining and completing all ages. That is why He is called the first and the last, Isa. 44: 6.

29. GOD PROTECTS THE WORLD

The Old Testament is familiar with the doctrine of Providence in two forms. God upholds the world by struggle and by direction. While for us the idea of providence is an inference and deduction from the idea of creation, in the Old Testament providence is the earlier attested. The Old Testament revelation always proceeds from the immediate and given circumstances backwards to that which inference shows is a reasonable and imperative presupposition of these given circumstances.

This then is given: that the stability of the visible world is continually menaced by the sea, the original waters. Moreover this sea includes the storehouse of the rains, the danger and the menace of which were particularly experienced on the lowland plains of Babylon. Here belong those mythical ideas of their power which also impressed the minds of the west Asiatic hill peoples. When in Genesis 1: 2 we read: Darkness was upon the face of the deep and the spirit of God (it should be translated) "hovered trembling" upon the face of the waters. And God said, Let there be light: and (then really) there was light, that is the remains of a myth which told that the gods in battle with Chaos wrested from it the theatre of human events. And when it is related that the Creator God bid the waters be gathered together into one place that the dry land, the scene of human life and history, might appear (Gen. 1: 9) that likewise is a last faint echo of the creation myth, according to which God wrests the dry land from the deep in dread combat. More colourful and more substantial traces of the myth occur. God shut up the sea with doors, prescribed for it a boundary, set bars and doors and said: "hitherto shalt thou come but no further": Job 38: 8-11, Prov. 8: 29; Ps. 104: 6-9; to end the Flood "God made a wind to pass over the earth, and the waters assuaged; the foundations also of the deep and the windows of heaven were stopped", Gen. 8: 1-2.

Even so God's pledge was required that never again would a Flood occur which would destroy the earth. God's explicit pledge was required because the waters which fled at God's rebuke (Ps. 104: 7) permanently surround and lie in wait for the earth on its uttermost edge, Ps. 139: 9. Here too a lively relic of polytheism projects itself into the Old Testament. Only where there are many gods can there be the idea of creation where one god wrests the land from the others with rebuke and in combat. Then also it is understood how the displaced waters should constantly have a mind for revenge and return. The world is constantly threatened by enemy powers. This tension cannot be appreciated however where only one single God, without opponents or limits, calls the world into being of His own free will and plans it and launches it according to His own mind. Here there is no place for tension or conflict.

The doctrine of God as the upholder of the world in conflict is taken quite seriously however. The sea, outlawed from the dry land, threatens the world and as the enemy of God would cover it and destroy it. The waters of the sea roar and are troubled, so that the mountains shake with the swelling thereof, but the God of Jacob is our high tower, Ps. 46: 3. He rules the pride of the sea: when the waves thereof arise He stills them, Ps. 89: 9. He has placed the sand for the bounds of the sea for ever; though the waves are stormy they cannot prevail; though they toss themselves, yet can they not pass over it, Jer. 5: 22. All that is neither poetical nor allegorical nor is it mere personification of an occurrence in nature. It is intended to be understood literally. God has won the world by fighting. Hostile, rebellious powers dispute it. The whole time-process stands under the threat of the clash and of annihilation by destroyers. God is engaged in a constant struggle for the defence of His work (see

Isa. 17: 12-14; Jer. 5: 22; Hab. 3: 10; Nah. 1: 4; Ps. 74: 13;
89: 10; 104: 7; Job 38: 8-11; Isa. 51: 9; Ps. 89: 11; Job 26: 12).
God upholds the world amid strife. *Here then is the place where
the picture of God the conquering hero belongs.* "Thou hast a
mighty arm; strong is thy hand and high is thy right hand",
Ps. 89: 13; "put on thy strength, O arm of the Lord", Isa.
51: 9. When Israel rejoices in her God who rebuked the Red
Sea and led them through the depths as through pasture land,
Ps. 106: 9 and other passages, it is not merely thanks for a time
dimly remembered, it is an expression of real assurance in the
power of God to help in present danger.

30. GOD UPHOLDS THE WORLD

God who created the world also maintains it. He gives it the
seasons, for He has made summer and winter, Ps. 74: 17, and
the sequence of day and night, for the day is His, the night
also is His, Ps. 74: 16. He makes the sun to rule by day,
Ps. 136: 8 and the moon and the stars to rule by night,
Ps. 136: 9. He bringeth out the host of the stars by number;
He calleth them all by name; and not one is lacking or
remains behind, Isa. 40: 26. This last statement shows how
the Old Testament revelation is set in a world where sun,
moon, stars and many other powers and phenomena of nature
are independent forces and gods. The God of the Old Testament, however, has put them all under Himself and made them
obey His commands. He it is who blesses the fruit of the body
and the fruit of the ground, corn and wine and oil, the increase
of the kine and the young of the flock, Deut. 7: 13. All fertility
comes from Him and there are no gods or spirits of fertility. It
is God alone who likewise at creation provides seed and fruit for
plants and beasts and men, Gen. 1: 11, 22, 28, and thus by
propagation He maintains the life He has called into existence.
He keeps away all sickness, Deut. 7: 15 and He alone is the
physician, Ex. 15: 26; the spirits of sickness of Babylon and
the gods of healing of Egypt are set aside; God alone is the
supporter of life. He kills and He makes alive, 1 Sam. 2: 6. The
underworld and destruction are also before Him, Prov. 15: 11.

The concept which in the Old Testament is particularly used
to present God as the sustainer of the world is the concept of
time. To-day we would answer the question of how God
maintains the world by pointing to the laws of nature: the
Hellenic world would have said by means of order, by means

of the cosmos; the Old Testament answers by means of time. Jahweh, our God, gives rain in its season, Jer. 5: 24. I will give you rains in their season, and the land shall yield her increase and the trees of the field shall yield their fruit, Lev. 26: 4; Deut. 11: 14; 28: 12. The tree—thanks to God—brings forth its fruit in its season, Ps. 1: 3. God gives all things their meat in due season, Ps. 145: 15. He has His time when He will work, Ps. 119: 126. He appoints the time when the wild goats of the rock bring forth, Job 39: 1. To everything there is—according to God's appointment—a season, Eccles. 3: 1, 17. He leads forth the signs of the Zodiac in their season, Job 38: 35, and the times of the faithful are in His hand, Ps. 31: 15.

God is the Lord of time. He has according to His plan and purpose established the order of sequence of things, how long they shall last, when their turning point shall be, and their end. Day and night come in their season, Jer. 33: 20. "I the Lord will hasten it in its time", Isa. 60: 22. There is a time of vengeance, Jer. 51: 6; a time of need, Isa. 33: 2; a time of misfortune, Amos 5: 13; of visitation, Jer. 8: 12; of healing, Jer. 8: 15; 14: 19; of terror, Ezek. 35: 5; of punishment, 21: 30, of the heathen, that is the time of judgment of the heathen, Ezek. 30: 3; for everything there is the acceptable time, the time God wills for it, Isa. 49: 8; Ps. 69: 13.

The world and all it contains, even the tiniest thing in it, is in good order and in safety, for everything has its time, is provided for, determined and defined. Everything is in God's time and therefore in God's will. God is Lord of the World, its guide and its sustainer.

31. GOD SHAKES THE WORLD

From the position reached in the preceding chapter it is but a short step to a world order completely inflexible and predetermined. One religion which bases itself on the Old Testament has followed this path. But the Old Testament revelation follows an entirely different one. God is so superior to His creation that He does not need it. He can destroy it just as easily as He can create it. The Creator is in no way bound by His creation. He can disturb His order, change His will, make an end of time, destroy His creation, withdraw His work, supersede His world with another. God is God of all ages, not just of time; of all worlds, not just of the world; of all eternities, not just of eternity.

While the earth remaineth, seedtime and harvest shall not cease, is God's assurance (Gen. 8: 22) to Noah when he leaves the ark and God smells the sweet savour of the sacrifices he makes. The earth has its appointed number of days but then it passes away, and until that day it owes its continuance not to any fixed law of nature but to the sheer grace of God. He roars from Zion and mourning covers the whole land, Amos 1: 2. He visits transgressions upon the transgressors and smites all houses, Amos 3: 14 f. He passes through the midst of His people and the voice of wailing is heard everywhere, Amos 5: 17. He causes the sun to go down at noon and darkens the earth in the clear day, Amos 8: 9. The mountains are molten under Him and the valleys are cleft, Mic. 1: 4. The heavens tremble and the earth is shaken out of her place, Isa. 13: 13; the mountains tremble and the hills move to and fro, Jer. 4: 24; the stars of heaven do not give their light, the sun is darkened in his going forth and the moon does not cause her light to shine, Isa. 13: 10. The whole of the Old Testament is full of this idea and it expresses it in ever new images. But it would be a mistake to treat these as merely rhetorical images. They are expressions of the truth that God is fearful (§ 15), a God at hand and a God far off, filling the heaven and the earth, Jer. 23: 23 ff., and a watchful God, Jer. 1: 12; 1 Kings 18: 27. God is ever ready to strike and where His holiness is neglected His wrath streams forth to punish and to destroy. *Since it is God's world in which man lives, the life of man is constantly and fundamentally uncertain.*

32. GOD DIRECTS THE COURSE OF HISTORY

One may treat the Old Testament as the document of revelation of a religion; one has to note, however, that it is no systematic document, on the other hand it is a document whose main subject from beginning to end is history. Of 39 books, 14 are pure history books: and to these could be added the books of Jonah and Ruth. In all the prophetic writings, and even in the apocalyptic writings of the book of Daniel, history is the subject; so also in the book of Lamentations and in a large number of the Psalms. The Song of Songs, the book of Proverbs and Job are the only possible exceptions and the book of Ecclesiastes is doubtful. The Old Testament knows only of a God who is active in history.[74]

What is history? It is the course of things on the human

plane with its innumerable individual acts related to one
another, by their relatedness making for greatness and from
their mutual relationship gaining their meaning and value.
What is important in history is important because it affects
something else; what is in itself unimportant has its value in
having the closest possible association with something else.
Two further characteristics must now be noted. The first is
this: *history moves towards a goal*. In the classic conclusion of
the elohistic historiography in Joshua 24: 1-28 and in the last
sentence there we read how Israel, reminded of all that Jahweh
had done for her, decides to serve Jahweh. The people is then
bound by the covenant and a stone is erected as a memorial
of what took place. "So Joshua sent the people away, every
man unto his inheritance", 24: 28. The covenant is concluded,
God has His people, the people its inheritance; the goal has been
reached.

The same thing is to be found in the priestly writings. Moses
fixes the borders of the lands east of Jordan, Josh. 13: 15-32;
Eleazar and Joshua fix them in the land west of Jordan, Josh.
14: 1-5; 15: 1-12, 20; 16: 4-8; 17: 2; 18: 11-20; 19: 1-31, the
cities of refuge are appointed; then comes the conclusion, Josh.
21: 41-45: "There failed not aught of any good thing which the
Lord had spoken unto the house of Israel; all came to pass."
The goal had been reached, the process had come to a happy
ending. Whoever reads these two passages, the one from the
time of the earliest prophets, the other from the time of the
Exile—whoever reads these with the eye of the theologian will
perceive in both the same lesson: history is movement towards
a goal, not a mere purposeless and endless series of events.

He will perceive also the other characteristic of the biblical
concept of history: *History is under God's management*. He sets
the process in motion by His promise. He sets its limits according to His will. He watches over it and beholds its course, Isa.
18: 4. He intercepts it when the situation demands it. All history
has its source in God and takes place for God. The whole Old
Testament is an endorsement in different ways of what has
just been said. The short story of Ruth ends with the genealogy
of David, bringing it into the main stream of divinely ordained
history. The lesson of the book of Jonah is that God purposes
the conversion of all the heathen. The postscript written to the
books of the Kings gives the work an ending which speaks of
hope in the grace of God. The canon of the book of Judges,

2: 6—3: 6, shows God training and educating His people, and
all the conflicting stories are pressed into this framework. The
two books of Chronicles, which say not a word about Creation,
the Fall, the Flood, the Tower of Babel, the stories of the
Patriarchs and the covenant at Sinai, lead on to the establishment of the true cult, the preparation and completion in Ezra
and Nehemiah lead on to the beginning of the true cult under
divine law. God chose David His trusted servant to feed Jacob
His people, Ps. 78: 70 ff. God gave them the lands of the nations
that they might keep His statutes, Ps. 105: 44 ff: "gather us
from among the nations that we may praise thee", Ps. 106: 47.
God is the God of history; history is His work, His will, His
revelation; "that they may know that I am the Lord", Ezek. 6:
14 and 62 times besides. God "brings things about", as it says
in 1 Kings 12: 15 and 2 Chron. 10: 15; that is to say, He is
responsible for that disposition which fulfils the announcements
of the prophets.

The prophets are publishers of the divine will. However
varied their motives, their concerns and their commissions they
always speak of what God has done in past history, of His
judgment on events of present history and what He announces
for future history. The injunction to observant recipients of
revelation to lift up their heads to behold the coming of the
kingdom can be traced back to the prophetic message. In the
prophets the Day of the Lord (§ 56) becomes the epitome of
history, when all the past and all the future will be seen to run
together into one meaningful unity. In the prophets therefore
we find also an ideal comprehension of God as the Lord of
history. We find it above all in Isaiah, from whose day on it is
mostly implicit presupposition.

There is a work of the Lord, Isa. 5: 12. One can see the work
of His hands, 5: 12, 19. The Holy One of Israel has a plan, 5: 19.
The fact that the prophet's opponents ridicule these ideas shows
that the ideas are new and revealed through Isaiah. What God
does not will, shall not stand, it shall not come to pass, 7: 7,
8: 10; but what God wills shall certainly come to pass: for He
is one who does things and fashions them from afar, 22: 11.
Whoever resists His will is like "the saw that magnifies itself
against him that shapes it", like "the rod that shakes him that
lifts it up", 10: 15. The proof of the fact that God makes history
lies in this: that He intimates the future and announces what
shall happen, so that one recognizes the happenings when they

begin, 41: 22 ff; the gods cannot do that and therein are they shown to be no gods, 41: 23. Israel is God's witness that He declares things to come and no one reverses them. "Only I have declared and I have saved", 43: 8-13. "Who, as I, doth tell the things that are at hand? Have I not declared them unto thee of old and shewed it?" 44: 7 ff. Only from the mouth of God goeth truth, a word that shall not return, 45: 23.

Between the assertions of Isaiah about the God who fashions history and those of Deutero-Isaiah about the same God there stands the sermon of Deuteronomy. It is historical preaching. Jahweh your God will fight for you as He did when He helped you in Egypt and in the wilderness, "where thou hast seen how that the Lord thy God bare thee, as a man doth bear his son, in all the way that ye went", Deut 1: 30 ff. History is the revelation of God, the fulfilment of His intimations, the proof that He is in and for Israel, a God that hides Himself, a Saviour, the God of history.

33. GOD GUIDES MAN

We shall say more in the section on anthropology (§ 41) about the belief that a man is important in the sight of God only as part of mankind, the individual is important only as a member of the people. Here we mention it because it explains why the attention of the Old Testament is directed so much to God's dealings with His people and His community. The picture changes only very gradually. First of all a few chosen individuals emerge: Enoch whom God takes, Gen. 5: 24; Noah who is blameless in his generation, Gen. 6: 9; Abraham of whom God wills to make a great nation, Gen. 12: 1; Moses who is to lead the people of God into the covenant; then there is Joshua, the judges, the kings and the prophets, all of whom God requires in His service. The next stage is where we have individuals in large numbers; nameless, inconspicuous individuals. The people, whose members because of their nationality have a place in the service of God, is replaced by the community of the faithful who acknowledge God through the decision which each has to make for himself. Ezekiel and the situation in his time marks the turning point. If Ezekiel does not warn the sinner, God requires the sinner's blood at the prophet's hand. If Ezekiel warns the sinner and the sinner does not turn from his wickedness, the prophet has nevertheless delivered his own soul. Again if Ezekiel does not warn a righteous man whom God permits to stumble, God requires his blood at the prophet's hand, but if he warns him and he does not sin, then the righteous man shall surely live and the prophet has delivered his soul; Ezek. 3: 18-21. Here everything depends upon the decision of the individual. Here a man stands immediately and individually before his gracious God. Here the "I" of the Psalms has its roots.

But the gospel of the guiding hand of God is older than this change. It is the main characteristic of the very ancient Joseph-saga. His father's favourite and object of his brothers' wicked jealousy, Joseph has a remarkable career. He is sold in the slave market, he gains rapid promotion as a servant, he is falsely accused and imprisoned, suffers the agony of being forgotten by his companions but becomes in time adviser to Pharaoh, he is then directly responsible for the preservation of the land and forgiving saviour of his father, his brothers and the whole future people of God. The brilliance of Joseph's career is not attributed to his own virtue, however, but to God's guidance. "God meant it for good, to bring to pass, as it is this day, to save much people alive", Gen. 50: 20. Perhaps an even older example can be found in the biography of David. There was that day when David fleeing from his own son has to face Shimei's battery of stones and refuses to permit his officers to harm him. "Let him alone and let him curse: for the Lord hath bidden him. It may be that the Lord will look on the wrong done unto me, and that the Lord will requite me good for his cursing of me this day", 2 Sam. 16: 11 ff. Here about the year 1000 B.C. a man in the Old Testament knows that he is led by God. It is not by chance that the Psalm "The Lord is my shepherd" was later attributed to him. The Jahwist also knows of faith in God's guiding. In his writings God says to Abram: "Get thee out of thy country, and from thy kindred, and from thy father's house, unto the land that I will shew thee", Gen. 12: 1. Old Testament revelation is mediated not only through history, therefore, but also through individual histories. From these the Hebrew who heard them learned and the modern reader still learns that God's guiding hand is to be found in the life of the individual.

There are, as we have said, first of all the great figures whose stories bear witness to God's guidance or who, like David, themselves acknowledge it. These include Enoch, Noah, Abraham, Jacob, Joseph, Moses, Joshua, David and the great

prophets. The prophet's call is divine guidance: Amos 7: 15;
Hos. 1: 2, 4, 6; 3: 1, Isa. 6: 9; 7: 3; Jer. 1: 4-7; Ezek. 2: 3.
Development thereafter is along two lines of different range.
One line, the shorter and narrower, leads to passionate argument with the God who guides. God's guidance in the Old
Testament does not imply the complete subjugation of man
nor the suppression of his will. In fact, as the prophets show, it
effects a conscription of all the human, all the individual
powers and gifts of the person being guided. The guidance of
God creates a life on a higher plane. One sees that clearly in
the words of the prophets. Even where they expressly designate
the word they speak "the word of Jahweh" and therefore
inspired (§ 37) their human style is not abandoned nor their
human outlook. Even in the word of Jahweh which he delivers,
Isaiah differs from Jeremiah and from Amos.

Not only so, but divine guidance does not mean the suppression of human will. God shows the fall of Israel to Amos in a
vision, the prophet protests and intercedes and God ceases.
The Lord repented. It shall not be! saith the Lord, Amos 7: 1-6.
Theologically Abraham's intercession for Sodom, Gen. 18: 16-
33, belongs to this category also. Though in these instances
intercession is for a third party, there are also examples of
supplication on the person's own behalf. The godly man
wrestles with God's guidance: "Thou hast made me a laughing
stock". The fearful revolt of the prophet Jeremiah (15: 10-21;
20: 7-18) is the forerunner of the book of Job, Job 31: 35 ff.,
and of Psalm 73; it is also the foreshadowing of what is almost
but not quite the disillusionment and renunciation of the pale
Ecclesiastes. The reason why the Old Testament could not
set aside the story of Jacob's wrestling, Gen. 32: 22-32, so
strange in its theology, is also to be found here.

The other line of development of the idea of guidance of the
individual reaches further and stretches out over a broad
plane. This is the line which leads from the lamentation poems
of Jeremiah[75] with their ring of personal piety to the Psalms of
complaint, prayer and trust. Here God is He who is concerned
for every detail of the individual's life. Everything comes from
His guidance, everything is laid in His hands and commended
to His sympathy. The godly are beset behind and before, He
understands their thought afar off and is acquainted with all
their ways; He leads the godly in the way everlasting, Ps. 139:
5, 2, 7, 24. The times of the godly are in God's hand, Ps. 31: 15;

God maketh poor, and maketh rich, bringeth low and lifteth up, killeth and maketh alive, 1 Sam. 2: 6 ff.; He keeps men from all evil, Ps. 121: 7, He leads them according to His plan. This great theme is found in every possible variation. The piety which has made the Psalter the world's hymnary and prayer-book is grounded in God's guidance—that piety which lives in the confidence that the godly under all circumstances and at all times (Ps. 73: 25 ff.) are hidden in God, out of whose mouth cometh good and evil, Lam. 3: 38.

VI. DIVINE REVELATION

34. REVELATION IN THE OLD TESTAMENT; THE ABSTRACT IDEA

Revelation implies for the Old Testament *the means God uses to make possible a knowledge of God for men.* In and by himself man does not have a knowledge of God: all knowledge of the kind must be granted to him by God, must be made known to him. This communication or notification where God is its author we call revelation. The Old Testament uses the following expressions: appear, נִרְאָה, Gen. 12: 7; make Himself known or recognized, הִתְוַדַּע, Num. 12: 6 and נוֹדַע, Ex. 6: 3 (here both expressions occur side by side: "I appeared unto Abraham, unto Isaac, and unto Jacob as El Shaddai but by my name Jahweh I did not make myself known to them": Ezek. 20: 5 "I made myself known unto them in the land of Egypt and swore unto them with uplifted hand: I am Jahweh your God"); shewed, made to know, הוֹדִיעַ ("God hath shewed thee all", Gen. 41: 39, "in the morning the Lord will shew who are his", Num. 16: 5), disclose Himself, reveal Himself, נִגְלָה ("because there God was revealed unto him", Gen. 35: 7); God comes to meet Balaam (וַיִּקָּר Num. 23: 3, 4.)

Concerning this revelation vocabulary then there are six things to note. 1. There is no one consistently used expression for revealing, rather there are several. 2. None of the words is a specifically theological word, they all have profane usages. 3. In order to know what the individual expressions mean, one must fix one's attention on their objects. One sees what (previously) was invisible, one comes to know what up till then was unknown: one discovers what was covered. Of these, the contrast between the hidden and the things that are revealed is the only one we find ever actually expressed, Deut. 29: 28. 4. Besides the words to which we have referred, which are not specifically theological but do have a certain solemnity by association, we find simple words like דִּבֶּר, speak, and אָמַר, say: "God spake all these words saying, I am the Lord thy God, which . . ." Ex. 20: 1. 5. Corresponding to this revelation vocabulary the words for receiving the revelation are רָאָה,

see; חָזָה, behold; שָׁמַע, hear, and particularly יָדַע, to perceive, understand, know. Wherever one of these verbs has a predicate of possible revelational content it can indicate revelation. יָדַע in particular very often means receive (a revelation), understand, apprehend something definite—any suggestion of asking or seeking or enquiring is excluded. This comes out very clearly in Ezek. 38: 23, "I make myself known in the eyes of many nations, נוֹדַעְתִּי, and they shall know"; cf. Ezek. 35: 11, 12, יָדְעוּ. 6. There is no suggestion anywhere in the Old Testament that the reception of revelation is dependent on any particular predisposition in man, faith or anything else.

35. GOD REVEALS HIMSELF IN HIS WORKS

God's works may be divided into five groups: *1*, the works which God has done at creation; *2*, the works which He goes on performing for the maintenance of the world; *3*, the works which He has done for His people; *4*, the works which He continues to do for His people and its members: *5*, the works which He will do for the final execution of His will. The effect of all these works is this: that whoever sees them, realizes the greatness of God's might. God reveals Himself therefore in His works.

1. "The heavens declare, סָפַר, the glory of God; and the firmament sheweth, הִגִּיד, his handywork", Ps. 19: 1. "Of old hast thou laid the foundation of the earth; and the heavens are the work of thy hands", Ps. 102: 25. *2.* "He that turneth the shadow of death into the morning and maketh the day dark with night, that calleth for the waters of the sea and poureth them out upon the face of the earth—the Lord is his name", Amos 5: 8. The remainder of the hymn is similar, the communication of a revelation. *3.* The Midianite knows that the Lord is greater than all gods, for He delivered Israel out of the hand of the Egyptians because they dealt so proudly against them, Ex. 18: 11. When the fire of the Lord fell and consumed the burnt offering and the wood and the stones and the dust and the water, then the people knew that the Lord, He is God, I Kings 18: 37-39. When God's people remember the answer that Balaam gave to Balak king of Moab, then can they know the righteous acts of the Lord, Mic. 6: 5. When Jahweh this once causes them to know His hand, הוֹדִיעַ, they shall know that His name is Jahweh, Jer. 16: 21. *4.* When Jahweh liberates Israel the Egyptians know that He is Jahweh, Ex. 7: 5. When

Israel receives the quails in the wilderness at even, then Israel knows that it was Jahweh that brought them out from the land of Egypt, Ex. 16: 6. When Naaman is cured by dipping himself seven times in Jordan he knows there is no God in all the earth but in Israel, 2 Kings 5: 14 f. When Jahweh gives King Cyrus the treasures of darkness Cyrus knows that it is Jahweh who has called him by his name, Isa. 45: 3. 5. When the Israelites may return home they will know that Jahweh is the one for whom one may wait and not be ashamed, Isa. 49: 23. When the slain lie round about the altar the Israelites will know the Lord, Ezek. 6: 13. When the false prophets disappear Israel will know that Jahweh is the Lord. When Israel becomes the least of the kingdoms Israel will know that Jahweh is God, Ezek. 29: 15 ff. The nations shall know that the house of Israel went into captivity for their iniquity, Ezek. 39: 23.

The dogma that God reveals Himself through His works, whether in nature or in history, is one attested by numerous examples. The content of the revelation is small. It amounts to not much more than the statement that Jahweh is God who governs the world according to His will, bestows His love on Israel, Deut. 11: 2-7, and punishes Israel when He must, Ezek. 39: 23. The works on the other hand, through which God reveals Himself, are legion. The number of those who receive revelation is also large: the people, the Egyptians, Ex. 7: 5; 14: 4; Pharaoh, Ex. 7: 17; Jethro, Ex. 18: 11; the stranger that prays in Jerusalem and all the peoples of the earth, 1 Kings 8: 43, 60; the enemies of Nehemiah, Neh. 6: 16. There is no bar to receptivity of God's revelation of Himself in His works. Anyone who witnesses them or experiences them is capable of the knowledge of God. From this there are a number of consequences.

a) Since God is known in His works of creation, it is possible conversely to investigate the aim and intention of the works of God in creation and nature in order to deduce from this aim the existence and nature and wisdom and providence of God. This is the origin of the teleological study of nature. b) If the historical experience of Israel indicates for Israel herself and to her neighbours a knowledge of God, as the books of Exodus, Deuteronomy and Ezekiel prove, then history as a whole is a revelation of God. History is meaningful, it serves God's purpose and can be explained in terms of God's counsels. Here a theological view of history as the pedagogue of salvation

takes root. c) Guidance of individuals also leads to a knowledge
of God. "Help me, O Lord my God . . . that they may know
that this is thy hand", Ps. 109: 26 ff. God does not merely guide
individuals, He guides them in a way that can be understood
and appreciated by anyone. Those who are to know that it is
God's hand are not believers but unbelievers. This is the
beginning of the theology of experience.

When individual acts are understood as works of God and
reveal Him they are called signs, אוֹת, omens, מוֹפֵת, and
wonders, פֶּלֶא, נִפְלָאָה, or mighty acts, גְּבוּרוֹת. Jahweh performs
signs through Moses among the Egyptians, whose heart He
has hardened, that Israel may know that He is Jahweh,
Ex. 10: 1 ff. Such signs, אוֹת, or omens, מוֹפֵת, are of course
of limited revelatory value. They may be performed by a
prophet who commends the worship of other gods; they do
not guarantee the trustworthiness of that prophet. It is God
who is responsible for the signs, and in the case just mentioned
He uses the sign to prove Israel's loyalty to Himself, Deut.
13: 1-3. Here we are presented with two conflicting types of
revelation: on the one hand this free revelation given immediately in the signs and on the other hand the ordered revelation
of true doctrine.

In the signs which God gives or causes to be performed He
reveals what He will do. Thus Isaiah walks naked and barefoot
because Egypt will go naked and barefoot, Isa. 20: 3 ff. The signs
in the heaven are however meaningless, Jer. 10: 2. The falling
of Hophra into the hands of his enemies is for the remnant of
Judah in Egypt a sign of their punishment, Jer. 44: 29 ff. The
siege-act which the prophet plays at God's command with tile
and pan is a sign for the house of Israel, Ezek. 4: 1-3. God makes
Ezekiel a sign, מוֹפֵת, for Israel: he must carry his belongings
on his shoulder in the dark, and dig through the wall, Ezek.
12: 6 ff. God turns the sun into darkness and the moon into
blood and reveals by this sign the coming of His day, Joel 2: 31.
Jahweh doeth wonders פֶּלֶא; and therein He makes known,
הוֹדִיעַ, His strength among the peoples, Ps. 77: 14. All the
people see God's marvels, נִפְלָאוֹת, Ex. 34: 10, for God
causes them to be seen intentionally, Mic. 7: 15, Ps. 78: 11;
they are "to us-ward", Ps. 40: 5. These marvels are sometimes
great events of history, Josh. 3: 5, Judg. 6: 13; sometimes
rescue at sea, Ps. 107: 23-31; sometimes delivery from sickness,

Ps. 118: 23; sometimes the might of God which expresses itself in the wisdom of His law, Ps. 119: 18. There is no god in heaven or in earth that can do according to God's works, מַעֲשִׂים, and God's mighty acts, וּגְבוּרֹת: in them God has shewed His servant His greatness and His strong hand, Deut. 3: 24. God reveals Himself in His works.

36. GOD REVEALS HIMSELF IN VISIONS

Not anyone by any means but only chosen individuals may see or hear God in apparitions. There are, however, a fair number of such individuals. "I will make myself known to him (the prophet) in a vision. I will speak with him in a dream." Only with Moses did God speak "mouth to mouth . . . and he beholds the form of the Lord", Num. 12: 6, 8. The Old Testament has accounts of a great many theophanies in which God reveals Himself, and it is possible to establish the following points.

1. There is no consistent form of appearance; it changes from one occasion to the next. *2.* There is also no hard and fast rule as to the time of a divine apparition. God appears when He wills. *3.* Likewise there is no human process, no prayer, sacrifice or technique of any kind, whereby man could induce a divine apparition. Man is always the recipient only, never the author of revelation. *4.* All accounts of apparitions have a peculiarly fluid and merely suggestive character. One may know to some extent how they begin, Isa. 6: 1; one does not discover how they end. From seeing Isaiah passes to hearing and in saying what he hears he quite forgets to say when and how the vision goes out. Did he himself perhaps not notice? The vision in Ezekiel is an exception; it is much more than suggestive, but everything points to the fact that in it there has been theological reflection. *5.* All apparitions are verbal and revelatory, i.e. the apparition in itself or in what it symbolizes is never sufficient, there is always a thought-content in addition expressed as a rule in plain words. "What seest thou? I see a rod of a juniper tree (*shaqed*). Thou hast well seen, for I watch (*shoqed*) over my word to perform it," Jer. 1: 11 ff. The visual part vanishes, the word remains. That is true of nearly all visions. Revelation in visions is also verbal revelation.

6. Revelations in visions can be divided into several groups. The first group are those which may be called "foundation-theophanies". Someone has a vision of God somewhere and the result is that the spot becomes a holy place, the anniversary of the founding of which is marked by the retelling of the story of the foundation-theophany. Gen. 16: 13 ff., 21: 22-33, Josh. 5: 2-9, Judg. 6: 11-24, etc., are of this category. Many of these theophanies were only subsequently attributed to Jahweh. 7. Theophanies in which God comes from far to fight for Israel His people: Deut. 33: 2, Judg. 5: 4 ff., Mic. 1: 3 ff. comprise a second group. What is involved in these is not history in the real sense but fearful natural phenomena, which because of their incidence in times of emergency testify to the presence and assistance of God. 8. A third group is formed by those visions in which God appears to those whom He calls into His service: Ex. 3: 1-7 ff., Isa. 6, Jer. 1: 11 ff., Amos 1: 2. The content of these revelations concerns in the first instance only those who are called. 9. A fourth group contains those visions through which God announces a judgment or a measure He proposes to take: Amos 7: 7-9, 8: 1-3, Ezek. 2: 8—3: 3. All four groups have this characteristic in common: that each vision stands by itself, needs no elaboration and points to nothing other than to its own content. 10. A fifth group contains visions which appear in series form and in such a way that the complete context alone gives sense and significance to the individual vision. The perfectly symmetrical series of visions in Zech. 1-6 belongs to this group, as do also the visions in Ezek. 1; the wheels which are the vehicle of the glory of Jahweh, 10: 1-22; the wheels bear the glory of Jahweh out of the Temple, 11: 22-23; the wheels bear the glory out of the city, etc. 11. Finally there is a sixth group which contains visions which are not incidental theophanies but foreshadowings of the one last great theophany which is the goal of all history. Isa. 40-55[76] is one such vision. The subject is stated right at the start. "The glory of the Lord is revealed and all flesh sees it together", 40: 5. The goal of earthly history is the revelation to all flesh of the glory of God.

37. GOD REVEALS HIMSELF THROUGH MEN

The Old Testament takes it for granted that there are *homines religiosi*, that is to say, men whose special gifts (this is as accurate as we can be) fit them to perceive the presence of God, hear His utterances, His commissions and His announcements, and convey them to their day and generation. These *homines religiosi* are mediators between God and men. There is no comprehensive name for them. The term man of God,[77] which sometimes occurs, is not an established usage. The word

נָבִיא can also mean something else. In view of the wording of Isa. 6: 8, Amos 7: 15, and Ex. 3: 10 the term ambassador or messenger would be appropriate, but in fact it never occurs in the Old Testament in that sense.

The fact remains, however, that God chooses men and sometimes women to make known His will to those about them. They speak in the name of God and their vocation really to speak in God's name is their only qualification, Jer. 26: 12, 15, 16. They are never officials, always freely appointed. Likewise their vocation to speak in the name of God is an inscrutable thing with no outward marks that might be examined.

What does it mean to speak in God's name? Formally it means that the prophet prefaces and validates his utterance with the oath חַי יַהְוֶה "as the Lord liveth", Jer. 4: 2. The speaker thereby makes God his witness and places himself under God's judgment. If he fails to speak the truth, then he forfeits his life in the sight of God, for he has played with God's life. And if one goes on to ask how God's messengers know that it really is God who sends them, it must be confessed that there is no answer whatsoever; for there are no outward tokens and signs. In fact the possibility has always to be reckoned with that God Himself may even put a lying spirit in the prophet's mouth because He has resolved on evil for his hearers, 1 Kings 22: 23.[78] There are no outward signs or characteristics by which God's revelation through men could be identified and distinguished from falsifications of it and imitations and perversions.

It is a fact nevertheless that men come forward with the claim that they have a message from God to deliver. They begin their message, as good messengers should, with the formula: "Thus saith the Lord".[79] They end it in order to make its limits perfectly clear, with the formula of conclusion: ". . . saith the Lord", Amos 1: 5, or: ". . . is the word of the Lord", Amos 2: 16. These and similar formulae separate very exactly the word spoken by the prophet from his own words. That is clear for example in the Book of Amos. The prophet is not one who speaks only as God's spokesman, he also speaks for himself. But he is one who leaves us in no doubt as to when he is speaking for God. All prophetic utterances to which a formula is attached and which are therefore made at God's command are clearly considered by the prophets to be inspired. Here and only here is the real foundation of the biblical doctrine of the inspiration of Holy Scripture to be found. In the Old Testament a passage is inspired which is marked by the formulae appropriate to a message or something similar as the word of God. But the converse of this must also be observed. Everything that is not marked[80] by such formulae is not inspired. The biblical doctrine of inspiration does not simply isolate the Old Testament as a whole from all other writings; it is defined along lines which cut across the individual books.

Certain observations must now be made on the inspired messages in which God reveals Himself through men. *1.* The revelation contained in these words is always particular. It is never in the form of a general, impersonal truth; rather what is said is always addressed to one particular individual or circle with reference to his time and circumstances. For those of a later time therefore it is not always easy to appreciate the individual revelation as such. *2.* A further consequence is that the individual revelations contained in the prophets' words do not necessarily form a consistent whole. They are not parts of a jig-saw puzzle; they are historical phenomena each with its own context in time and place. *3.* For that reason two revelations may not match like the halves of a broken flagstone. They may even contradict one another. Jonah reveals to Nineveh that in forty days the city will be overthrown, 3: 4. But then God reveals to the prophet that He has compassion on the city, 4: 11. Isaiah announces that God will hiss for the bee that is in the land of Assyria and it shall be as a chastisement upon the whole land, Isa. 7: 18 ff. Assyria, the rod of God's anger, intended to destroy and is punished for his high looks, 10: 5 ff. The husbandman is not continually threshing, for Jahweh is wonderful in counsel, Isa. 28: 29; the message which He sends changes with the time and with the circumstances, it is not fixed and irrevocable.

4. It would be wrong to conclude, however, that the Old Testament view was that God's revelation through the prophets was transmitted in separate, sporadic, unconnected and purely incidental acts of revelation. There is a linguistic argument against this which is frequently overlooked. That which the prophets have to declare is always called *the* word of God. It is never called *a* word of God. Indeed, this latter expression would seem never to have occurred. Each individual revelation is called not *a*, but *the* word of Jahweh. Any number of individual messages may follow one another therefore and each be introduced by the formula, "Then came the word of Jahweh".[81] In every single revelation it is always the whole word of God that expresses itself. Each part stands for the whole as a ball rolling through a thicket when each part of its surface that is visible conveys an impression of the whole ball. This totality of the revelation that is made through God's messengers cannot be written off as merely an insignificant peculiarity or inadequacy of language. On the contrary, God's revelation is such that from the Exodus to the Exile, and beyond, God was continually speaking with His people through men. "These three and twenty years the word of the Lord[82] hath come unto me, and I have spoken unto you early and late . . . and early and late hath the Lord sent unto you all his servants the prophets", Jer. 25: 3 ff. Through the centuries the succession of men continues through whom God reveals Himself to His people.

38. GOD REVEALS HIMSELF IN THE LAW

Revelation in the works of creation, providence and history shows that God exists and that He is wise and mighty: these three predicates constitute more or less the whole of that revelation. Revelation in visions shows that God is present, that He is alive and that He actively involves Himself in the life of man. Revelation of this kind contains moreover many media of revelation which are not easily reduced to a common denominator. This is especially true of revelations through men. In this category we find a whole series of variations. Through Moses God tells Israel that He has heard their cry and will deliver them, Ex. 3: 7-10. Through Isaiah God tells Shebna that he is to be thrust from his office, Isa. 22: 15-19; through Jeremiah He announces to Hananiah that he will die within the space of a year, Jer. 28: 15-17. Good and evil, misfortune and progress, punishment and grace, rebuke and call to repentance—there is nothing that is not mentioned. But when one asks where God tells Israel and tells man what he should do in order to fulfil God's will, then the answer is: God reveals Himself in the law.

The actual law as we have it bears clearly the marks of its earthly and human origin. It is based on the common conception and codes of law of the ancient east.[83] It arose out of the needs and circumstances of Hebrew civilization and was adapted to them. The various collections of laws show the changeableness of Old Testament law through the centuries.

But all of that does not prejudice the validity of the claim that the law is a revelation of God. The idea of divinity in the sense of an objective impersonal quality is entirely foreign and repugnant to the Old Testament. It is, however, familiar with the idea of divine in the sense of coming from God and belonging to God; and in this sense one can say that in the Old Testament the law, each law, is something divine, for every law has as its ultimate object the community desired by God. In every law the individual must sacrifice something of his claims and advantages for the sake of the whole. Every law serves to make clear the rightness and the value of community as the thing for all individuals. In every law moreover there is the attempt to achieve justice which looks on all with an impartial countenance. Law is always the struggle for the universal, binding, deep and real things of life. In this respect law is always God's affair and not man's. God speaks in law. Law too is a divine medium of revelation.

We may divide the legal material which we find in the Old Testament into four groups. This division is relevant but of course it is not present in the record of revelation.

The first group is made up of a small number of self-evident moral instructions, without attention to which the life of man is not possible. The Decalogue[84] represents that group. The greatness and godliness of the Decalogue is abundantly apparent; it is even more apparent that here it is not man who is expressing himself but God who is revealing Himself. The second group contains those laws which are no longer the ultimate axioms of human community life but do have an undoubted moral character, in virtue of which, once formulated, they bring to bear an influence that is not merely external, resting on authority, but is inwardly constraining, based on conviction and consent. He that killeth shall surely be put to death, Ex. 21: 12, is clear evidence,[85] but there are no books of law made up of laws of this type. In fact these laws are as a rule intermingled with those which belong to the third group. The third group contains laws whose moral core is clear but whose appearance and form are closely related to a particular time and place. The fourth group finally contains those laws which are concerned essentially not with morals but with cult, so that if this cultic concern was not present or if it was differently arranged then all occasion for that particular law disappeared.[86] Were there only this fourth group or even only the third and fourth group, it would scarcely be possible to say that God reveals Himself in law; but certainly it holds for the first and second group. Because of this the claim is extended to everything that is law and therefore to the third and fourth groups. In law God speaks. Everything that is law is revealed by Him. "Cursed be he that confirmeth not all[87] the words of this law to do them", Deut. 27: 26.

The importance of revelation in law is appreciated when we examine more carefully the individual aspects of this phenomenon. The development of the idea of law in the Old Testament is limited and slow. תּוֹרָה=law occurs very often with the limiting demonstrative adjective "this (law)", Deut. 27: 26, or in the restrictedness imposed by a series of related terms "my commandments, my statutes and my laws". Gen. 26: 5, or, and this applies until the time of the deuteronomic reform, it does not yet mean law but has still the vaguer connotation of teaching: "the teaching of our God", Isa. 1: 10; "for out of Zion shall go forth instruction", Isa. 2: 3; "they reject the teaching of Jahweh", Isa. 5: 24, "I seal the teaching among my disciples", Isa. 8: 16; "ye will not hear the teaching of Jahweh", Isa. 30: 9. This Isaianic usage of the word explains a great deal. Above all it shows that תּוֹרָה is something which is now coming into being—God gives the instruction at the time. It is living and new; it is not tradition, to which one refers. The fact that Jahweh is the lawgiver who instructs men in living is here more important than what He gives as instruction. Isaiah has no thought of a complete, written, traditional and absolutely fixed law; indeed, a hundred years after Isaiah, Jeremiah is found saying: "The priests say not, where is Jahweh? They that handle the law (the teaching) know me not", 2: 8. "The teaching shall not perish from the priest", says the same Jeremiah, 18: 18.

The Old Testament itself bears witness therefore to the fact that the law is historically conditioned and questionable, and is very far from attributing to the law the comparative uniformity which characterizes it in Paul's thinking. It would be wrong, however, to conclude that it is possible to distinguish true and just law from false law, law that has been added, the product of human genius, either by standards of historical criticism or of theology and ethics. That is impossible. God is the lawgiver. In the law He reveals His will and gives form and purpose to the life of man. Without God's law the life of man would be utterly impossible, for life cannot be without form, but to determine which among the laws and ordinances before us are divine revelations and which are the chance and arbitrary decisions of men is quite out of the question. To-day one would therefore probably not venture any opinion on the origin of the law. The Old Testament faced with this same situation had no hesitation in referring the whole of the law back to God and calling it all God's law. On the other hand, the Old Testament makes no attempt to arrive at a complete system of law, at least for the main spheres of life; and even concerning sacrifice, the most important part of the cult, it contains only occasional and by no means fundamental statements.

It is symptomatic of the slow development of the idea of the law in Old Testament history that only at a late date are any statements made about the meaning and significance of the law. When a son asks his father what the testimonies and the statutes and the judgments mean—in the time of Deuteronomy the law is still made up of these three parts—then the answer should remind him of the redemption out of Egypt and go on to say that God demands obedience to His law "that it may always go well with us and he may preserve us alive", Deut. 6: 20-24. "And it shall be righteousness unto us if we observe to do all this commandment before the Lord our God", Deut. 6: 25.

There are three motives for observing the law. One is *gratitude*:[88] The lawgiver is He who led them out of Egypt, Deuteronomy; this recurs again and again as a basic principle. Another is *the fear of God*. "The Lord commanded us to do all these statutes and to fear the Lord our God", Deut. 6: 24. Whoever knows about God knows also about His "right", that it has to be obeyed. What the New Testament calls obedience the Old calls fear, יִרְאָה.[89] The third motive for observance of the law is *the promise*—"that it may ever go well with us". The fulfilment of the law is a matter of life and death. "See, I set before thee this day life and good, and death and evil"; "I lay before thee life and death, blessing and cursing: therefore choose life that thou mayest live", Deut. 30: 15, 19. This law is neither too hard nor is it far off; it is very nigh and asks to be observed, Deut. 30: 11, 14.

In the law God reveals Himself decisively. Man's hearing or not hearing of this revelation is a matter of life and death.

39. GOD REVEALS HIMSELF THROUGH THE SPIRIT

1. The one word רוּחַ is used in four different connexions. Firstly, it means the wind, air in motion, the breeze. With this meaning the word properly belongs to the realm of cosmology; it is mentioned here only because this physical meaning is the original from which the other three meanings have arisen: the spirit is originally called after the wind as in Latin *anima* is derived from *animus*, Greek ἄνεμος. Secondly, the word רוּחַ means spirit in the sense of breath of life, Hab. 2: 19; vital energy, Josh. 2: 11; soul, Job 7: 11; mind, Ezek. 11: 5; will, Ex. 35: 21, Num. 14: 24. Here therefore it is an anthropological and psychological term. As such however it always refers to something that is only the possession of the individual, not his nature: it remains impersonal.

A third meaning which רוּחַ can have is the sphere and effect of spirit. Spirit is an effective power whose proper location one never rightly knows. Spirit, as a power, assumes various characters and pursues various aims; there is for example a spirit of life, Gen. 6: 17; of experience, Ex. 28: 3; of wisdom, Isa. 11: 2; jealousy, Num. 5: 14; of evil, 1 Sam. 16: 23; of deception, 1 Kings 22: 22; of judgment (or arbitration), Isa. 4: 4; of understanding, Isa. 11: 2; of counsel and might, Isa. 11: 2; of knowledge and of the fear of the Lord, Isa. 11: 2; of perverseness, Isa. 19: 14; of deep sleep, Isa. 29: 10; of unchastity, Hos. 4: 12; the spirit of grace and of supplication, Zech. 12: 10; of willingness, Ps. 51: 14; of arrogance, Ps. 76: 12. Others could be added, for there is plurality among the forms of spirit but there is not plurality of spirits. The differentiation is always in attribute; there is not (yet) any question of individualization of spirit. The pneumatology of the Old Testament is therefore an unsolved problem. There is not sufficient material on which to work, and therefore there can be no satisfactory insights into the question.

Fourthly and finally, spirit is the nature and possession of God. Indeed, it is nowhere explicitly stated that God is spirit, but that God lives in the realm of spirit or that spirit is God's world is clearly implicit in the words of Isa. 31: 3; "The Egyptians are men and not God; and their horses flesh and not spirit". Which of the alternative statements is the more correct? One cannot say, there is just no means of determining whether it is more in accordance with the Old Testament view to say that God lives in the realm of spirit or to say that spirit is God's world. Where the Old Testament speaks of spirit its language approximates more than anywhere else to the language of the philosophy of religion, and spirit and the spiritual tend to become something impersonal in terms of which God almost ceases to exist. The spirit claims an existence separate from God. This is nowhere explicit, but the tendency is in this direction.[90]

2. The Old Testament speaks of the spirit of Jahweh (some 30 times) and of the spirit of God (some 15 times) in a striking variety of expressions which bear witness to a similar variety of conceptions.

The form in which the spirit communicates himself to a man or to men is sometimes clearly described and sometimes only hinted at, and from the multiplicity of these descriptions it is obvious that there is no adequate language of description. The spirit of God clothes Zechariah the priest's son, 2 Chron. 24: 20, and Amasai, who was chief of the thirty (1 Chron. 12: 19); the spirit of Jahweh clothes Gideon, Judg. 6: 34. In these references the spirit appears as a sphere which enwraps the recipient as with a garment; it is as if the person were suddenly caught in an encompassing wind. In Ex. 31: 3 Bezalel is filled with the spirit of God; and similarly Isaiah 63: 11 speaks of God's putting His holy spirit into Moses, and Ezek. 36: 27 of God's putting His spirit within the Israelites. In these references the spirit is thought of as a power—not a substance—but a power of inspiration within the recipient. This is perhaps the description best fitted to the nature of the spirit. In some references the spirit is much more substantial and easily recognizable, e.g. God pours out, נָסַךְ, His spirit (a spirit of deep sleep) on the prophets, Isa. 29: 10; He pours, יָצַק, His spirit upon the seed of Israel, Isa. 44: 3; He pours out His spirit on Israel, Ezek. 39: 29, upon all flesh, upon Israel's sons and daughters, שָׁפַךְ, Joel 2: 28 ff. All three usages see a certain fluidity in the spirit and in the person a receptacle—one thinks of the *gratia infusa* of Christian dogmatics. The same conception is present in Isa. 32: 15; the spirit from on high will be poured out, יְעָרֶה, upon us.

Among all the various metaphors of the spiritual one can distinguish two groups: one group contains those which are more perceptual and belong therefore to the sphere of physics, the other group contains those which are more "spiritual" and belong to the sphere of ethics. The proper context of the Hebrew word צָלְחָה, Judg. 14: 6, 19; 15: 14; 1 Sam. 10: 10; 11: 6, because of its etymological homelessness, cannot be determined. But clearly the undernoted belong to the ethical group: God sends an (evil!) spirit, Judg. 9: 23; the spirit of Jahweh comes upon Jahaziel, 2 Chron. 20: 14; the spirit of Jahweh comes as an evil spirit upon Saul, 1 Sam. 19: 9; Jahweh puts a lying spirit in the mouth of the prophets, 1 Kings 22: 23; there is a spirit in the king of Assyria, 2 Kings 19: 7; the spirit of God comes on Balaam, Num. 24: 2; on Saul's messengers, 1 Sam. 19: 20; and on Azariah, 2 Chron 15: 1.

Other references speak not of the coming of the possession of the spirit but of the existence of such possession. The spirit begins to move Samson in the camp of Dan, Judg. 13: 25—the dynamic of the spirit is nowhere given such clear expression as in this passage. The spirit of God is in Joseph, in Pharaoh's opinion, Gen. 41: 38. The spirit is upon Moses, Num. 11: 17; it rests on the seventy, 11: 25. The spirit of Jahweh speaks in me, declares נְאֻם David (in his inspiration); and that means that Jahweh's word, מִלָּה, is upon David's tongue, 2 Sam. 23: 2. This same inspiration means that Jahweh's words, דְּבָרַי, are in Israel's mouth and in the mouth of Israel's seed, Isa. 59: 21. The spirit of Jahweh is therefore upon the servant of Jahweh, for Jahweh has anointed the servant, Isa. 61: 1. A man of the spirit, אִישׁ הָרוּחַ (Hos. 9: 7 only and there equivalent to a prophet) is one who has received the spirit. He has received the spirit because Jahweh has given it to him. This phrase, that Jahweh puts the spirit upon someone, נָתַן, Num. 11: 25, 29, Isaiah 42: 1 (puts it in a person's mouth, 1 Kings 22: 23; 2 Chron. 18: 22); puts it in someone, 2 Kings 19: 7; Isa. 37: 7; puts it within someone, Isa. 63: 11; this phrase, whatever preposition is used, is the most interesting of all, for in it the clearest possible expression is given to the thought that *the spirit of God is always a free gift to men by grace.* It cannot be claimed, however, that the usage is a common one. Indeed, we have probably quoted all the instances of it.

3. It is plain that there can be no question of claim or desert in the matter of possessing the spirit of God; for the possession can come to an end. "Take not thy holy spirit from me", cries the Psalmist, 51: 11, and when he prays "let thy good spirit lead me in a plain way", 143: 10 (cf. Neh. 9: 20) he is thinking primarily of the way he will be led but also of the spirit he hopes to possess and keep to lead him. For the spirit of God can depart

from a person, סוּר. The spirit of God departed from Saul,
1 Sam. 16: 14. 1 Kings 22: 24 would suggest that it can also go
from one prophet, עָבַר, to speak to another; but that is
hardly so, for the prophets' contradiction of one another arises
from the fact that the spirit of God is in the one and a lying
spirit commissioned by God is in the other. But certainly God
Himself takes of the spirit that is upon Moses and puts it upon
the seventy elders, Num. 11: 25. What exactly does God take?
One hesitates to say God takes some, or a part, of the spirit,
for spirit is indivisible and if by the act of God the seventy
have the spirit it does not mean that from then on Moses has
the spirit of God in a lesser degree. It is rather different in
the case of Elisha's prayer that he might receive a double
portion of Elijah's spirit when Elijah is taken away, 2 Kings
2: 9. When the prophet is taken from his work the spirit that
dwelt in him is free. Thus Moses, before he dies, transfers to
Joshua the spirit of wisdom by laying his hands upon him,
Deut. 34: 9. The spirit of God can dwell in a man if and for as
long as the grace of God wills it. It is never the natural possession
of an individual. Man is never more than a temporary receptacle
for the spirit of God.

4. We have been concerned with the question of the form in
which God communicates His spirit to man; but there are two
questions of even greater importance. One concerns the effect
of possession of the spirit, the other concerns the context and
purpose of God's imparting His spirit to men.

To the first question, the question what happens when a man
receives the spirit of God, the Old Testament gives not one but
many answers. a) There is a purely *dynamic operation* of the
spirit of God. Samson is moved or stirred in the camp of Dan,
Judg. 13: 25; he rends a young lion, 14: 6; he smites thirty
Philistines, 14: 19; he bursts the ropes with which he had been
bound as if they were burnt thread, Judg. 15: 14. If the Samson
stories are perhaps saga merely taken over by the Hebrews it
may be that what we have here is an ethnic view of the spirit,
but the spirit has the same effect on Othniel, Judg. 3: 10, and
on Jephthah, Judg. 11: 29—they also do mighty deeds in war;
their deeds are however for the salvation of the people of God,
3: 10. Saul too is roused to burning anger by the spirit of God
that God may work salvation in Israel, 1 Sam. 11: 6, 13.

b) There is an *ecstatic operation* of the spirit of God. It came
upon Saul's messengers and immediately they were seized with

an ecstatic frenzy—"they prophesied", 1 Sam. 19: 20. God gives of His spirit to the seventy and they "prophesy", and Moses wishes that it would happen to all the people, Num. 11: 25-29. When God pours out His spirit upon all flesh, then men will prophesy, dream dreams and see visions, Joel 2: 28 ff. In this last passage the transition to the inspirational operation of the spirit is clear, but the other two passages speak of an excitation which does not manifest itself as a commission to make any definite proclamation. It is merely ecstasy without any inspiration. Nevertheless when one speaks of ecstasy it should be carefully noted that the Old Testament never violates the boundary between God and man; not even when it speaks of that ecstatic frenzy in which men "prophesy". Any sort of mystical intercourse of God and man is entirely foreign to the Old Testament.

c) There is a *work of guidance done by the spirit*. When God puts His spirit in the King of Assyria he hears a rumour and returns to his own land and perishes, 2 Kings 19: 7. The spirit of God can carry Elijah "whither I know not", 1 Kings 18: 12, and likewise Elisha, who has the spirit of Elijah, i.e. the spirit which formerly rested on Elijah; 2 Kings 2: 16. While the two passages quoted involve only an incidental leading—the translators speak with some justification of a leading away in 1 Kings 18: 12 and 2 Kings 2: 16—we do find elsewhere a consistent and carefully planned guidance. God's spirit leads Israel to her rest, Isa. 63: 14. "Thou gavest them" (the Israelites wandering in the wilderness) "thy good spirit to instruct them", Neh. 9: 20; "may thy good spirit lead me in a plain path", Ps. 143: 10.

d) There is *an operation of the spirit wherein one is endowed with earthly wisdom*. The above-mentioned passage, Neh. 9: 20, belongs to this category. Bezalel is filled with the spirit of God and the result is the gift of artistic ability, Ex. 31: 3; 35: 31. Joseph has the spirit of God—the writer puts the opinion in the mouth of Pharaoh—that is why he can cope with the famine that threatens the Egyptians, Gen. 41: 38. Moses has the spirit of wisdom and hands it on to Joshua, Deut. 34: 9.

e) There is an *inspirational activity* of the spirit. The spirit of God comes upon Balaam and he takes up his parable, Num. 24: 2 ff. A prophecy is spoken because the spirit comes upon the speaker; cf. Jahaziel, 2 Chron. 20: 14; Zechariah the priest's son, 2 Chron. 24: 20; Ezekiel, Ezek. 11: 5. The possession of the spirit may give rise to a sermon, cf. Azariah, 2 Chron. 15: 1, or to an inspired song, cf. Amasai (Abisai?) 1 Chron. 12: 19; cf. also 2 Sam. 23: 2. *This is clearly acknowledged inspiration.* We shall have more to say about it later (p. 118). Suffice it for the moment to give two further examples of this clear inspiration. God sent instruction and words by His spirit through the former prophets, Zech. 7: 12. The detail of the expression "by His spirit through former prophets" deserves attention. It betrays the conflation of two ideas. According to the one, God sent instruction and words by the former prophets. That is the older of the two. According to the other, God sent instruction and words by His spirit. That is the later idea, as we shall presently show (p. 117.). The other example is Neh. 9: 30: "thou didst admonish them by thy spirit through thy prophets." Here we see again the same conflation of the same two ideas.

In all the passages we have mentioned, the inspiration is given as the situation arises. When God wills that a pronounce-ment should be made He makes it possible, if He chooses to do it this way—this necessary qualification will be discussed below—by giving His spirit on the occasion and for the duration of this one pronouncement. Each message, prophecy, song or sermon is therefore, in virtue of a temporary inspiration, an inspiration confined to the content of the one utterance. It is a quite different sort of inspiration that we find in Deutero-Isaiah. It happens only once and it remains; the number of pronouncements and other manifestations of it is unlimited. "I have put my spirit upon him; he shall bring forth judgment to the nations. . . till he have set judgment in the earth, and the isles shall wait for his law", Isa. 42: 1, 4. This same view of inspiration as a lasting gift is found also in Trito-Isaiah. "The spirit of the Lord God is upon me: because the Lord hath anointed me to preach good tidings unto the poor; he hath sent me to bind up the brokenhearted, to proclaim liberty to the captives, and the opening of the prison to them that are bound; to proclaim the acceptable year of the Lord . . . to comfort all who mourn . . .", Isa. 61: 1-3. Here the anointing is the pre-condition of the possession of the spirit, the person concerned is a chosen individual, the outcome is the preaching of salvation and the duration of the possession is obviously unlimited.

f) There is *an operation of the spirit which disposes people to be well-pleasing to God.* When God pours His spirit on Israel's seed, they spring up and confess that they belong to God,

Isa. 44: 3-5. God will gather Israel from among the nations, bring them into their own land and put a new spirit within them and cause them to walk in His statutes, Ezek. 36: 26-27. The outcome of the change caused by the spirit is obedience. The spirit of God is within the whole people as well as in its leader. Hagg. 2: 5 and the revelation formula "fear ye not"[91] is there to confirm that this is revelation.

5. When one surveys these statements one feels bound to ask how great, how comprehensive or how select the number is of those to whom the gift of the spirit is granted. This question coincides to some extent with the other question concerning the compass and accuracy of statements about the spirit of God in the Old Testament revelation. The two questions can be answered together, therefore, and we begin by making certain points which narrow the field of enquiry. In the book of Jeremiah there is no mention whatever of the spirit of God; nowhere in the whole vast document does the concept appear, neither in the prophet's actual words nor in his biography nor in any of the other parts. Similarly in Amos it is lacking. Hosea does not have it except in the solitary designation for the prophet— "the man of the spirit", Hos. 9: 7. Micah knows of the spirit of Jahweh as the medium of the divine emotions, 2: 7.[92] In Isaiah from 11: 2 to 32: 15 the spirit is seven times spoken of in such a way that it may fairly be construed as the spirit of God.[93] Isa. 31: 3 is the classic passage for the difference between the spiritual and the material world. The spirit here is a quality of God, not His gift in revelation. Isa. 30: 1 emphasizes God's warning of woe to the rebellious children who take counsel without God and make agreements without His spirit. This is clearly a reference to spiritual guidance, but how does this guidance operate? Do the Jews have the spirit of God as a permanent possession, or do they know of a means of acquiring a moment's inspiration of the spirit, or should they have waited until an inspiration of the spirit would come to tell them what was to be done? These are three possible answers, but one can never be certain which is correct. Isa. 11: 2 says in four ways that the saviour out of the stock of Jesse will receive the spirit of Jahweh; he will be inspired. There remains—though it is disputed[94]—Isa. 32: 15: the spirit shall be poured out upon us from on high. Who are the recipients? The Jews? Their careless wives? Why is the spirit called the spirit from on high? The description seems to be a current one, but this is the first (authentic)

appearance of it and it is infrequent because it is so strangely formalistic. Moreover this outpouring of the spirit has no clear and carefully described effect. The passage remains also questionable.

Our finding up to this point then is that with the exception of Isaiah the pre-exilic prophets do not speak of the spirit of God. That does not mean that when these prophets from Amos to Jeremiah have to deliver a word of the Lord they do not claim inspiration for themselves, for they do. Isaiah does so also, and Isaiah likewise does it without connecting his prophetic inspiration with the gift of the spirit. *For the early prophets the gift of the spirit of God and prophetic inspiration have no connexion one with the other*—theologically a very important point.

Isaiah is the prophet of the spirit of God. Isaiah is the theologian *par excellence* among the prophets and the father of Old Testament theology. There are allusions to the spirit of God in the Old Testament that are older than Isaiah, but they are of popular origin and of no theological significance. They are predominantly those referring to the dynamic and ecstatic operations of the spirit, his work of guidance and his power of imparting wisdom. What then does Isaiah have to say about the spirit of God? He too makes no assertions which could be said to be central, exhaustive or theologically fundamental. In fact there is no such statement anywhere in the Old Testament. There can therefore be no systematic Old Testament doctrine of the spirit of God.

In the six or seven relevant passages in Isaiah he takes the popular statements and gives them a theological turn. Even so we find there no consistent point of view which could be called the Old Testament doctrine of the spirit of God. One is dealing with theological units, not with a theological unity. This is confirmed by the fact that the prophets succeeding Isaiah show no sign of his influence in this matter. Jeremiah can deliver his message without any reference to the spirit of God. Ezekiel is the first to speak of him, and then Deutero- and Trito- Isaiah. These latter two know of an endowment with the spirit of men specially commissioned by God, while Ezekiel knows of an endowment of the whole people, which effects the great conversion in those able to obey and to receive salvation. But Ezekiel too utters the word of the Lord as the earlier prophets did, conscious of inspiration, without necessarily mentioning the spirit of God. The same is true of the later prophets.

6. God reveals Himself through the spirit, and the operations of the spirit are manifold. Sometimes they permit of being

classified; sometimes they are entirely isolated cases. There is certainly no one group, like the prophets, of which the possession of the spirit of God was characteristic and for which it was indispensable. The spirit of God is an essentially undefined quantity in the Old Testament and the manner and scope of its operation is only very vaguely outlined.

7. *Appendix.* It may be convenient here to draw attention to several other Old Testament allusions to the spirit of God which have no real connexion with one another or with those previously mentioned. "Who hath directed the spirit of the Lord or being his counsellor hath taught him?" Isa. 40: 13; here the spirit which Jahweh has is meant, not the spirit which He communicates. "Spirit" sets the prophet on his feet, Ezek. 2: 2, 3: 24; and brings him in a vision to a place, 11: 24; certainly it is to spirit from God that this strange mode of expression refers, but not so certainly to the spirit of God. "Make you a new spirit", Ezek. 18: 31: he means merely obtain for yourself a new spirit; his language is rather loose. Zech. 4: 6: God will bring salvation, not by might nor by power but by His spirit. One can scarcely understand this spirit as "the other-worldly power granted by God to the whole social order of a theocracy";[95] surely it is the transformation and conversion effected by endowment with the spirit the writer had in mind. Gen. 1: 2: "the spirit of God moved upon the face of the waters"; an unconnected relic of a cosmogenetic myth which proves eloquently how improper it is consciously to build a conception of the spirit of God within Old Testament teaching. Job 33: 4: "The spirit of God (אל) hath made me, and the breath of the Almighty hath given me life": he might as easily have said, God hath made me by His spirit (Gen. 2: 7). The spirit of God in this case is an organ, not an independent power. Gen. 6: 3: "my spirit shall not abide in man for ever"; this is a reference to the spirit of God as the supporter of human life (§ 44). Finally it is to be noted that twice the spirit is designated the Holy Spirit: in the one instance the spirit is the spirit whom God has and whom men grieve, Isa. 63: 10; in the other instance he is the spirit whom God puts within Moses, 63: 11.

40. GOD REVEALS HIMSELF THROUGH REPRESENTATIONS: THE ARK, THE MESSENGERS, THE FACE AND THE GLORY OF GOD

1. It is difficult to find the right word to define these four things mentioned in the title. They are certainly not hypostases,

independent modes of being limiting God's true nature, which
He assumes in order to have intercourse with the world and
with human nature. Still less are they emanations, parts of His
nature which God permits to detach themselves from His
nature in order that they may exist and operate as beings with
their own life, as mediating intermediaries between Himself
and the world. Again, they are not substitutes—i.e. things
which without being God Himself take His place when there is
to be an encounter with men. The word representation remains
therefore the only adequate word. It indicates that under certain circumstances God approaches man, not in His full nature,
because God is too exalted and holy and great—one cannot in
the context of the Old Testament with its realistic thinking
say too spiritual—but in order to represent Himself intimately
to man He turns only one side or operation of His nature
towards him by entering a certain condition. This condition
is no more than a temporary agent of revelation, and there is no
suggestion that it detaches itself from God to have a separate
existence. Therefore it is better to speak of representations
than of forms of apparition, since the former always contains
as part of its meaning the idea that the representation is always
only meant to serve a particular purpose.

2. One must not imagine that the representations were
particularly late forms of revelation, the result of a theologizing
of the language of divine appearances. On the contrary, they
are old, and indeed a declining form in later times. When the
Jahwist says that Jahweh spoke with Abraham as together
they went, Gen. 18: 16ff., and the Elohist says that God came
to Abimelech in a dream of the night and spoke to him, Gen.
20: 3, 6, there we have theologizing. The Elohist does not use
the Jahwist's expression because it does not appear to him
theologically adequate. God does not speak with a man as one
traveller with another. Indeed, God rarely speaks to men—a
line of thought which the priestly material pursues to the logical
conclusion where all "novelese" divine speaking is excluded
and God speaks without anyone's responding (Gen. 17: 1, 3, 9,
15 is an admirable example of this) and where the instances of
God's speaking are reduced to the absolute minimum—and
when He does speak to men He speaks only from the distance
which night and dream-consciousness ensure. That is clear and
conscious theologizing. But when Jahweh's messenger, not
Jahweh Himself, accosts Balaam on his ass (Num. 22: 22 ff.)

the change is accidental. This can hardly be theologizing; it is much more likely to represent an inclination to avoid an anthropomorphism. It may be that the representations are to be partly explained in terms of this same inclination. Where God is only partly involved, His activity will not be typical of His whole nature. Where His visible presence is given through things like the ark and the glory and the brightness, His whole nature is not brought to bear. But it is significant that, as we have said, representations of God have no place in the late parts of the Old Testament. Those writings refer exclusively to God Himself. His whole yet completely imperceptible being is present and acts, and this is possible because in the course of the history of the Old Testament revelation the conception of God has been heightened. God has become, so to speak, more Himself, truly God, and it is found best to speak of Him simply as God.

There are four distinct divine representations in the Old Testament.

3. The oldest, most materialistic, and therefore most quickly abandoned representation of God is *the ark of Jahweh.* It has its historical context in the time of Samuel. The prophets have nothing to say about it; only Jeremiah mentions it as something that will be superfluous, 3: 16. All cognizance of it ceases with the Exile. The ark appears under a variety of names: the ark of God 34 times, the ark of Jahweh 31 times, the ark of the covenant of Jahweh 27 times and simply the ark 47 times. Besides these it has the following incidental names. It is called the ark of the God of Israel 7 times, the ark of God's covenant 5 times, the covenant ark 5 times, etc. The original name is the ark of Jahweh; in the two books of Samuel alone there are 20 instances of it. It is also called there 22 times God's ark. Later it came to have a place in the Temple and is therefore mentioned frequently in the first book of Kings (12 times) and in Chronicles (48 times). Because it found a place in the Temple it is also considered a requisite of the "Tabernacle" and therefore is mentioned in Exodus and Numbers 24 times and also in Joshua (3: 3—8: 33) 29 times. These frequent references should not, however, mislead us into exaggerating the importance of the ark. It really played only a very small part.

Whether the ark of Jahweh was a throne (the later view) or a chest with a particular content (the older view) cannot be determined[96] from the knowledge we possess. It is sufficient for us that it serves, particularly in time of war, as a vessel which guarantees the presence of God. When the people at war with the Philistines fetch the ark from Shiloh Jahweh comes among them and saves them out of the hand of their enemies, 1 Sam. 4: 3. When in the wandering in the wilderness the ark set forward Moses would say, "Rise up, O Lord, and let thine enemies be scattered", and when it rested a different word was addressed to Jahweh; Num. 10: 35. One sees the materialism of this representation. To the student of the history of religion this is most welcome; the theologian is grateful that already at an early date it sits in the Temple merely as an ornament and that the prophet expressly speaks of the time when it will be entirely forgotten (Jer. 3: 16).

4. The second representation in which God reveals Himself is the מַלְאַךְ יַהְוֶה, *the messenger of the Lord.* This representation also is of limited currency. It does not appear at all in the prophets. The messenger of the Lord who stands among the myrtle trees, Zech. 1: 11 ff., and he before whom the high priest stands, Zech. 3: 1, 5, 6, is an ordinary angel only with a special function. Zech. 12: 8 therefore is the only possible instance in the prophets, and it is a simile, really a gloss,[97] attenuating what goes before. There are also a few narratives in which we find the messenger of Jahweh[98] also called the messenger of God: a name which in the present state of the sources is sometimes interchangeable with the other, Judg. 6: 20; 13: 6, 9. The story of the flight of Hagar is one such. The messenger of Jahweh speaks with her, Gen. 16: 7 ff., he gives her the promise that he will multiply her seed, v. 10, but then he goes on to speak of what Jahweh, not he himself, has heard, v. 11.

Other instances can be found of a transition of this kind from the messenger of Jahweh to Jahweh Himself, and vice versa. The messenger of the Lord calls to Abraham out of heaven and restrains him from putting Isaac to death; then He calls to Abraham a second time out of heaven and says: "By myself have I sworn, saith the Lord, that I . . ." Gen. 22: 11, 15 ff. Elsewhere it seems possible to maintain a clear distinction between God and His deputy. Does the story of Moses and the burning bush perhaps belong to that category? The messenger of Jahweh appears to Moses in the burning bush, and then when Moses draws near does Jahweh Himself see him coming and speak, Ex. 3: 2, 4, 7? One hesitates to say. The situation is clearer in the Balaam incident. The messenger of Jahweh accosts Balaam, as he rides on the ass, as a Satan=an adversary. The ass, on seeing the messenger of Jahweh, turns aside. When Balaam smites the ass a third time Jahweh Himself opens the ass's mouth, Num. 22: 22-28. Here Jahweh and His representation in the messenger, who holds a drawn sword in his hand, v. 23, are clearly and deliberately distinguished. That is confirmed by v. 31 where Jahweh opens Balaam's eyes so that he may see the messenger of Jahweh standing in the way. Then comes the inversion; it is the messenger of Jahweh who speaks to Balaam in v. 32 and to whom Balaam replies in v. 34. The messenger of Jahweh is the representation of the invisible God. Similarly in Judg. 13: 9 God hearkens to the voice of Manoah and then the angel of God comes again to Manoah's wife.

These examples will suffice[99] to help us form certain conclusions. When in the Old Testament it is desired to avoid anthropomorphism, God revealed and visible is replaced by the messenger of God as His representation. But the inclination to avoid anthropomorphism is not strong; it is certainly not universal. There is no situation in which Jahweh's messenger must necessarily be spoken of instead of Jahweh. The use of the representation is irregular, one might almost say arbitrary. That is particularly significant for Old Testament angelology. Were this a clear-cut angelology, to which importance was to be attached, this inconsistency between Jahweh and the messenger of Jahweh would be impossible. The fact that it is possible shows how reticent the Old Testament revelation is in the matter of a proper angelology.

5. The third representation under which God reveals Himself is the *face of God*. A number of texts which speak of the face of God might be regarded as merely figurative. Thus, when one wants to say that one appeases the angry God, one can say that one makes His face relaxed, weak, benevolent; חִלָּה, I Sam. 13: 12, Zech. 7: 2; 8: 21, 22, Ps. 119: 58. The *religionsgeschichtliche* origin of this is probably that one rubs with oil a monumental stone that somehow embodies God, Gen. 35: 14. When one seeks out a holy place in order to come in prayer and sacrifice into closer contact with God, one can say that one seeks God's face, 2 Sam. 21: 1, Hos. 5: 15, Ps. 24: 6; 27: 8; 105: 4, I Chron. 16: 11, 2 Chron. 7: 14, or that one comes before His face with a sacrifice, Ps. 95: 2. Similarly one can also say that mercy and truth go before God's face to express that they have His attention, Ps. 89: 14.

But the explanation that they are figures of speech does not hold for all the passages involved, e.g. where God hides His face from someone. "When he hideth his face, who then can behold him?" Job 34: 29; His revelation is obscured. God hides His face so that He may not see something, Ps. 10: 11; then He is withholding His grace. In a little wrath He hides His face for a moment, Isa. 54: 8; because of man's iniquity, 57: 17; so that He does not hear; 59: 2, to make known His anger, 64: 7; because of the wickedness of His people, Jer 33: 5; because they have trespassed against Him, Ezek. 39: 23; He forsakes them because they have broken the covenant, Deut. 31: 17; because they have wrought such evil things in their doings, Mic. 3: 4, Isa. 8: 17, Deut. 31: 18, 32: 20, Ps. 13: 1, 22: 24, 27: 9, 30: 7, 44: 24, 51: 11, 69: 17, 88: 14, 102: 2, 143: 7, Job 13: 24. When God hides his face all His creatures are afraid, for every creature lives by the grace of God. *The face of God is the revelation of the grace of God.*

It is a wonderful privilege therefore to be able to pour out one's heart before the face of the Lord, Lam. 2: 19, but it is terrible when God turns His face against those that do evil, Ps. 34: 16, or when He sets our secret sins in the light of His countenance, Ps. 90: 8; then His countenance rebukes, Ps. 80: 16. But where He makes his face to shine, Ps. 31: 16, 67: 1, 80: 3, 7, 19, 119: 135, Dan. 9: 17, where one walks in the light of His countenance, Ps. 89: 15, there is blessing and victory, Ps. 44: 3. Thus the man of faith prays that God will lift up the light of His countenance upon us, Ps. 4: 6, and the benediction in Num. 6: 25 is that Jahweh will make His face to shine upon thee, that he will not turn it away from thee, 2 Chron. 30: 9, but lift it up upon thee, Num. 6: 26.

It is noteworthy that this also is scarcely mentioned by the prophets; Hos. 5: 15, Mic. 3: 4, Isa. 8: 17, Jer. 33: 5, Ezek. 39: 23, 25, 29, Zech. 7: 2, 8: 21, 22 are the only passages where reference is made to it.

6. The fourth representation in which God reveals Himself is *the glory of God*. There is adequate proof that כְּבוֹד יַהְוֶה means the brightness or glory of God: linguistically (the Septuagint renders כָּבוֹד 177 times out of 201 δόξα and a further 5 times uses a word in which the stem of δόξα occurs; also in passages such as Luke 2: 9, Rev. 21: 23 δόξα means clearly brightness or glory) the line of development of the

meaning leads from weight through importance and gravity to brilliant appearance. The glory of God is an expression belonging to a perceptual context: that is also evident in certain passages.[100] It stands alongside the idea of the light of God's countenance therefore. It is of limited currency but the instances of it are ancient, clear and important.

When Isaiah sees Jahweh sitting upon a throne, high and lifted up, the seraphs cry one to another that the whole earth is full of His glory, Isa. 6: 3; the prophet does not see this, only the seraphs. Amos, Hosea, and Micah do not mention God's glory, nor does Jeremiah. But Ezekiel sees a form so wonderful and intricate that it almost defies description; its brightness round about is as the brightness of the bow that is in the day of rain; "this was the appearance of the likeness of the glory of God", Ezek. 1: 28; as is his custom, Ezekiel seeks by his mode of expression to avoid the perceptual. The glory of Jahweh raises itself (read בְּרוּם) from its place, 3: 12; it stands in the plain, 3: 23. Then the glory of the God of Israel is there in the inner court of the Temple, 8: 4. It rises on high and gives a command, 9: 3, and then quite suddenly, 9: 4, Jahweh takes its place—one thinks of the observations made on the messenger of the Lord (pp. 122 ff.). It mounts up from the cherub and the brilliance of the Lord's glory fills the Temple court, 10: 3. It goes forth from over the threshold of the Temple and the cherubs hold it over the east door of the Temple, 10: 18 ff. It rises over the Mount of Olives, 11: 22 ff. When the new order begins then the glory of the God of Israel comes from the way of the east into the Temple and fills the house, 43: 2, 4, 5; 44: 4. Ezekiel makes it quite clear that the glory of God is the representation of God through which the omnipresent God, who is present in Babylon just as much as in the holy land, displays His—shall we say special?—presence in the Temple. One might say this revelation form serves to reconcile the idea of the omnipresence of God with that of His having His abode in the Temple: it should also be observed however that the glory of God serves no other purpose; it is accorded no inordinate honour and in particular there is no suggestion that it promotes a mystical union between God and man. The glory of God in the Old Testament is a form of the divine presence and nothing else.

1 Kings 8: 11 and 2 Chron. 5: 14 also state that the glory of Jahweh fills the Temple: these passages are perhaps older than Ezekiel. One may not associate them with Isa. 6: 3, however,

for there the glory of Jahweh fills the whole earth; it is—so to speak—a cosmic, not a cultic, phenomenon. The glory of the Lord is likewise cosmic when in the great eschatological theophany of the last time[101] it reveals the return from the Exile and all flesh sees it together, Isa. 40: 5. At the return the glory of the Lord is the rereward, 58: 8. It rises upon Israel when the darkness is ended and the nations come to Israel's light.

All other references belong to the priestly writings and Chronicles. It is seen in the wilderness by the Israelites who have murmured against Jahweh, Ex. 16: 7, 10. It abides upon mount Sinai and its appearance is like devouring fire on the top of the mount in the eyes of the children of Israel, Ex. 24: 16 ff. It fills the tabernacle, Ex. 40: 34, as in 1 Kings 8: 11 it fills the Temple. When the cult is initiated and Aaron, with his sons, has prepared the first sacrifices, all the congregation stands before the Lord in order that the glory of the Lord may appear unto them; the people is blessed and then, in this festive moment, the glory of the Lord appears unto all the people and fire comes forth from the Lord and consumes the offering; with that the cult is inaugurated (Lev. 9: 6, 23, 24). When the congregation wants to stone Moses and Aaron, the glory of Jahweh appears—apparently as a warning and as a defence—to all in the tent of meeting, Num. 14: 10. So also it appears when Korah and his faction gather at the tent of meeting with the forbidden cult fire, Num. 16: 19; and when the congregation rebels against Moses and Aaron, Num. 17: 7. Again when Solomon completes the Temple and the first sacrifices are ready, fire falls from heaven which consumes the sacrifices and the glory of Jahweh fills the Temple, 2 Chron. 7: 1-3.

There are no personal manifestations of this representation. Only at the great events in divine history, at the giving of the Law, at the inauguration of sacrifice, when the cult and the guidance of the people are threatened, before sacrilege in the Temple, and at the world theophany—then and only then is the glory of Jahweh seen. One would expect to find it at the restoration of the Temple and in Ezra and Nehemiah, but it is not there. Even Haggai, Zechariah and Malachi do not speak of it any more. The period when it is taken seriously is the period from Ezekiel to the priestly writings. 2 Chron. 7: 1-3 is an echo. Otherwise it figures only in Isa. 6: 3 and in the prophecy of Hab. 2: 14 that the earth shall be filled with the knowledge of the glory of the Lord, as the waters cover the sea.

Part Two

MAN

41. MEN

THERE is neither a word for man nor for mankind in the Old Testament's vocabulary. The Hebrew word אָדָם means rather men taken as a whole, and it is only late and slowly that the individual idea replaces the collective. When one wants to say "man" one says בֶּן־אָדָם, Ps. 8: 4. Let us, so it runs in the Creation Narrative, make אָדָם and *let them* . . . Gen. 1: 26; and God created הָאָדָם . . . male and female created He *them*, Gen. 1: 27. This collective sense of the word אָדָם, where it coincides with the individual proper noun Adam, causes obvious confusion. "He called *their* name (collective) man אָדָם in that day when they were created. And Adam (the individual)=אָדָם lived an hundred and thirty years", etc., Gen. 5: 2-4. Of the 510 times that the word אָדָם occurs, only a very few times does it with any certainty mean the individual man or an individual man and not men.

The fact is theologically important in various respects. *1.* The Old Testament revelation deals not with the concept man but with flesh and blood men. *2.* As far as the Old Testament revelation is concerned a man is automatically in a sociological context; it thinks of man only in the plural and the relationships between every man and his neighbour are not accidental historical social contracts, they are part and parcel of the true life of man. In other words, *a* man is no man; man is man always reckoned only within and as a member of a group. *3.* Since the Old Testament is not familiar with the idea of a man isolated and individualized, it is also ignorant of the fact and the manner of the individual's relationship to his God. The individual is always member, co-partner, co-sufferer of a group. A man's individuality and his withdrawal from his group, whether for a time or gradually, is always the new, astonishing, unusual thing in the Old Testament, the thing that must be spoken of and received with astonishment. If for the man of the New Testament the basic question is: how shall I be a real and living member of the community? the question for the Old Testament man is the opposite: how is it possible and legitimate to step out of the community? When in the Old Testament a man is separated from his community it is a matter for complaint, Jer. 15: 17, Job 19: 13-19. Even in relation to their God, men stand always within and as members of the group to which they belong.

42. GROUPS AND CLASSIFICATIONS OF MEN

For the Old Testament the family is the unit from the point of view of which the origin of the peoples is explained. Just as the people of Israel, stemming from one man Abraham through Isaac and all the succeeding generations, i.e. by natural descent and increase, are to become as the stars of the heavens in number, so also all nations are of one blood and originate in one ancestor; the nations belong together to a certain extent as kindred, for their ancestors were related. Moabites and Ammonites are related, for they have a common ancestor Lot and their female ancestors were sisters. Blood binds and separates the nations, draws them together and keeps them apart: but in the last resort all nations belong to one family, for they can be traced back in three main groups to Noah, and the obligations laid upon Noah are binding for all of them, Gen. 9: 1-17. In Noah "all flesh that is upon the earth" is a unity.

The thing that divides the nations so that they are strangers to one another, distrustful, even enemies, is language. Jahweh confounded "the language of all the earth", Gen. 11: 9, that they might "not understand one another's speech", 11: 7. Those who cannot speak with one another also cannot share experiences, or business, or faith.

The efforts in Gen. 10 to enumerate the nations of the earth and to group them according to similarity of type or language or situation or history have no theological merit: the only thing that is important for us is that no man in the Old Testament is without nationality. The stranger, גֵּר, is landless because he has had to leave his native land or because his village or his clan have disappeared owing to plague or war or some similar catastrophe, but he does not cease to belong to a people. The stranger moves in communities where he has no rights either in matters of land, religion or law, but he moves among the members and within the tradition of his own people. There is no such thing in the Old Testament as a man without nationality. There is scarcely such a thing as a man who belongs only to a tribe. The individual stands over against all other peoples and over against his God within and together with his people. His people is the largest unit he knows—there is no such thing as mankind—and also the most natural unit since he is born into it. David was driven from his own people and told to go and serve other gods. Thereby he was being denied a share in the inheritance of Jahweh, 1 Sam. 26: 19. Jahweh, the God of Israel, has divided unto all the peoples under the whole heaven the sun and the moon and the stars, even all the host of heaven, that the peoples might worship and serve them, Deut. 4: 19— the gods belong to the peoples and individuals worship their people's gods. The Syrian Naaman, healed by the prophet of Jahweh, takes with him a quantity of earth from Jahweh's land in order to bring burnt offering and sacrifice upon it even in his heathen homeland to Jahweh and no longer to other gods. But when in Syria he goes to the temple of Rimmon with his king and like his king bows himself before the god Rimmon, then—may the Lord pardon him in this thing; 2 Kings 5: 15-18.

Men exist only as members of the social units: the peoples and their subdivisions, the tribes, clans and families. There are no men outside these units. Every man belongs to a people. The variety of peoples is due to the variety of languages. The variety of languages is a punishment by God on originally "unilingual" humanity. Yet, however different the peoples now are, originally they were all related. All the peoples are descended from ancestors and these ancestors were blood relations, sons of one father.

43. THE ORIGIN (CREATION) OF MAN

The Old Testament revelation offers two quite different accounts of the origin of man, Gen. 1: 26-30 and 2: 4-7, 18-22, accounts which have very little in common.

The one account, the older, 2: 4-7, 18-22 is to-day mythology —it always was, as certain elements in it clearly show. The original myth tells of a god earth made by the God Jahweh and joined to the serpent earth to make a pair. Both are created not for the earth but, as it is expressly stated, as dressers and keepers of God's garden, 2: 15. Also they are not meant to produce children, because the tree of life, i.e. that tree whose fruit, when one eats it, gives new and lasting life is not denied them. They are forbidden to take of the tree of life and eat it, 3: 22, only after their disobedience. It was in no way God's intention that this Adam and this Eve should be the parents of man[102] and it is only when the passage is set alongside the other that the idea emerges.

This other passage, Gen. 1: 26-30, is of a quite different sort. God resolves to make "man", not simply a man. Here it is not a question of creating a male and then forming the woman subsequently as the complement of the male, corresponding to him and serving as a suitable companion[103] for him. God means to make "man" in the plural. From the start therefore he will make men and women, "male and female". Theologically expressed: the sexual differentiation is inherent in earthly[104] man and not an accident. A human being is either male or female. Whoever is not male or female is not man. The woman in this passage is created neither after the man nor for him. She is created concurrently and as an equivalent. Man and woman are created for one another and alongside one another, and the commission is addressed to both in the self-same way: "Be fruitful and multiply and replenish the earth and subdue it." It is usually assumed in exegesis that Genesis 1 is an account of the creation of one pair, an assumption which stems from a naïve reading in of elements of the account in the next chapter. In fact there is nothing to hinder the assumption that God created men and women in considerable numbers, a whole series of pairs. Indeed this assumption has much to commend it in that it avoids the misfortune which the assumption of one original human pair involves, namely marriage of brothers and sisters amongst the children.

The creation narrative in the first chapter of Genesis knows nothing of Paradise lost, or of the Fall, and one may not say it merely omits to speak of them. On the contrary the silence is intentional. God created man for this earth of ours and not for Paradise, and men are on the earth not as a punishment for the sin of their first parents but because God willed that they should be. The origin of man's earthly existence is in the will of God and not in the guilt of man. God wills that men and women together should produce children and replenish the earth with them. It would probably be wrong however to conclude that the procreation of children and the replenishing of the earth with men was really God's ultimate purpose. When plant life is created it is explicitly and deliberately stated, 1: 11, 12, that the plants should yield seed. God creates them in such a way that they possess in themselves the means of reproduction by seed and God does not have to create them afresh from generation to generation. The gift of fertility is similarly given to all animals, 1: 22. And man shares this capacity with plants and animals, he has this gift of life by fruitfulness, received at creation, the ability to go on reproducing his species. God's ultimate purpose for man is therefore not expressed in the command "be fruitful and multiply" but in the elaboration of it, "replenish the earth and subdue it and have dominion" (over the animals). It is a purpose which is quite clearly aimed directly at the earth as it is without reference to Paradise. Life on earth is not punishment. Man's work is not under a curse. *The life-work of man is civilization.* And in God's own judgment it is all very good, "God saw that it was good", 1: 25, 31.

One cannot say that the author of Genesis 1 realizes that the story of Paradise and the Fall must necessarily be inserted between his account of creation and historical earthly man. Even the champion of the pre-Adamite doctrine[105] saw that that would be wrong. It is historical earthly man as he is whose creation is narrated in Genesis 1. Likewise one cannot deflect the unmistakable optimism with which God judges His creation from the world as it is by interposing a disturbance of creation. Where would it come? Gen. 1: 1—2: 4a, 5: 1-28, 30-32, 6: 9-22, etc., is a continuous story. In it the flood is not caused by a corruption of the created world or of mankind that one could call a fall—cf. the classic Jahwistic expression: *cuncta cogitatio cordis (hominum) intenta . . . ad malum omni tempore*, Gen. 6: 5 —in the eyes of the priestly writer the flood is obviously a difficulty. Were it not for Noah and the covenant with Noah which belongs so naturally to the whole system of covenants (§ 9) it would not have been necessary to relate the story of the flood at all. At a later date the author of the book of Chronicles "wrote" the history of the time from Adam to David without saying one word about creation, fall, flood, promises to Abraham, exodus or covenant at Sinai (1 Chron. 1: 1—2: 15). But since the story of the flood is told a reason is also given for it, a reason has to be given for it. And it is a vague and slender reason that is given: "the earth was corrupt before God, and the earth was filled with violence. And God saw the earth and, behold, it was corrupt; for all flesh had corrupted his way upon the earth", 6: 11-12.

What does this say? And why are we not told the most

important thing, namely, why it was that "all flesh had corrupted his way"? As soon as one ventures this question one
feels the embarrassment in the priestly reasoning concerning
the flood. So also the conclusion of the story of the flood in the
priestly account, 8: 14-19, 9: 1-17, is weak (in the Jahwistic
account it is otherwise, there the flood is a complete and self-
explanatory tale). Here in the priestly conclusion there is
again nothing to indicate what the purpose of the flood was.
Things remain as they were. The flood does not alter anything
in the world or in men. The one new thing in it all is that
whereas before the flood men commit violence, after the
flood the first covenant is effected, the first prohibitions are
uttered, the *first law* is laid down. It is undoubtedly following the line of what the priestly writer is aiming at with his "all
flesh had corrupted his way upon the earth" when one says
that the flood is the result of lawlessness. Where law is lacking
there is violence. The priestly writer does not actually say this,
but he opens his mouth as it were to say it, for the whole
underlying tendency of the priestly account is to advocate the
thesis that God-given law must be added to God's creation in
order that God's people may live in God's land a life that is in
accordance with God's will. Since this is the main stream of
thought, the reason for the flood is not the corrupt nature of
man but his lawlessness. In the Jahwistic writings there stands
after the account of the flood the expression of divine resigna-
tion: *sensus enim et cogitatio cordis humani in malum prona sunt
ab adolescentia*, 8: 21—a pessimistic critique of man. In the
priestly writings this has no equivalent. The blessing from
creation is repeated: "be fruitful and multiply and replenish
the earth! And the fear of you and the dread of you shall be
upon . . ." 9: 1-2. The critique of man remains optimistic.

The fact that revelation in the Old Testament has clear and
unmistakable limitations is perhaps nowhere so obvious as
here. Not merely in details and .incidentals but in cardinal
issues there is divergence. Man was made for Paradise; he was
made for earth. The life of earth with its labour and toil is God's
punishment for sin: it is God's will and in His original ordering.
The life of earth stands under the divine curse: it stands under
the divine blessing. These statements do not admit of being
combined; one can only reject both or choose one or other of
them. One falls into a real difficulty, however, if one feels
bound to accept the accounts of Paradise and the Fall because

of their place in the thinking of Paul. There can be no doubt that the Apostle did see revelation in these two stories and in their whole "pessimistic" outlook. But it is equally indubitable that the priestly writer had no hesitation in replacing the stories of Paradise and the Fall with his completely different representation and opinion of the situation. To him the two stories were not binding revelation. Nor is the hope of finding a clue to the resolution of this dilemma somewhere in the Old Testament ever fulfilled.

When finally one tries to ascertain what is common to the two points of view, in spite of all their differences, in order to identify it as Old Testament revelation one reaches the following conclusion: Man is God's creature. God, his creator, has given man life, a way of life and a mission. God his creator has also prepared for man the locus and circumstances of his life: the creation. By the will of God, His creature man is independent of all other parts of creation and superior to them. The created world is the servant of man. Man is lord of creation. By the will of God, his creator, man remains under the power and lordship of God: man is God's creature and only but also continually dependent on God.

44. THE NATURE OF MAN, I

In the later account of creation there are only two assertions made about the nature of man: one that man is male or female and the other that man is created in the image of God, *imago Dei* (see § 47). The latter assertion has been of particular theological importance. In the older account of creation we are told first that Jahweh forms man of the dust of the ground. Man is, to begin with, merely body, consisting (as 2: 23 shows) of flesh and bones. Into the nostrils of this body God then breathes the breath of life and man thereby becomes—not receives—a living soul. These are the anthropological and psychological elements of the creation narratives. It is worth taking them together with whatever other material on the subject may be found elsewhere in the Old Testament and trying to understand them in detail in order to arrive at a complete picture of what they tell us of the nature of man.

1. Man is Dust. God formed him of the dust of the ground, Gen. 2: 7, therefore he is dust and to dust he returns; he lives a certain time and then he returns to the ground from which he was taken, Gen. 3: 19. God it is who turns man back, Ps. 90: 3, who takes away man's breath so that he returns to dust, Ps. 104: 29, Job 34: 15, and to his earth, Ps. 146: 4. That man is dust means that he is frail and mortal. Dust returns to the earth as it was, Eccles. 12: 7; all are of dust and all turn to dust again, Eccles. 3: 20.

2. Man is Flesh. Where we speak of man's flesh and blood the Old Testament speaks of man's flesh and bone, Gen. 2: 23, 29: 14. Bone, עֶצֶם (especially in the plural), is also used by itself, but it may be that in cases where this happens the basic physiological sense still shines through; it is not clear whether it is an "I" that is represented by עַצְמִי עַצְמוֹתַי or whether on the other hand something is being said literally about "my bones".

The situation is different in the case of the word בָּשָׂר, flesh. This frequently means man in the physical sense, e.g. in the phrase כָּל-בָּשָׂר, "all flesh". One must be careful to observe that the phrase "all flesh" can be meant quite literally, i.e. it can mean men and beasts, in fact every living thing, יְקוּם (Gen. 7: 4, 23), that is flesh. In the flood all flesh wherein is the breath of life is to be destroyed from under heaven, i.e. men and all beasts, Gen. 6: 17; 9: 11. In other passages all flesh means only the beasts: "and all flesh died . . . and every man", Gen. 7: 21. The scope of the phrase varies. When all flesh shall see that it is God who acts, Ezek. 21: 4; 20: 48, when all flesh shall see the glory of God, Isa. 40: 5, when all flesh shall know that the Lord hath drawn forth His sword out of its sheath, Ezek. 21: 5, does all flesh mean only man or does it mean man and beasts together? The question cannot be easily answered, Rom. 8: 22. When in Deut. 5: 26 the writer asks who of all flesh hath heard the voice of God speaking out of the midst of the fire and lived, then clearly all flesh means man. It comes to this, then: that all flesh means sometimes merely man, sometimes merely beasts, sometimes men and beasts together, because flesh is the stuff of which their bodies are made. The single word "flesh" can stand for man, therefore; Ps. 56: 4 (cf. v. 11).

Flesh is the stuff of man; man is flesh. But flesh is only the corporal stuff of man; man is not only flesh. To flesh the breath of life must be added, Gen. 6: 17; 7: 15, before you can have a living being, a living soul; Gen. 9; 15. Flesh is only the lifeless stuff of man. Man consists of two things: soul, נֶפֶשׁ, and body or flesh, בָּשָׂר, Isa. 10: 18, Ps. 63: 1. Body is the human (or animal) form which the stuff flesh assumes. Soul and flesh, the combination in the two passages cited, is a wrong combination, for soul (as we shall show) is the form assumed by spirit whereas flesh is stuff not yet having a form (body). The contrast is clearer where the two stuffs stand alongside one another: "the Egyptians are men and not God; and their horses flesh and not spirit", Isa. 31: 3. Here one can establish a clear relationship: flesh is related to spirit as man is to God. Flesh is grass, Isa. 40: 6, it passes away. Without spirit flesh perishes, Job 34: 15, it is the victim of death. Therefore the man is cursed who trusteth in man and maketh flesh his arm, Jer. 17: 5. The fleshly arm has no power against God.

Because man is flesh, he is transitory and weak and stands in need of spirit. God, who alone does not have eyes of flesh, Job 10: 4, would have to destroy man if He wanted to measure him by His standard, but He forgives him because He remembers that man is flesh.

The idea that flesh is the seat of lust—$\epsilon\pi\iota\theta\upsilon\mu\iota\alpha$ in Paul, *concupiscentia* in Luther—and that this lust operates against the spirit, Gal. 5: 16-17, is not expressed in the Old Testament.

3. Man has the Breath of Life in Him. "He breathed into his nostrils the breath of life; and man became a living soul", Gen. 2: 7; man is he who has breath in his nostrils, Isa. 2: 22; in the sick (1 Kings 17: 17) and in the weak (Dan. 10: 17) there remains no breath; and if God gathers again unto Himself His breath which He has given to man then man must perish, Job 34: 14 f. Thus breath is the life and being of man, so that no breath means no man, Josh. 11: 11, and all breath means all that lives, Josh. 10: 40.

It would be wrong, however, to suppose that in the Old Testament breath of life can be identified either in respect of content or effect as a particular thing. Rather breath of life, which can be shortened to breath, Isa. 11: 4, Ps. 150: 6, Josh. 11: 14. 1 Kings 15: 29, Deut. 20: 16, is itself an abbreviation for breath of the spirit of life (Gen. 2: 7, cf. 7: 22). Breath, נְשָׁמָה, can equally mean spirit, רוּחַ, the breath of God—the spirit or blast of His anger, Job 4: 9; the breath that is in me—the spirit of God in my nostrils, Job 27: 3; the breath of the Almighty giveth me life—the spirit of God hath made me, Job 33: 4. It is by the operation of the spirit of God that the fleshly body[106] of man, formed of dust, lives. The breath of life is the spirit of God dwelling in living man.

4. Man as the Recipient of the Spirit of God. What we call spirit, רוּחַ, means first of all air in motion, and therefore also the wind. The breath of God, i.e. the cold wind, makes ice, Ps. 147: 17. A wind comes forth from the Lord and brings quails, Num. 11: 31. In such cases the two meanings, wind and spirit, are still almost involved in one another. Certainly the natural, meteorological element from which the whole idea of the spirit is derived is still present. To mention this here in a theological connexion is justifiable in that only a glance at the whole scope of the meanings enables one adequately to determine an individual meaning.

From a meteorological context where things are visible on a large scale the concept turns to a physiological context where things are visible on a small scale. It remains perceptible, however: one can still detect it. With the blast of thy nostrils the waters were piled up, Ex. 15: 8. Thou didst blow with thy wind, a breathing, the sea covered them, Ex. 15: 10. The breath (or spirit?) of the Lord began to move him, Judg. 13: 25. When he had drunk, his breath (or spirit) came again and he revived, Judg. 15: 19. When he had eaten, his breath (or spirit?) came again to him, 1 Sam. 30: 12. Life is breathing, and breath is observed as wind. Hunger and thirst take it away, food and drink help it to return; excitement such as Samson's displays itself in agitated breathing, Judg. 13: 25. Likewise the physiological can give place to the psychological and the apperception of wind, and breath is gone. In its place is the apperception or rather the concept of spirit; we say the concept because one can only speak negatively of spirit at first. Spirit has no perceptibility, it is not something which has form or locus, it can be known and described only by its effects and its manifestations. It is a particular kind of tension, excitement, state of mind and capacity. It is that which is added to the corporal to make the living. There were bones, sinews, flesh, and skin, Ezek. 37: 6, 8; but spirit had to be added before the whole could be life. Without this initial corporality there can be no spirit according to the Old Testament. It knows of no independent realm of the spirit. But also it knows of no life without spirit. It would be wrong, however, simply to equate spirit and life, since the Old Testament speaks advisedly of the spirit of life because spirit and life are not identical.

It is typical of the unsystematic nature of the Old Testament revelation that its spirit terminology is extensive. Only when it has been reviewed will it be possible to understand what is meant by saying that man appears in the Old Testament as the recipient of the spirit of God. When Samson is travelling to Timnah with his parents he meets a young lion that roars against him. Then the spirit of the Lord forced its way through (as through a cleft) in him and he rent the lion, Judg. 14: 6. In the same way the spirit of the Lord comes upon him and he smites thirty men. The same thing happens to Saul and he prophesies among the prophets, 1 Sam. 10: 10. Here the spirit of God (so it is expressly in 1 Sam. 10: 6, 10) comes on him like a fit, quite suddenly and with a marked, extraordinary but transitory effect: the spirit dwells in the man as in a shell. It is quite the reverse in Judg. 6: 34, 1 Chron. 12: 19, 2 Chron. 24: 20, where we find the spirit of the Lord clothed the person. Here the spirit is the shell, or rather the sphere which envelops the man.[107] One cannot form any conclusion about the length of time a person retained the spirit, however; in the case of Gideon, Judg. 6: 34, it was a long possession: in the case of Amos in 1 Chron. 12: 19 and Zechariah in 2 Chron. 24: 20, short.

Besides the above two clear and significant usages there are others which are quite colourless. Joshua is "a man, in whom is spirit", Num. 27: 18; that is evidently a permanent attribute of Joshua, and his qualification to be Moses' successor, 27: 19-23. According to Deut. 34: 9 Joshua is full of the spirit of wisdom, "for Moses had laid his hands upon him". Here are two variations; in the one it is a question of a spirit of a particular sort, and of these particular kinds of spirit we shall have more to say later; in the other the spirit is transferred to Joshua by Moses and from himself. The spirit is also upon (it was *in* Joshua) Moses, Num. 11: 25. God takes of this spirit and puts it upon the seventy elders so that the spirit rests upon them and they begin to prophesy. Moses wished, however, that God would put His spirit upon all the people, Num. 11: 25-29. Note the variation in terminology! Joshua has "spirit" "in him"; Moses has "the spirit" "upon him". When God took away a part of the spirit that was upon Moses and laid it on the seventy this part was called roundly "the spirit"; Moses indeed calls it "his", i.e. "God's", spirit. These variations in expression are neither inaccuracies nor weaknesses in style; rather they show that it is not possible to speak clearly and precisely about the spirit since the spirit cannot be adequately perceived. One can say the spirit is upon a person; one can say equally well the spirit is in him. It is equally accurate whether one says a person has spirit or the spirit or the spirit of God in or upon him. Therefore it is possible to take away a bit of the spirit, as if it were a quantum, and likewise it is possible to speak of this bit when it is given to the seventy as if it were the whole and call it "the" spirit. For in fact spirit is in its very nature neither upon nor in, neither a whole nor a part nor a quantum at all. One can say a great variety of things about it because really one can say nothing, or at least very little, about it.

What can one say about it? We started off above with the meteorological meaning because obviously the word רוּחַ, air in motion (like πνεῦμα from πνέω) has its origin there and both the physiological and the psychological sense of the word are derived from it, for the phenomena of life, all emotions and life itself are accompanied by breathing of one kind or another. Where the essentially spiritual (*pneumatische*) takes the place of the psychological[108] sense is hard to say. The following points can, however, be made.

a) When the Old Testament speaks of spirit, it means a quite definite and particular kind of exertion and direction of the powers and faculties of a being. b) Spirit always comes from God: He alone has the ability to give spirit or a spirit to a being. Even an evil spirit comes from God. God sent an evil spirit between Abimelech and the men of Shechem, Judg. 9: 23. When the spirit of the Lord had departed from Saul, an evil spirit from the Lord troubled him, 1 Sam. 16: 14; 18: 10; 19: 9. c) The spirit upon a man or in him can be a transitory experience, a condition lasting some time, or the disposition of a life-time. It is a transitory thing when the spirit of God comes upon Saul so that his anger is kindled and he liberates Jabesh, 1 Sam. 11: 6, or upon Azariah so that he preaches, 2 Chron. 15: 1. A longer possession is indicated when Joseph has the spirit of God so that he can interpret dreams, Gen. 41: 38, or when the contemporaries of Moses have the spirit of wisdom, חָכְמָה, and can make the priestly garments, Ex. 28: 3, or when the Messiah has the spirit of wisdom and understanding, the spirit of counsel and might, the spirit of knowledge and of the fear of the Lord, Isa. 11: 2. A life-long condition is meant when God gives the spirit of life (so also in Gen. 6: 17, 7: 15) to the dust of the earth in order that man may have life, which ceases when God takes back this breath of life—carefully called breath of the spirit of life, Gen. 7: 22—Job 34: 14.

d) When the Old Testament speaks of a spirit of life, Gen. 6: 17; of skill, Ex. 28: 3; of wisdom, Deut. 34: 9; of counsel, Isa. 11: 2; of lying, 1 Kings 22: 22, 23, etc., it does not mean that there are several spirits of which one has life as its particular attribute, another skill, a third wisdom, so that when a man is given one particular spirit he receives that spirit's particular gift of life or wisdom or whatever it may be. This conception of a plurality of spirits is not merely foreign to the Old Testament, it is also repugnant. A spirit is called a spirit of life in the Old Testament not because it is distinct from other spirits in alone having the power to impart life; rather it is so called because God invests this particle of the spirit with power to give life. As far as the Old Testament is concerned there are no individual spirits with special functions and provinces, there is only the One spirit, of which particles (whether spatial or temporal we know not) according to their God-given commission produce results of different kinds—now life, now wisdom. If subsequently they are called spirit of life or spirit of wisdom it is not intended that the name should make any real differentiation. The scriptural warrant for this assertion is in Isa. 11: 2: "The spirit of the Lord shall rest upon him, the spirit of wisdom and understanding, the spirit of counsel and might, the spirit of knowledge and of the fear of the Lord". Here the true Old Testament view is easily comprehensible: this does not speak of four different spirits but of the one spirit of the Lord manifested in this case in three or, if you like, six operations.

Man, therefore, who possesses the spirit of life does not possess the spirit whose nature (and therefore whose limit) it is to call forth life; he possesses the spirit who in this case and in this mission is commissioned to give life and who may be commissioned on another occasion to give wisdom or lying or the fear of God. The life of men is derived not from the spirit that is in him; the life of men is derived from the gracious will of God. Man owes his life to the circumstance that God's spirit fills him.

Two questions immediately arise. If the fact that a man lives is proof that God's spirit fills him, how can the spirit of God be said to come upon a man in particular cases? And how likewise can we speak of a spirit in man that is obviously not God's spirit? These two questions will be answered later (§ 50, section 3). Meanwhile we must turn to the sentence which says that man, when God had breathed into his nostrils the breath of life, became a living soul, Gen. 2: 7. What does that mean?

45. THE NATURE OF MAN, II

5. Man is a Living Soul. This sentence, which corresponds exactly to Gen. 2: 7, says three things. It says first of all that man became a living soul and now is a living soul. It does not say man has a living soul. Soul is the nature of man, not his possession. A dependence is therein stated. What I have I can do with as I like. What I am made, however, I am accountable for to the one who has made me this thing. God made man a living soul. The existence of man goes hand in hand with his being soul. Whoever is not soul is not man. Whoever is man is a soul.

The second thing the sentence says is that man is a soul. Were man only flesh made from the dust he would be only body. Were man only spirit without body, he would be formless. For spirit is by nature without form. In that man is spirit-filled body, he is soul. Soul is equivalent here to being with form, one might almost say personality. The aesthetic element—in the philosophical sense—in the soul concept should not be overlooked. The Old Testament with all its inclination towards realism has a marked liking for (bodily) beauty. Notice is not seldom taken of the fact that a man or a woman is comely to behold. When David's qualities are being rehearsed it is expressly stated that he is "a comely person, and the Lord is with him", 1 Sam. 16: 18. The two things stand together, for the two are interdependent. If a man is comely God is with him, and to whomsoever God is well-disposed, that man becomes and is comely. Form in the Old Testament does not play the same important rôle that *kalokagathia* played among the Greeks, but it is not a matter of indifference. Form is essential to soul.

What then does soul mean in the Old Testament? The Hebrew word for it is נֶפֶשׁ, which is nearly always (more than 650 times out of a possible 756) rendered in Greek *psyche*. This word נֶפֶשׁ has a great variety of meanings. The more original like "throat", Isa. 5: 14; "perfume", Isa. 3: 20; "greediness", Isa. 56: 11, Ezek. 7: 19, do not affect the issue—there remains variation enough.

The נֶפֶשׁ is the seat of the will. "They lift up their soul to return" is equivalent to "they long to return", Jer. 22: 27; "their bread is for their נֶפֶשׁ" means "for their appetite", Hos. 9: 4.[109] The נֶפֶשׁ is also the seat of the feeling. The נֶפֶשׁ of a stranger is the way a stranger feels, Ex. 23: 9. "My נֶפֶשׁ shall rejoice in . . .", Isa. 61: 10. "My נֶפֶשׁ shall weep", Jer. 13: 17. "My (God's!) נֶפֶשׁ was alienated from her", Ezek. 23: 18. The נֶפֶשׁ is likewise the seat of life; one can very frequently translate the word "life". "Deliver my life from the sword". Ps. 22: 20, "Your life from death", 33: 19. "As her נֶפֶשׁ was in departing" is "as her life was in departing". Gen. 35: 18. "My נֶפֶשׁ is yet whole in me" is equivalent to "my life is yet in me", 2 Sam. 1: 9. God himself swears "by his life", Jer. 51: 14, Amos 6: 8; God also has a נֶפֶשׁ therefore.

Since נֶפֶשׁ is often almost the same as life it can also stand for people, an individual, I, thou, her. "The totality of נֶפֶשׁ" means "all the people", Josh. 10: 28; 11: 11. "Sixteen נֶפֶשׁ"=sixteen people, sixteen men, Gen. 46: 18. "Abraham got נֶפֶשׁ" is equivalent to "he acquired (or took) people, slaves", Gen. 12: 5. "If a man steal a נֶפֶשׁ"="if a man steals a man", Deut. 24: 7. "That my נֶפֶשׁ may bless thee"="that I may bless thee", Gen. 27: 25. "My נֶפֶשׁ hateth them=I (God!) hate them" Isa. 1: 14. "When a נֶפֶשׁ"="when any one", Lev. 2: 1. "She hath kept her נֶפֶשׁ from blame"="she hath kept herself from blame", Jer. 3: 11. If one deplores the fact that the English word "soul" has fallen into misuse and is used in ways that are wholly inappropriate and cheap, one can appreciate what has happened with the Old Testament word נֶפֶשׁ—in one place it means something, in another it means practically nothing. The only difference is that one cannot observe as in English a gradual decline from an original lofty concept, theological and philosophical. One can say what soul really and properly and originally is. Can one do the same with נֶפֶשׁ?

Man became a living נֶפֶשׁ, Gen. 2: 7. That is the starting point. Jahweh made us this נֶפֶשׁ, Jer. 38: 16. That obviously refers back to Gen. 2: 7, although it changes the concept somewhat since in Gen. 2: 7 man *is* what in Jer. 38: 16 he *has*. But

what does נֶפֶשׁ mean here, and נֶפֶשׁ חַיָּה? The latter expression
occurs not only in Gen. 2: 7, it is found in the incomprehensible gloss of Gen. 2: 19, still in the priestly narrative.
There it means creatures—creatures of the water, Gen. 1: 20;
beasts of the earth, Gen. 1: 24; every living creature that is with
man, 9: 12. In Gen. 9: 15 God makes a covenant with man and
with "all living souls of all flesh" and 9: 16 speaks of a covenant
of God's "with all living souls of all flesh that is upon the earth".
Here clearly the beasts have a living soul like men: the passages
Gen. 1: 30, 21; 9: 10, Lev. 11: 10, 46 and also Ezek. 47: 9 are
merely formal but not different: "all living souls" are in the
priestly writings either the beasts or beasts and men together.

Between the expression as it is used in Gen. 2: 7, where man
becomes "a living soul", and the expression in the priestly
writings where it corresponds exactly to the modern expression
"a living creature", there is a space of five hundred years and a
wide cleavage in point of view. We reach therefore some important negative conclusions. *1*. The expression Gen. 2: 7 did
not become standard for the Old Testament world; the priestly
writer did not adopt it. *2*. The expression "living soul" is not
unequivocal and therefore not clear as used in Gen. 2: 7, since
there are no other passages to explain it. It probably states no
more than that man by receiving the breath of life became a
living being. *3*. Since the passage Gen. 2: 7 is not clear and
since—in spite of its antiquity and its claim to instruct—it did
not become standard for the Old Testament one may not build
any anthropology on it.

What is meant then when the Old Testament speaks of a
man's נֶפֶשׁ? The most we can do is to make a number of
important points. And as a preliminary let us say נֶפֶשׁ means
soul, with the reservation that it is *the soul as it is known in the
Old Testament* that is involved and that all Greek and modern
conceptions must be excluded.

a) The soul is not the I. In the Psalter the word occurs 144
times, 105 times in the form "my soul". But one may not simply
replace it with "I", rather "my soul" is the I as it were in a
special context and degree and in a particular respect—the I
in a private and unitary capacity. This is expressed in a phrase
like Job. 14: 22, "his soul within him", or Ps. 42: 5, 6; 131: 2,
Job 30: 16, "my soul within me". The soul is not the I, it is
added to it. b) The soul dies when the man dies; the Old

Testament knows nothing of the immortality of the soul. "And it came to pass as her (Rachel's) soul was in departing, for she (Rachel) died . . ." Gen. 35: 18; "she breathes out her soul" (gives up the ghost) Jer. 15: 9; "let my soul die" Num. 23: 10, Judg. 16: 30; "God taketh away the soul", 2 Sam. 14: 14. It might have been imagined that when the soul is once separated from the body it continues to exist somehow in some other place. Such an idea never occurs. c) Soul exists only in connexion with body. It does not exist before body, receiving body as a garment to put on. Soul comes into being when God breathes the breath of the spirit of life into flesh, Gen. 2: 7. When soul quits the body, it dies. d) *Soul is therefore the (individualized) spirit, delimited by its connexion with a body*, which animates the body.[110] e) The seat of the soul is the blood, "the blood is the soul", Deut. 12: 23, Lev. 17: 14. The blood is the sustainer of life; the soul ends with life; the identification of blood and soul is therefore not far off. Furthermore, it is demanded by the fact that in the Old Testament the blood of a man is not just one thing among many. It is something which forms a oneness. Blood as something common to all men and soul as something common to all men are combined in the one word life. f) Body-soul dualism does not occur in the Old Testament, because of course the soul always presupposes the body. It cannot exist without the body. g) For this reason also the soul does not measure up to being the seat of the spiritual life as, under the influence of Greek ideas, some have suggested; it has too little autonomy.

46. THE NATURE OF MAN, III

6. Man has Feeling, Understanding and Will. Of the three physiological organs of the human body to which the moderns[111] mostly attribute mental and spiritual functions—brain, heart and bowels, the Old Testament knows only the last two. The brain[112] and its significance are entirely unknown in the Old Testament. The result is that the heart is treated as the seat of the understanding, the bowels as the seat of the feelings, and aspiring and willing is divided between the two according to whether deliberation or inclination is involved.

Concerning feelings there is little to say, since they follow much the same pattern in all men. The most striking thing is great excitability. The Old Testament man is alarmed, trembles, shudders very quickly; astonishment and overwhelming amazement (שְׁמָמָה, the θάμβος of the gospels) come easily to him and judging from the threats in the divine pronouncement of judgment they certainly should. Man is destined to excitability in the face of the vicissitudes of life. Then one must mention the great range of emotions stretching from the loudest jubilation and the boldest confidence right to the desire to die, Num. 11: 15, 1 Kings 19: 4, Jonah 4: 8. The fact that the expressions for the emotions originated mostly in material contexts (wax red for be afraid, Nah. 2: 11; my bowels boil and rest not, Job 30: 27) shows that these expressions are popular and possess no deeper insights.

The sphere of knowledge is preponderantly pragmatic. חָכְמָה means first of all skill, Ex. 36: 2, then wisdom in all things gained from experience, 1 Kings 10: 3-4, and only in Prov. 11: 2 the state of mind which is able to face all the questions and difficulties of life. Even the knowledge of God is of a pragmatic character; it tells what God wills, it does not explain God; its aim is righteousness not theology. Moreover, enquiry is not the right way to knowledge. The Old Testament man does not approach things with questions and answers as does the Greek. The Hebrew בִּינָה, insight, means examination of and research into circumstances like the Greek critique, but with this difference—that critique is an activity and a self-imposed task, but *the Hebrew insight is a gift*. With God is wisdom and might: He hath counsel and understanding, Job 12: 13; and to the man that pleaseth Him He gives wisdom and knowledge and joy, Eccles. 2: 26. The most important submission in the whole Old Testament theory of knowledge is this, that all true knowledge comes from God.

It follows from that, as will be shown later (§ 50) that God grants His revelation to certain people in order that they may teach others. It also follows that the Old Testament revelation has nothing to say of the prospect of man's investigating the world. Even the considerable knowledge of nature in the book of Job is not concerned with details and is not bound up with any theory on the subject of how man knows and whether he should know.

47. THE NATURE OF MAN, IV

7. *Man is created in the Image of God.* In the priestly account of creation, Gen. 1: 26, God declares His intention to make man "in our image, after our likeness",[113] and the intention is

carried out. "God created man in his own image, in the image of God created he him; male and female created he them", 1: 27. The third of these clauses is not without importance; it precludes from the start any thinking about the outward form, for that is not the same in both man and woman. But what does the whole sentence mean? Dogmatics builds on it the doctrine of the *Imago Dei*. What does the Old Testament revelation actually state?

The concept appears only in the priestly narrative. The Jahwist knows nothing of a plan or image according to which Jahweh had created Adam. And no other Old Testament source knows of it. Also the priestly writer's statement is not repeated or utilized in any other passage which could be consulted. One is confined to the priestly material. Of these 5: 1 takes up the phrase "in the likeness of God" without adding anything that would help, and 9: 6 likewise refers back in the sentence "for in the image of God made he man" without offering anything new. The biblical meaning of the phrase must therefore be discovered from Genesis 1 or it cannot be discovered at all.

It is widely accepted that the image of God consists in man's right to have the animals, the plants and the earth at his disposal and to rule over them, 1: 26, 28. As God rules over the whole world, so men should rule over the earth and all that is in it. Man, only a little lower than the angels, is made to have dominion over the works of God's hands, Ps. 8: 6. And as the appraisal of God's creation is good, very good, so also civilization is given a positive appraisal. It is the fulfilment of God's command: "replenish the earth and subdue it", Gen. 1: 28. Only on linguistic grounds can the explanation be offered that God creates man in such a way that he alone in contrast to the beasts has an upright form. In this respect man is clearly distinguished from the beast and with the additional words "in our form, to look like us" is raised above the beasts and made to approach nearer to God. The ancient classical world in earliest times made much of the fact that man alone has an upright form; a fact which underlies the concept of the *Imago Dei*, which in its turn has given rise to far-reaching speculation in the field of systematic theology.[114]

48. THE LIFE OF MAN

1. Birth. To man as to beasts and plants is granted the gift of fertility with all it involves. "Give me children or else I die", Gen. 30: 1. The woman shall be saved through her childbearing, 1 Tim. 2: 15. But the man is not in God's stead who withholds the fruit of the womb, Gen. 16: 2; 30: 2. Sons are a gift of Jahweh and the fruit of the womb a reward. When God wills He shuts up a woman's womb, 1 Sam. 1: 6, or gives to the barren the promise of a child, Judg. 13: 3, exactly as He wills; not however in such a way that God determines all man's actions. The sinful man can defy God's ordinance, though he pays for it with his life, Gen. 38: 9 ff. Procreation and child-bearing are fulfilment of the divine ordinance; fruitfulness and barrenness come from the hand of God. A woman's pregnancy is by the will of God. The pain she suffers in childbirth is the result of her sin, Gen. 3: 16.

2. Death. Where there is birth there must also be death: birth and death are the two corresponding extremities of life, and both have their appointed time. Eccles, 3: 2. In Old Testament narratives death, at least when it comes in old age, plays the rôle of a friend. Job died, old and full of days, Job 42: 17. Abraham gave up the ghost, and died in a good old age, an old man and full of years; and was gathered to his people, Gen. 25: 8. Accounts of this kind are numerous and death appears in them as that which should be. The same is true of those passages which speak of the span of life. The days of man's life shall be 120 years, Gen. 6: 3; the days of our years are threescore years and ten or even by reason of strength fourscore years, Ps. 90: 10; in the day of salvation he shall be called a child who dies an hundred years old and whoever does not reach an hundred years shall be accursed, Isa. 65: 20; the fear of the Lord prolongeth days but the years of the wicked shall be shortened, Prov. 10: 27; but all must die. The Old Testament thinks of an early death as punishment for godlessness, 1 Sam. 2: 32; it sees sudden death as a divine judgment, Jer. 28: 16-17; it views the end with terror, Ps. 73: 19; it knows that because of his disobedience the tree of life is denied to man, Gen. 3: 22; but *it knows nothing of the idea that the death of man is punishment and a breach of God's original order.* The story of the Fall itself shows that man's punishment consists in the laborious nature of his work. His toil shall last till he dies, Gen. 3: 17-19. Man's death is the necessary and tacit assumption behind "till thou return unto the ground", 3: 19; and in order that man may not frustrate the divine arrangement the way to the tree of life is barred, 3: 22-23. Any attempt to read something else into the story of the Fall is idle.

"Thou turnest man to destruction", Ps. 90: 3; "The Lord killeth and maketh alive", 1 Sam. 2: 6.

3. Death as the End. With death, the life of the individual ceases for ever. In Jesus' day the Sadducees still say there is no resurrection, Matt. 22: 23, and however much they may be contradicted they are nevertheless not accused of heresy. Their view is possible, for it is in accordance with the Old Testament revelation. It is true there is in Dan. 12: 2 a resurrection of the dead with a double purpose, "some to everlasting life, and some to everlasting contempt". Again there is the statement in Isa. 26: 14, "dead shall not live, shades shall not arise" with 26: 19 in strong contrast speaking of a partial resurrection: "thy dead shall live, my dead bodies shall arise".[115] Finally Ps. 49: 15 should be mentioned: "But God will redeem my soul from the hand of Sheol: for he shall receive me". Some see in this a "removal to heaven without previous death", others "a receiving by God of the soul of man after death (a uniting of the righteous with their God)", others "rescue from imminent death in the hour of danger", others "persuasion of the personal immortality of the individual, and especially of the sufferer".[116] It is well to note from such confusion how uncertain the interpretation is and how bold the interpreters. Further passages relating to resurrection are not to be found. Ps. 16: 10, "thou wilt not suffer thy holy one to see the pit", speaks of being spared death, not of resurrection; Ps. 73: 24 is incomprehensible in the second half (R.V. "and afterwards receive me to glory") and seeks as does the entire Psalm (verse 19) the settlement in this life; Job 19: 25-29 expresses, as even Chrysostom saw, the expectation "that God will vindicate Job here on the earth during his life".[117] The Old Testament betrays only the humblest beginnings of resurrection hope. It knows of (temporary) deliverance from death: thou hast delivered my soul (my life) from the pit of corruption, Isa: 38: 17, but what is dead is dead and remains dead. Sheol cannot praise thee, death cannot celebrate thee. They that go down into the pit cannot hope for thy truth. The living, the living, he shall praise thee, as I do this day; Isa. 38: 18-19.

In the providence of God death follows on life and in the providence of God death is the end. There is nothing more than what we know here on earth. Only with difficulty and half-heartedly were the righteous of the Old Testament able to relate death and the underworld and its forms and powers to the living God; the dead are unclean, Lev. 21: 1, removed from God's sphere.

4. Translation instead of Death. As belief in the resurrection is only vaguely hinted at in the Old Testament when it is expressed at all, is but in embryo and appears as only a partial and not a general resurrection, Isa. 26: 19, Dan. 12: 2, so this other idea, of translation, affects only selected individuals. Enoch walked with God: and he was not; for God took him, Gen. 5: 24. Elijah is parted from his companion by a chariot of fire and goes up by a whirlwind into heaven, 2 Kings 2: 11. But this substitute for death is rare. Even Moses dies; only God Himself buried him and no man knoweth of his sepulchre, Deut. 34: 5-6. Translation in the Old Testament is the exception.

5. Life between Birth and Death. We are concerned here not with details, of which there would be an infinite number, but with the basic principles governing the Old Testament view of the life of man between birth and death. Four points are important.

a) The whole of life and every part of it comes from God and is under His guidance. The Lord directeth the steps of a man, even against man's intention, Prov. 16: 9; power and weakness, hunger and plenty, poverty and riches (1 Sam. 2: 4-7) and good and a curse (2 Sam. 16: 11-12) come from His hand. He delivers a man into another's hand though the man did not lie in wait for him, Ex. 21: 13. b) There is however that which just happens, that is to say impersonal fate, which has no connexion with God. The Philistines, 1 Sam. 6: 9, are not alone in reckoning with the possibility of a chance; for Ruth also "her hap was" to light on the portion of the field belonging to Boaz, Ruth 2: 3, and Ecclesiastes speaks readily of fate as something to which both the wise man and the fool are subject, Eccles. 2: 14, which he has indeed in common with the beasts, 3: 19; yes, that is the evil in life—that all share the same fate, 9: 2-3. These would be the passages from which to develop a biblical doctrine of chance. c) The opinion of human life is in the main somewhat unfavourable. The man who enjoys the normal span of life has his fill of life. Unusually long life is labour and sorrow, Ps. 90: 10, for it is soon gone. Man that is born of a woman is of few days and full of—trouble, Job 14: 1. Ecclesiastes chants very clearly and sadly the dirge of labour and vanity. The reason for this melancholy outlook, that the life of man is under the wrath of God, we shall deal with later.

d) Prominence should now be given to the prayer which arises from the knowledge of the depressing results of the divine wrath: "make us glad according to the days wherein thou hast afflicted us, and the years wherein we have seen evil", Ps. 90: 15. The divinely ordained content of human life is joy. There is hardly a word so characteristic of the Old Testament as the word joy. Israel's task is to serve the Lord her God with joyfulness and with gladness of heart, Deut. 28: 47. The reason for such joyfulness is the abundance of all things which God gives, i.e. gratitude. Ideal historical pictures show how Israel came over to this view. Eating and drinking and making merry, 1 Kings 4: 20, are the characteristic occupation of Israel and Judah in the time of Solomon. That must be God's will; ye should be merry before the Lord "in all that ye put your hand unto, wherein the Lord thy God hath blessed thee", Deut. 12: 7. Joy arising from gratitude for God's goodness is the characteristic of human life. And when the day of salvation comes God increases men's joy: "they joy before thee", Isa. 9: 3. The author of joy is God. But the form, it should be noted, is worldly: joy according to the joy in harvest, Isa. 9: 3; with the mouth filled with laughter, Ps. 126: 2. That in the streets of Jerusalem the voice of mirth and the voice of gladness, the voice of the bridegroom and the voice of the bride should no more be heard, is for the prophet the most painful proof of mankind's deviation from that which God intended; Jer. 7: 34.

6. *Work and Profession.* The Old Testament knows neither the word profession nor the idea behind it. The activities which may give men their names and which we are wont to regard as professions are in reality either social functions, as in the case of the king, the judge, the priest, or they are particular crafts like that of the potter, the smith and the surgeon. But they are not professions; by vocation almost all men are without exception husbandmen; even the priests, as Luke 1: 23, 39, 40 shows. Profession is a concept introduced by the Reformers.[118]

Work too is a modern concept. Of course the Old Testament man labours and "does all his work", Ex. 20: 9, but the labour has the exclusive purpose of providing what is necessary for life: work as moral testing or as a means of arresting a person's attention is unknown. The Old Testament censures the lazy, but only because by his laziness he is reduced to want. Work in the Old Testament is not a blessing, it is a necessity; it is toil and it is under a curse, Gen. 3: 19.

49. THE WORLD OF MAN

The Bible knows of only one present world, but since it speaks of it constantly in its relation to man one may call it the world of man. One understands man only when one has reviewed the main features of his world.

1. The Structure of the World[119]

a) The world consists of heaven earth and sea, Ex. 20: 11. The bipartite formula earth and heaven as it is in the earlier passages, Gen. 2: 4b, heaven and earth in the later passage, Gen. 2: 4a, is only an abbreviation of the tripartite. The word "sea" in it is a rather inadequate substitute for a much more extensive kind of realm of water: the earth, the heaven and the deep (תְּהוֹם) that coucheth beneath, Deut. 33: 13. The earth is here—in contrast to the original but isolated cosmogony of Gen. 2: 5-6—surrounded by the waters, Gen. 1: 9, and they are not merely round and under the earth but also above it. A fixed expanse, the "firmament of the heaven", Gen. 1: 15, holds back the waters above the firmament, Gen. 1: 7, only in times of flood do they break out together with the fountains of the great deep, Gen. 7: 11.

The earth is therefore merely a small space with the tiny vault of heaven above it, the whole being enclosed on all sides by mighty and menacing (§ 29) waters. But it is perhaps only to the modern person that the creation appears small and tiny. The Old Testament betrays no such impression. On the other hand it does have something which is lost to us—a strong sense of the constant insecurity of the world.

b) The strangest thing of all in this to the modern mind is the picture of *heaven*, for this reason: that it does not lose itself in azure infinity but is strictly limited. Heaven in the Old Testament, in all passages that are clear—a fixed and dogmatically accepted world picture is out of the question, ideas probably remained in a state of flux—is the small space that stretched out above the earth but beneath the firmament. It is only what we call the air; the fowl of the heaven in Gen. 1: 26, Matt. 6: 26 are the fowl in the air.

It is only late and gradually that heaven acquires significance therefore in the Old Testament. The title for Jahweh, "the God of heaven", 2 Chron. 36: 23=Ezra 1: 2, Neh. 1: 4, 5; 2: 4, 20, Jonah 1: 9,[120] is apologetic and polemic. It is addressed to an age which saw divinities in sun, moon and stars, the chief luminaries of heaven. The same purpose is served by the expression: Jahweh is God in heaven above and upon the earth beneath, Deut. 4: 39, Josh. 2: 11. It makes clear also that "in heaven" indicates a sphere of influence more than a habitation. This is true also of Ps. 136: 26, God of heaven, of Ps. 14: 2; 33: 13; 80: 14; 102: 19; 148: 1; Lam. 3: 50, God looks down and beholds from heaven, and Jer. 23: 24, God fills heaven and earth. It is likewise apologetic and polemic when it is claimed expressly and vigorously that God made the heavens: Ps. 33: 6; 96: 5; 102: 25; 136: 5; Neh. 9: 6; 1 Chron. 16: 26; Prov. 3: 19. The heavens which are made are a created thing, not an independent being and certainly not a divinity. On the same basis heaven is called that on which God rides, Ps. 68: 33, and God's throne, Isa. 66: 1; Ps. 11: 4; 93: 2; 103: 19. And on account of the variety of these expressions, which are all possible because none of them contains a pre-eminent idea, and on account of the nature of the theological intention that underlies them, one may doubt whether the statement that heaven is God's habitation (Deut. 26: 15; 1 Kings 8: 30, 39, 43, 49=2 Chron. 6: 21, 30, 39; Ps. 2: 4; 123: 1; 2 Chron. 30: 27; also in the form "God in heaven", Ps. 115: 3, 2 Chron. 20: 6, Lam. 3: 41, Eccles. 5: 1)—one may doubt whether this statement says anything about God at all or whether its real purpose is not to take from heaven its claim to divinity by asserting that it serves to house God. In any case heaven as the dwelling of God does not play the theological rôle which the pious imagination of later times assigned to it.

c) There is a further point of cosmology to be made about heaven, and that is that it rests on foundations, 2 Sam. 22: 8, on the pillars of heaven, Job 26: 11; that it spans the face of the deep like a vault, Prov. 8: 27 and that, spread out like a curtain (Isa. 40: 22) and like an awning (Ps. 104: 2) it stretches to four corners (Jer. 49: 36) or as four winds (Zech. 2: 10; 6: 5, Dan 8: 8; 11: 4). This last assertion may be only a contribution to the ancient *mappa mundi* or to the space-consciousness of

Old Testament man, but certainly the assertion about the foundations of heaven is more valuable. If the earth quakes, the foundations of which cannot be fathomed, Jer. 31: 37, the heaven quakes also; this is not metaphor but reality and the Old Testament man's attitude to the world is one of anxiety and disquiet and apprehension.

d) Like the heavens, the earth also extends to four corners, Isa. 11: 12, Ezek. 7: 2; its pillars and boundaries are found in the uttermost parts of the sea, Ps. 139: 9, in the coastlands of the nations, Gen. 10: 5, Zeph. 2: 11. The expression is interesting —whether the אִיִּים[121] were regarded as the coasts of the continent or the peninsulas of Asia Minor or the islands of the west does not matter—to its furthermost edge the earth is full of nations of men; the terrifying and grotesque creatures of Greek geography are not found in the Old Testament. The earth also rests on foundations, Isa. 24: 18—the mountains, Mic. 6: 2; that is why at the creation of the earth they were first to be formed, Ps. 90: 2; that is why also it is the end of the world when the mountains subside. No indication is given as to what it is on which the mountains rest that bear up the earth and the vault of heaven.

e) In the innermost parts of the earth lies *Sheol*, שְׁאוֹל, the underworld, the precursor of Hell and companion realm of Hades. When anyone wants to flee from the earth and from God he seeks the heavens, the uttermost parts of the sea and Sheol, Ps. 139: 8-9, Amos 9: 2-3. The heavens are the heavens of the Lord and the earth He has given to the children of men. But the dead praise not the Lord, neither any who go down into silence. Praise ye the Lord! Ps. 115: 16-18. Sheol is the place of the dead, the realm of silence. Man descends to it, Isa. 14: 9, 1 Sam. 2: 6, Job 21: 13; the Rephaim, the weak, the powerless, the shades dwell there, the former chiefs of the earth, pale kings of the earth upon their thrones, Isa. 14: 9. Sheol is in the lowest part of the earth, indeed according to some passages even under the deep, Job 26: 5; 38: 16 ff. Korah's whole band is swallowed up alive by it—the ground clave asunder, the earth opened her mouth and then closed upon them, Num. 16: 31-33. This is something unheard of, as Jahweh is the one who does not suffer His saints to see Sheol, Ps. 16: 10. Jahweh has therefore power over Sheol also. But since God is not praised in Sheol, Ps. 6: 5, and since the godless and all people who have forgotten God return there as to their home, one can see clearly that God only subsequently took the realm of the dead into His control. This is *religionsgeschichtliche* material, not theology. Sheol has been taken over in the interests of completeness from another Lord. God is a God of the living, not of the dead, Matt. 22: 32. In Sheol, however, whither man goeth, there is no work, nor device, nor knowledge, nor wisdom, Eccles. 9: 10. Note also that the Old Testament knows nothing of suffering and torment there. Shades, the silence of the depths, nothingness, that is Sheol. It is the no-world.[122]

f) In the heavens, that is to say in the expanse which divides the air from the ocean of heaven, are the heavenly bodies, Gen. 1: 14—the sun, the moon and the stars, Jer. 31: 35; the host of heaven, Isa. 45: 12. They are called lights, Gen. 1: 14, and their purpose as expressed in this late passage is threefold. They serve as signs, but this is not a passport to the realm of astrology, for the signs occur only at infrequent and exceptional times. The earth quakes, the heavens tremble, the sun and moon are darkened and the stars withdraw their shining; then man knoweth that the day of the Lord is at hand, Joel 2: 1, 10. The heavenly bodies serve to date seasons. By them is calculated the new moon, 1 Sam. 20: 5, and the time when the Passover is to be celebrated, Ex. 12: 6. The heavenly bodies serve in the computation of days and years, that is to say the calendar is regulated by their courses and through the calendar the whole of life. In addition the sun has a particular function—to rule the day, and likewise the moon has the function of ruling the night, Gen. 1: 16, Jer. 31: 35. How important this is can be gauged from the fact that these functions of chronology are called ordinances, חֻקִּים, and that their inviolability is the guarantee of the continuance of Israel as a nation; Jer. 31: 35 ff. All these heavenly bodies are God's creations, only creations: to worship them would be gross sin. They that worship the host of heaven upon the housetops will be destroyed, Zeph. 1: 5. For it is God who has ordained the moon and the stars, Ps. 8: 3. The moon itself hath no brightness, the stars are not pure in His sight, Job 25: 5; it were an iniquity to be punished by the judges to kiss the hand before them, Job 31: 27 ff.

2. Man and the Beasts

a) As already stated, there are no *monsters*, no creatures half man and half beast. The Rephaim[123] belong to the realm of the

dead, they are shades; nothing of any significance is said about
them. In antiquity there were giants, the offspring of the sons
of gods and the daughters of men, Gen. 6: 1-4, Num. 13: 33,
and Emim, Deut. 2: 10, and Anakim and other giants, Deut.
2: 11; finally the wicked Og of Bashan; all these however are
insubstantial relics of a forgotten past. Old Testament man and
therefore man in general as the Old Testament presents him
has no beings about him other than his fellow men and the
beasts.

b) The *beast*, according to the oldest account of creation, is a
creature that failed to fulfil its purpose. God wanted to make a
help meet[124] for Adam for whom it was not good that he should
be alone. Had God then formed the woman out of his rib there
would have been no beasts. But God meant one of the beasts to
be the counterpart to man. Man gave every beast a name, i.e.
he knew the nature of the beast but he found no beast that was
a help meet for him, Gen. 2: 18-20. The beast is not on the same
level as man.

c) According to the later account of creation, Gen. 1: 20-25,
God creates the beasts according to His plan and by His will,
though no specific purpose for the beasts is mentioned. He
creates them after their kind and to each kind He gives, in the
blessing of fertility, the power to preserve the species. The
modern kinds are the same as those that existed at creation;
there are no species not created by God. One group of species is
called בְּהֵמָה; this comprises cattle and domestic animals in
contrast to חַיַּת הָאָרֶץ, 1: 24, 25. There is no domestication,
tame animals are created tame. To the beasts God gives the
plants for nourishment; even beasts of prey feed on plants at
the eschaton, which represents creation under perfect conditions; Isa. 11: 7. Why certain beasts are carnivorous is not
explained any more than why the beasts also must suffer in the
flood. To suppose that they share in the general guilt because
they are flesh like men—"all flesh had corrupted his way upon
the earth", Gen. 6: 12—would be to attribute to flesh in itself
a corruptibility and rebellion against God which is quite foreign
to the Old Testament concept of flesh. The one ground given for
the inclusion of the beasts is this: that Jahweh repents of
having made man and beast and creeping thing and fowl of the
air, Gen. 6: 7. The beast lives according to the Old Testament
revelation under a fate shared with man. What God does to

man must have significance, but not what He does to the beast. The beast goes with man.

d) *The beasts are under man's dominion*; man may make use of them, from the time of the flood on he may also eat their flesh so long as he does not eat flesh with the blood thereof, Gen. 9: 1-5, Ps. 8: 7-9. What happens in the day of salvation when the carnivorous animals cease to be beasts of prey and the cow and the bear feed together and the lion eats straw like the ox is not indicated. Perhaps even then the eating of flesh is permitted, for the attitude to beasts in the Old Testament is entirely objective and dispassionate. The continual slaughter of animals for sacrifice is passed over without a word, and similarly Job in his recitation of wrongs that he might have committed mentions a misdeed against his lands, 31: 38-40, but nothing against his cattle. Admittedly God is extolled for preserving man and beast, Ps. 36: 6, and a righteous man is one who regardeth the life of his beast while the tender mercies of the wicked are cruel, Prov. 12: 10. The good shepherd is esteemed, Ps. 23; woe to the evil shepherds, Jer. 23: 1 ff., Ezek. 34: 2 ff., Zech. 11: 4 ff. There is no trace, however, of a personal or friendly relationship between man and any beast.

e) On the contrary we are told of *enmity between the seed of Eve and the seed of the serpent*, Gen. 3: 14 ff. It is to be observed that this is a curse on the serpent. The serpent is deprived of legs and made to go on his belly as punishment. Likewise as punishment the serpent is denied all other food and must eat dust. As punishment God puts enmity between man and the serpent; men shall lie in wait for serpents, serpents for men, nor are we told of any end of this enmity or of any victory. The three elements of the punishment continue, they are marks of the enmity which are explained in this way: the passage is therefore a piece of aetiological myth—a story to explain an existing state of affairs.[125] To regard it as "protevangelium" is unscriptural.

3. Man and Spirits

The world of man, peopled only by man and the beasts under him, is almost rationalistically empty. Only occasionally do we hear in the Old Testament of beings between God and man, binding the two together and separating them, beings for whom there is no proper name—a sign that we are dealing with a vague subject.

"Thou hast made man", says the eighth Psalm (v. 5) "a

little lower than the angels", but it is not improbable that the translation should be "lower than God", since elsewhere that is what the word which is used means. *Angels* in Hebrew are מַלְאָכִים which can also mean messengers, so that one is often in doubt as to whether angels or messengers[126] are meant. The figures on the ladder set up to heaven, Gen. 28: 12 (admittedly a dream!), the companion of God when He visits Abraham, Gen. 18: 2; 19: 1, the man whom Joshua beheld before Jericho, 5: 13, the man who appeared to Gideon, Judg. 6: 11, 12, and to Samson's parents, Judg. 13: 3 ff.—these are undoubtedly angels in the true sense. They look like ordinary men (there are no female angels in the Old Testament) and they have no wings or they would not have required a ladder. They appear later also occasionally, 2 Sam. 24: 16, Isa. 37: 36, but very occasionally and at a distance from the earth. This characteristic is also found earlier when the angel of God calls to Hagar "out of heaven", Gen. 21: 17, or when the angel of the Lord calls unto Abraham out of heaven, Gen. 22: 11. One may question of course whether the angel of the Lord (58 times) and the angel of God are appropriate terms at all or whether what we have is not much more a particular form of divine presence (§ 40). When to the prophets, Isa. 44: 26, 2 Chron. 36: 15, 16, or to the priest, because his lips keep knowledge and one seeks the law at his mouth, Mal. 2: 7, is given the name מַלְאָךְ of God, one may wonder whether to translate the word messenger or angel, but at least one is clear how indefinite the concept of angel is on the borderland between man and spirit.[127] Clearly however the angel that destroyed the people, 2 Sam. 24: 16, and the angel of destruction of 1 Chron. 21: 15, together with the angel of the covenant, Mal. 3: 1, must be taken as supernatural beings. And is the "angel that talked with" the prophet Zechariah, 1: 13, 14, etc., to be included? Then there is the ancient tradition of God's court of beings, the host of heaven, 1 Kings 22: 19, which He assembles from time to time; Job 1: 6.

One wonders, in view of such allusions, at the reserve and hesitation shown by the writers of the Old Testament in this whole realm of ideas. It produces neither a hierarchy of angels nor those frequent and intimate appearances of angels that are found elsewhere. Only in the book of Daniel do the holy ones, that is the angels, speak to one another, 8: 13; the "man

Gabriel" flies to Daniel, 9: 21; another angel is called Michael, 10: 13, who is "one of the chief princes" in the angelic hierarchy, and the kingdom of Persia as well as Greece has one of these angel princes (10: 13, 20) as patron saint. In this respect therefore the book of Daniel lies on the outermost edge of the Old Testament revelation and bears the unmistakable marks of the influence of Persian angelology.[128]

Angels in the plural occur very infrequently in the Old Testament. God can give His angels charge over His own, Ps. 91: 11, Matt. 4: 6, as also, if this interpretation of the passage is correct, He could send upon the Egyptians "a band of angels of evil", Ps. 78: 49.

There is an angelic group of a higher order, namely the *Seraphs*, שְׂרָפִים, who stand before God when He appears high and lifted up upon a throne. They have three pairs of wings—one pair for flying, another for covering their face so that they may not look on God, and the third pair to cover their legs, for they are naked and nakedness is unfit for God's eyes. Their service is to proclaim the holiness of Jahweh, Isa. 6: 2-3. This is all perfectly clear but one is mistaken if one expects to learn anything from it, for the passage is quite unparalleled. Seraphs are not known anywhere else, and not once are we told how they are related to "ordinary" angels.

There is yet another angelic group which similarly we suppose to be of a higher order. These are the *Cherubs*, כְּרוּבִים. Jahweh rides through the air upon them—though at the same time He is soaring on the wings of the wind!—2 Sam. 22: 11, Ps. 18: 10. The cherubs bear up the firmament above which the glory of God appears; they have feet, for they walk, and wings, for they fly—Ezek. 10: 1, 5, 16. Each of them has four faces, four wings and "the likeness" of the hands of a man was under their wings, Ezek. 10: 20 ff. They serve as covering, protecting but also expelling forces in God's garden, Ezek. 28: 13, 14, 16: Jahweh places "the" cherubs at the east of the garden of Eden to keep the way of the tree of life, Gen. 3: 24. Are these Seraphs and Cherubs something in process of becoming and not yet clearly defined, or are they the last indistinguishable receding echoes of an ancient tradition? The latter suggestion is obviously correct. The Old Testament has borrowed something here which in the context of its revelation, rightly viewed, is embarrassing and alien.

There are still other beings who are not borrowed and
tolerated but inherited and suppressed. Such are the *demons*
in the form of he-goats, שְׂעִירִים, which appear dancing in
fallen cities, Isa. 13: 21; 34: 12-14 where also the female demon
Lilith and others are found, for whom priests are sometimes
appointed, 2 Chron. 11: 15, and to whom sacrifices are offered,
Lev. 17: 7. From these cult arrangements it is clear that originally and also later where fixed forms of worship appear, these
were gods (of the field, of fertility, of the underworld, of death)
supplanted by Jahweh. Another sort, שֵׁדִים, called "the black
ones"[129] received sacrifices although they are not gods, Deut.
32: 17; even sacrifices of children, Ps. 106: 37.

All these belong to a realm of uncertainty. We do not know
what part angels, spirits and demons played in the life and faith
of Old Testament man. We see only that they have a much
greater proximity, a firmer reality and a more precise form for
the New Testament man and that there they are therefore of
much greater theological importance. In the Old Testament
Jahweh stands alone save for the angels (concerning Satan
see § 51) who draw near to serve Him. All other gods have
yielded to Him. We can barely imagine the feeling of distinc-
tiveness and freedom this must have aroused when the Jew
compared himself with Egyptian or other contemporaries.
There are no gods around Jahweh. Therefore there are also no
spirits around Him, for all spirits, demons and intermediate
beings are originally part of the band and retinue of the great
individual gods. When they go the others go also. They are
banished and lead only a forbidden shadow-existence in the
twilight of superstition.

According to the revelation of the Old Testament, man deals
with God and only with God.

50. MAN IN THE COMMUNITY,
AS INDIVIDUAL AND AS DISTINCTIVE PERSON

There remains one aspect of man's life to describe: his
personal relationships.

1. Man is grouped with his family and with his contemporaries.
That is the context in which his character is estimated, Gen.
7: 1; he shares with them the reputation that he knows the
Lord or does not know Him, Judg. 2: 10; instead of saying "all
thy descendants" one says "all thy seed according to their

generations", Gen. 17: 9. There is a unity and community of man both horizontally with his contemporaries and vertically with his forefathers and descendants. When a man dies he is gathered to his people, Gen. 25: 8; to his fathers, Judg. 2: 10; he sleeps with his fathers and is buried with them, 1 Kings 14: 31 (never said of a woman).

A man's mental and spiritual activity is also a community affair, however; it is not confined to his temporal activities. We read in the Old Testament: "all souls are mine" (though one cannot avoid individualizing in this phrase), we read "deceive not yourselves", Jer. 37: 9, but—and this is characteristic—we read: "their soul" (singular) for "them" (in the plural), Isa. 3: 9; 46: 2. We find "our souls", Num. 31: 50, but also "our soul", Jer. 17: 21. We find "the soul of thy wives", 2 Sam. 19: 6, "the soul of thine enemies", 1 Kings 3: 11, "the soul of the priests", Jer. 31: 14, "the soul of them that hate thee", 2 Chron. 1: 11. In other words, where it remains feasible, unity of soul is assumed and expressed both for several or for many individuals; only where there is reason for it do we find plurality of souls. The same is true of לֵב and לֵבָב, the word for heart, intellect, attentiveness, understanding. Your heart—of God and his two companions, Gen. 18: 5; their heart—the courage of Joseph's brethren, Gen. 42: 8; their heart made them willing —all the men and women of Israel, Ex. 35: 29; the heart of the Israelites, Num. 32: 7; the heart of the people, Josh. 14: 8; the Egyptians and Pharaoh hardened their heart, 1 Sam. 6: 6; indeed the plural, for all the frequency of the word, hardly ever occurs.

Let all this act as a brief indication[130] of the fact that in the Old Testament it is taken for granted that *man lives in a community*, comprehensive to a degree we can scarcely imagine. The community of the individual with the unit to which he is by nature assigned is unquestionable and is capable of settling a whole series of questions, theological questions included, which trouble us to-day. One can posit indeed that the theological concern of the Old Testament is not with the question of creating a community but with the question of the emergence within the community of individuals with personal value and personal responsibility.

2. *The emergence of the individual from the anonymity of the community* is accomplished at various points and in various

LII

ways. In earlier Old Testament times man lives completely in
family and group solidarity. Achan dies for his theft and his
whole house with him, Josh. 7: 10-26. In this case we are
clearly told that the bond of community extends to the guilty
man's sons, daughters, oxen, asses, sheep, his tent and all that
he had. We are also told (v. 15) that it is an elaboration of a
divine ordinance that the man should be burnt with fire, he
and all that he hath. Korah and all that pertained to him, with
their families, their households and all their goods were
swallowed up by the earth, Num. 16: 32; and the whole community was bidden depart from the two hundred and fifty
wicked men, 16: 26, 35.

The bond between the individual and his group has a distinct
direction and a clear limitation. The direction can be seen in
the fact that the sinner does not drag the righteous to destruction, Num. 16: 18-35, but the righteous rescue the sinners from
destruction. "I will not destroy it (the population of Sodom
and Gomorrah) for the ten's sake" (the ten righteous that I find
there), Gen. 18: 32. The bond is set in a context of grace. The
sinner does not involve the righteous in destruction, but the
righteous involves the sinner in salvation. The clear limitation
is this: that the bond does not work in terms of proportion. God
visits the iniquity of the fathers upon the children unto the
third and fourth generations of them that hate Him, but He
shews mercy unto the thousandth generation to the children of
them that love Him, Ex. 20: 5 ff. The visitation of punishment
lasts for only a fraction of the time of His loving grace. God is
much more a God of grace than a God of judgment.[131]

Later the bond is still further relaxed.[132] Amaziah slays his
father's murderers but not their children, 2 Kings 14: 5 ff. The
law is now in operation which says that every man shall be put
to death for his own sin, Deut. 24: 16. That will be the situation
under the new covenant, Jer. 31: 30. Thus Ezekiel is commissioned to proclaim the word of God that the son shall not
bear the iniquity of the father, neither shall the father bear the
iniquity of the son. "The righteousness of the righteous shall be
upon him, and the wickedness of the wicked upon him",
Ezek. 18: 1-20. One should not overlook the historical situation
referred to here. This word is spoken in a time in which a whole
generation—the good Jews in exile—takes it very ill that they
are encumbered with the sins of the fathers. This is therefore
absolution by the sheer grace of God.

There is, however, no attempt in the Old Testament to reconcile systematically the fact of the bond uniting those who as family, people or community belong together, and the fact of the detachment of those who have received a divine command. The whole affair is rather indefinite and can afford to be, as the bonds are too strong for the individual to drift too far from the unit. It is only the man whom God leads in the ways of an individual, the man who is directed to a particular task, only those special people who are alone. And they count it suffering to be so. "I sat alone because of thy hand", Jer 15: 17.

3. In a people and religious community whose characteristic is really an absence of differences in matters mental and spiritual we have to recognize nevertheless the fact of *the specialist, the distinctive person.* One cannot hope rightly to understand the anthropology of the Old Testament without taking note of these contrasting and complementary persons. For the power in virtue of which these men stand out from the others is not natural endowment and still less human effort; it is God's free choice. And because it is God's free choice it is a possibility for every man in one form or another. The distinctive ones are always God's people. They are not, however, an aristocracy. They are and remain closely bound up with all others.

It will be sufficient to survey quickly these distinctive callings, for we are not concerned with the spiritual condition of the men involved, nor with their personal experience, but only with the fact that God has set them apart from the others and again for the others.

There are first the *seers* or *prophets,* 1 Sam. 9: 9. Separated from the rest of mankind, they stand between God and man. But the eye that was opened, Num. 24: 3 ff., and the ear to which he communicates his secret, Amos 3: 7—such eyes and ears are intended by God for all men. "God hath spoken—who can but prophesy?" Amos 3: 8. "Your sons and your daughters will prophesy . . . your young men shall see visions", Joel 2: 28. Prophet and seer are not merely media of God's word, they are also the prototype and foreshadowing of that which really ought to be. Man's remoteness from God is thrown into relief by the directness of their relation to Him.

The position of the *priest* among the people is different. His station is early and strictly regulated[133] and designated as a calling that passes from generation to generation in certain families. The priests' duties were variously interpreted in the course of time. Originally any man with a knowledge of the cult could sacrifice, Gen. 4: 3 ff.; 8: 20; Judg. 13: 19-23, etc.; the priest has to watch over the propriety and due observance of rites, to decide in all questions of rites and cult, Hagg. 2: 11-13, and to maintain the difference between the holy and the profane and the observance of the Sabbath, Ezek. 22: 26; he is the keeper and mediator of the Torah, and of counsel, Jer. 18: 18, Ezek. 7: 26; 22: 26, how one should live and how in one's life one should treat this one and that one. The priest's lips keep knowledge and one seeks counsel at his mouth, for he is the messenger of the Lord of hosts, Mal. 2: 7. The ever-increasing and burdensome preoccupation of the priest with sacrifice, however, caused the emergence of another distinctive group alongside him: the wise, the Scribes. Yet, in spite of this historical development, the priest is to those in whose midst he lives a reminder of God's holiness expressed in quite definite habits of life, and demanding a constantly renewed effort to reach that condition in which one may draw near to God. The priest is what all one day will be, for all together shall be a kingdom of priests, Ex. 19: 6. The priesthood of the Old Testament is the prototype of the priesthood of all believers.

For a certain time, indeed until the time of the kings, there are distinctive persons usually called *judges*, though this term is false and should be replaced by the true name *champions*. Their function is not to make legal pronouncements in Israel but rather to champion the just cause of a tribe or group of tribes against its enemies. They are therefore called saviours and helpers, Judg. 3: 9, 15; 12: 3; 1 Sam. 11: 3; 2 Kings 13: 5; Isa. 19: 20; Obad. 21; Neh. 9: 27; an honorary title given also to God, 1 Sam. 10: 19; 14: 39; Isa. 43: 3, 11 (He is the only saviour), Jer. 14: 8; Hos. 13: 4. The significant thing about the human saviour is, however, that his office is a charismatic office. The saviour does not offer himself of his own free will; God raises him up, Judg. 3: 9, 15; God gives him, 2 Kings 13: 5; God sends him, Isa. 19: 20. God causes His spirit to come upon Saul, 1 Sam. 11: 6, and he becomes a saviour. Anyone can be a saviour: but only he is a saviour whom God appoints and invests.

Saul the saviour becomes Saul *the king*. The kingship in Israel, so long as it has God's sanction, is a charismatic and not a political office.[134] When men set up kings but not by God,

Hos. 8: 4, then it is to no purpose. Because the king is what he is by the grace of God he is called the Lord's anointed, 1 Sam. 24: 6, 10; 26: 9, 11, 23, on whom even in bitterest strife David will not lay a hand. The anointing is the sign of the charismatic separation that falls to the king, to the high priest (only Lev. 4: 3, 5, 16; 16: 15); to the priesthood as a whole, Num. 3: 3, Ex. 28: 41, etc.; to the prince, נָגִיד, over "my people Israel", 1 Sam. 9: 16; to the patriarch, Ps. 105: 15=1 Chron. 16: 22. It is explicitly the sign of the appointment to the rôle of saviour, "and he shall save my people out of the hand of the Philistines", 1 Sam. 9: 16. Thus even the heathen king Cyrus can be called the anointed of God or Messiah, Isa. 45: 1, since God uses him as a saviour for His people. When the kingship becomes hereditary its charismatic character recedes into the background; David's successor is still the anointed of God, Ps. 132: 10 and Dan. 9: 25 ff.

When at the Exile the ancient scriptures become holy scriptures with the meaning of which one wrestles, Dan. 9: 2, 2 Chron. 36: 22, and when the attention of priests is claimed more and more for sacrifice in Judah in the Temple, and when outside Judah, since one cannot sacrifice, the study of the scripture is becoming a substitute for sacrificial worship of ever-increasing importance—there appear again in a new form individuals separated off from the mass of men: the *Scribes*, who murmur the law day and night, Ps. 1: 2. There is nothing more to say about them here.

We may summarize all this in the following five points. *1*. The life of man in the Old Testament both outward and inward is bound up with the lives of others, and the community is therefore much more important than the individual. *2*. As time goes by, the individual does become to some extent independent of this bond, so that a sort of equilibrium comes about. *3*. Always at will, God in His grace calls individuals out of this bond into a charismatic existence. *4*. This charismatic existence never leads to mystical enjoyment of God's presence, rather its purpose is always the service of God for the salvation of His people. *5*. This setting apart serves constantly as an indication to the whole people of a future order that God intends, in which all shall prophesy, Num. 11: 29, and see visions, Joel 2: 28, and be priests, yea a kingdom of priests, Ex. 19: 6;[135] and no man teaches his brother any more, "for they shall all know

me, from the least of them unto the greatest of them", Jer.
31: 34.

*Thus the doctrine of man in the Old Testament becomes an
announcement of God's salvation.* This gains even greater validity
when we turn to what the Old Testament has to say about good
and evil and about the expedient by which men seek to create
their salvation.

51. GOOD AND EVIL; SIN; SATAN

1. Job was perfect and upright and one that feared God and
eschewed evil, Job 1: 1. That is the judgment of this old
Volksbuch. And in conformity with this judgment Job is
prosperous: he is rich in cattle and servants, the greatest of all
the children of the east, and he has seven sons and three
daughters, 1: 2-3. God's judgment of him also is that he is a
perfect and upright man, one that feareth God and escheweth
evil; there is none like him in the earth, 1: 8. Job himself says
so in the poem, "I am perfect . . . he (God) destroyeth the
perfect and the wicked", 9: 21 ff. Another word with the same
root and meaning as תָּם is תָּמִים. Noah is righteous and
perfect, Gen. 6: 9. Abraham is required to walk before God and
be perfect, Gen. 17: 1. "With the perfect thou wilt show thyself
pefect" says the Psalmist to God, 2 Sam. 22: 26. And in Ezek.
28: 15 God says to the King of Tyre; "Thou wast perfect in thy
ways from the day that thou wast created, till unrighteousness
was found in thee." The noun for the adjectives תָּם and תָּמִים
is תֹּם. "Let integrity (perfection) and uprightness preserve
me", Ps. 25: 21. "As for me, thou upholdest me in my perfection," Ps. 41: 12. Examples of descriptions of moral worth
and words used in this connexion could be multiplied, but it is
not necessary. It is necessary to ascertain, however, what is the
exact meaning of these commendations. When it is said of
someone that he is upright and God-fearing or that he eschews
evil, then the meaning has that same clarity that the concepts
themselves have, popular concepts, naïve and artless. But what
does "righteous" mean as a judgment of a man in the Old
Testament, and what does "perfect" mean?

The word צַדִּיק usually translated righteous originates in
legal parlance, and means first of all a man who has been
accused and who has proved that the accusation is unjustified.
Righteous here then is equivalent to "proved innocent of a

charge" in that "thou establishest the innocence of the innocent and treatest him according to his innocence", I Kings 8: 32. In this passage the opposite of צַדִּיק, namely רָשָׁע, also occurs. This is often translated godless, wicked, etc., but its original fundamental and indubitable meaning is guilty; "in that thou establishest the guilt of the guilty and bringest his way upon his own head". The true meaning of צַדִּיק when it is used in a pronouncement about the conduct of man is "proved guiltless of charges"; the corresponding meaning of רָשָׁע is "proved guilty of charges". There arise therefore the meanings, one who is in the right and one who is in the wrong, Ex. 23: 7. The verbs צָדַק הִצְדִּיק, רָשַׁע and הִרְשִׁיעַ also have these meanings; to be innocent, to be without guilt, Job 10: 15; declare innocent, Deut. 25: 1; to be guilty, be in the wrong, I Kings 8: 47; to declare guilty, condemn, Isa. 50: 9. The statement that a man is innocent occurs often in the Old Testament both in the limited sense of innocent of a particular charge and in the wider sense of innocent of all possible charges.

What is meant when in the Old Testament it is said that someone is תָּם or תָּמִים, perfect? These two words are not taken from legal parlance but arose in practical evaluation. תָּם is primarily that which is true to type, which is as it is meant to be. They went לְתֻמָּם (2 Sam. 15: 11) means, they went undisturbed by anything, without any apprehension or suspicions; likewise I Kings 22: 34. Job, Noah, and Abraham are תָּם, תָּמִים in that they are as one ought to be—perfect.

The Old Testament knows therefore the moral condition of man where no guilt can be proved and no reproach or blame can be brought against him. That is not the same as saying he is guiltless. But that he can be without guilt or blame—that certainly is claimed for him. To avoid misunderstanding, however, attention must be paid to the important fact that freedom from guilt and from blame is bound up inseparably with the setting of a norm outside of man. a) It is thought of as a fixed norm; the two words do not permit any dispensing with morality, and this norm b) being outside of man, is free from any modification as to considerations of utility or from dependence on a general ethical position or from any other such things. The Greek could say the same; his standard is the Ideal. But *the Old Testament knows no Ideal, only relationship to God the Lord.* According to the Old Testament that man is guiltless and perfect who is so in God's judgment. God is the norm of the ethical, and that gives rise to the issue in the book of Job whether a man can be guiltless and perfect before God.

2. There is no story in which the psychology of temptation is so briefly and vividly demonstrated as in the story of the Fall, Gen. 3: 1-7. The serpent says to the woman: "Hath God really said, ye shall not eat of any tree of the garden?" In so saying the serpent exaggerates the prohibition·and puts the woman into the position of being proud to know better. "We eat of the fruit of the trees of the garden." The Septuagint says "of all the fruits"—that is meant. The serpent is discomfited but—and this is what it wanted, because the woman is thereby made to feel that this is a limitation—the woman must add "but of the fruit of the tree which is in the midst of the garden, God hath said: Ye shall not eat of it, neither shall ye touch it, lest ye die." The last phrase helps the woman to recover from her humiliating admission. It is true God has limited their rights; they may not eat of all the fruits. But this limitation is for their own good. It saves them from death. Then the serpent lies (or does it not lie?): "ye shall not surely die." The serpent awakens curiosity and mistrust in the woman: "God doth know that in the day ye eat thereof, then your eyes shall be opened and ye shall be as God, knowing good and evil." The woman looks, desires, takes and eats, and having once ignored the prohibition she seeks someone to share her guilt. Therefore she gives the fruit to the man. He, though he is not the first to be beguiled, 1 Tim. 2: 14, nevertheless eats also. Then they see that they are naked. They know what is good and what is evil.

What is here good and evil? Certainly it has nothing to do with sexual intercourse.[136] There is not a word about that or any allusion to it. The consciousness of nakedness is no indication of it; if it were, God would have asked Adam: "Who told thee (you) that ye were naked?" The mutual nakedness would then be the essential thing. But instead Adam says: "I was afraid, because I was naked"; and God asks: "Who told thee that thou wast naked?" Individual nakedness is stressed; it is the personal expression for guilt consciousness which every man knows who is guilty whether he belong to the ancient world or to the present day.

What do good and evil mean?[137] The answer is simple. Good is that which is produced by obedience, evil is the result of disobedience; "one man's disobedience", Rom. 5: 19. It is God who determines good and evil. He commands and man must take heed, Gen. 3: 17. Man is disobedient—"since thou hast done what I forbade". Man is from the beginning in duty bound to obey. If he does not, God questions him and he must answer. Man is responsible to God. If he cannot answer for himself he is a sinner. Sin is disobedience. Here then we have two fundamentals of the Old Testament revelation. The one is God's command. The command, the order under which God places man is as old as man himself. Immediately He created Him God gave man His command, Gen. 2: 16. The command holds in the world of men both before and in spite of the Fall. *The command is a divine preparation for the salvation of man.* It therefore belongs to the sphere of soteriology (§ 53).

3. Sin is part of man; it belongs to his nature, the nature he has acquired through disobedience; it therefore is a part of anthropology. The terms for sin found in the Old Testament are numerous: they are from different contexts and they are of varying degrees of profundity. We shall therefore review them one by one.

a) The commonest word for sin is חֵטְא (34 times), חֲטָאָה (7 times), חֲטָאָה (twice) and חַטָּאת (155 times)—the verb is חָטָא to sin (more than 200 times). While "sin" in English is a word that is entirely comprehensible, but purely theological, חָטָא clearly means in Hebrew to fail, miss and חַטָּאת and its variations equally clearly mean failure. The verb still occurs in its non-technical sense: "Thou shalt visit thy fold and shalt miss nothing", Job 5: 24; "Whoso findeth me findeth life, he that misseth me wrongeth his own soul", Prov. 8: 35 ff. Thus חָטָא means sin in the sense of failure, i.e. that sin which is recognized as a clear violation of a given command or prohibition. It corresponds exactly even in etymology to the Greek ἁμαρτία.

b) The word עָוֹן is of quite a different origin and has quite a different shade of meaning. It is used 231 times (in Ezek. 44, Lev. 18, Num. 12, Jer. 24, Hos. 11). Its meanings are: crime or iniquity 55 times, guilt 159 times, and punishment 6 times. Its origin shows that it indicates an action or omission which is not straight, or not right.

In other words, while חָטָא designates a sin which can consist simply of a man's doing something which is forbidden or failing to do something which is commanded, without knowing or comprehending the reason for prohibition or command, עָוֹן designates a sin that originates in wrong intention. חָטָא indicates that there has been an offence against the divine order of things. עָוֹן on the other hand indicates that the sins of commission or omission are sins of men with a wrong intention, an intention not in accord with God's will. There are also sins committed in error. Lev. 4: 2, 27, Num. 15: 27 "if any man shall sin unwittingly", but this is called חָטָא בִּשְׁגָגָה. עָוֹן always presupposes consciousness of guilt. Thus Jeremiah can say, 30: 14, 15, "Because of the greatness of thine iniquity thy sins are increased" and "their iniquity whereby they have sinned against me" (one would never find עֲוֹנָם בִּשְׁגָגָה unwitting iniquity).

In brief one could almost say חָטָא and its kindred forms mean failure, error, blunder. עָוֹן means crime or iniquity. We have not yet exhausted the sin vocabulary, however.

c) The true profundity of the Old Testament sin concept is found in the word פֶּשַׁע, which occurs 86 times.[138] The verb פָּשַׁע means to revolt or to rebel against someone—Israel rebelled against the house of David, 1 Kings 12: 19; they have rebelled against me, Isa. 1: 2. They rebel against my wisdom (תּוֹרָה) Hos. 8: 1. פֶּשַׁע means therefore rebellion. It is the disobedience, παρακοή, of Rom. 5: 19. "In the day that I shall visit the rebellion of Israel upon him", Amos 3: 14; "for the rebellion of Jacob is all this", Mic. 1: 5; "their rebellions, even all their sins", Lev. 16: 16: "forgiving iniquity and rebellion and failure", Ex. 34: 7 (so also in the plural Lev. 16: 21, Ezek, 21: 29, Ps. 32: 5, Dan. 9: 24). This, the Old Testament's most profound word for sin, occurs relatively few times but this is explained by the fact that in the Old Testament more and more the individual circumstances of the rebellion are described in legal terms. Reference is made more to sins, therefore, than to sin. Individual sins have more prominence than sinfulness. But the word פֶּשַׁע does show clearly that essentially and in the last resort in the Old Testament revelation sin is not the violation of objective commandments and prohibitions and not the iniquities of men which demonstrate their weakness and folly (1 Chron. 21: 8!) and perversity. *Sin is revolt of the human will against the divine will*: men are θεοστυγεῖς (haters of God), Rom. 1: 30.

d) There are also other terms which express or paraphrase or concern what we call sin. מַעַל is one such, with its verb מָעַל. It means something like disloyalty, acting contrary to one's duty.[139] A divine sentence is in the lips of the king, he will not be undutiful in judgment; Prov. 16: 10; if any one act contrary to duty and sin unwittingly in the holy things of the Lord, Lev. 5: 15; in your answers there remaineth only faithlessness; for their undutifulness they were carried away captive to Babylon, 1 Chron. 9: 1. The word occurs first in Ezekiel and presupposes a law of fixed wording which one may not transgress. Like the חָטָא group of words, this word judges the act by the norm of a law, not by the intention. A whole collection of expressions for disobedience against the formulated commandments of God is found in Lev. 26: 14-40: will not hearken unto me, v. 14; will not do all those commandments, v. 14; reject my statutes, v. 15; abhor my judgments, v. 15; break my covenant, v. 15; walk contrary unto me, v. 21; be unwilling to hearken unto me, v. 21; will not be reformed unto me, v. 23; most of these expressions occur elsewhere as well but nowhere in this profusion. The word translated "walk contrary" unto me—in v. 24 it is used of God walking contrary to the Israelites —occurs only in this passage, Lev. 26: 21-41. This shows that even in the later periods of the Old Testament men are still trying to find new and more accurate and more comprehensive terms to describe sin, man's disobedience to God.

The commonest word for sinner is not חָטָא, which in 1 Kings 1: 21 still has the secular meaning "offender" and occurs elsewhere only 18 times; the commonest word is רָשָׁע, which is found 261 times.[140] This means originally one of the community proved guilty of a charge. The word therefore concerns primarily an individual instance, not general wrongdoing; it concerns indeed wrong that has been committed, not a tendency or inclination to wrong: he who (in fighting) did the wrong, Ex. 2: 13. Mostly, however, the word has a more general sense describing character rather than individual action: "Woe unto the wicked! the reward of his hands shall be given him", Isa. 3: 11; "wherefore doth the way of the wicked prosper?" Jer. 12: 1. In such contexts the word means one who is seen to be a sinner by his conduct and his character both, and the translators are in doubt whether to translate wicked or godless. This flexibility which the adjective possesses holds also for the nouns רֶשַׁע and רִשְׁעָה. They mean guilt, then wrong (treasures won by wrong, Mic. 6: 10, deceitful weights or weights which create wrong, Mic. 6: 11) but also sin, godlessness. Only in the case of this latter translation the fact should not be overlooked that the two words do not belong to the vocabulary of theology as they do in English; they have their roots in secular life and they do not therefore, like the word godlessness, contain within themselves any references to God.

The most exact word for guilt as something that must be made good is אָשָׁם and אַשְׁמָה: "thou shouldest have brought guiltiness upon us", Gen. 26: 10; "my guiltinesses are not hid from thee", Ps. 69: 5. The masculine of this word, however, later comes to mean almost exclusively "trespass offering", and the feminine is late and uncommon.

e) One must now attempt to map out, even sketchily, the area covered by what the Old Testament calls sin and guilt. The great and fundamental requirements of the Decalogue and all possible discussion and elaboration of them, being self-evident, are not our concern here. A reference to the *Männer-beichtspiegel* (Faulhaber) of Job 31 is more important. There looking upon a maid with covetous eyes, despising the cause of a manservant or maidservant, lack of concern for the poor, the widows and the fatherless, reliance on gold, malicious joy at an enemy's misfortune, are sins. In Ps. 15 there is an even nobler, finer and more sensitive consciousness of sin—the Psalmist speaks of blameless walk and conversation, of working righteousness, speaking truth in the heart, slandering not with the tongue, doing no evil to another, abusing not a neighbour, despising a reprobate, honouring them that fear the Lord, persevering even in a hurtful duty undertaken under oath, putting no money out to usury and bribing not for the sake of the innocent—this is almost entirely an ethic concerning the intentions. The early prophets felt constrained to teach that the true knowledge of the will of God belonged to the context of "social righteousness", Isa. 1: 17; 5: 7; Amos 2: 6; 5: 7, 10-12, 24; here is a noble result of that prophetic teaching—a knowledge of sin entirely in terms of a God-fearing intention.

On the other hand, Ezek. 18: 5-9[141] provides a not isolated example of another view which exists alongside this one. In these verses it is sin if a man does not do righteousness, if he gives forth upon usury, if he does not execute true judgment, etc. But it is likewise sin if a man lifts up his eyes to idols or eats upon the mountains or comes near to a woman in her separation. Alongside the ethical is the cultic, alongside the general there is the particular, conditioned and bound by place or time, and alongside the revelational there is—as the catalogue of forbidden animals in Deut. 14: 3-20 shows—the ethnic. The following are all under the same curse: the man that removeth his neighbour's landmark, he that maketh the blind to wander out of the way, he that taketh reward to slay an innocent person, he that lieth with his sister, the daughter of his father or the daughter of his mother, or with his mother-in-law, Deut. 27: 17-25. On the one hand there is a line in the Old Testament revelation on sin running from the grossness of the visible act to purity of intention. On the other hand there is a line obliterating all distinctions and in staggering simplification linking together everything that is termed sin in the one unconditional pronouncement. "Cursed be he that confirmeth not the words of this law to do them. And all the people shall say, Amen", Deut. 27: 26.

While here sin and the law are interrelated, there are also Old Testament passages which speak of sin and guilt without and before the law. Israel is bidden avoid unnatural prostitution. Before the Israelites came to Palestine the nations (heathen) there committed this sin, and the land became defiled, it incurred guilt, Lev. 18: 25. This guilt Jahweh visited upon the land in that the land vomited out her inhabitants. Here is a case of guilt without law; unnatural sin is recognizable even through natural religion. Sodom is Jerusalem's young sister. This was the iniquity of Sodom; pride, fulness of bread and prosperous ease was in her, but she did not strengthen the hand of the poor and needy. She was haughty and committed abomination, Ezek. 16: 49. Sodom too has sin without law.

f) On the questions whether there can be only individual responsibility or whether there is community liability, and whether and how far the one could exempt the other from guilt in vicarious atonement—on these questions the statements made are conflicting.

There is communal guilt and collective guilt: the transgressions of the Israelites, Lev. 16: 21; the guilt of Ephraim, Hos. 7: 1; of the house of Israel, Ezek. 4: 4; of Israel, Jer. 50: 20; of the people, Num. 14: 19; of the congregation, Lev. 10: 17; of the Amorites, Gen. 15: 16 (they have their time and when it is full the seed of Abraham will return to the land); the iniquity of us all, Isa. 53: 6; the iniquity of the inhabitants of the earth, Isa. 26: 21. The collectiveness becomes somewhat loose when it is seen as a succession of different generations. Job's reference to the iniquities of his youth does not yet belong here, but certainly the reference of Ps. 79: 8 does—it asks God not to remember against us the iniquities of our forefathers. Above all, passages like Isa. 65: 7 belong here: "your own iniquities and the iniquities of your fathers"; Jer. 14: 20, "our wickedness רֶשַׁע (and) the iniquity עָוֹן of our fathers", and Neh. 9: 2 —where the variation in the word used is noteworthy— "confessed their sins חַטָּאת and the iniquities עָוֹן of their fathers" (see Dan. 9: 16; both are prayers). It is even more strongly stressed that each generation lives for itself, though they are all bound together by sin, when Jeremiah says that they have turned back to the iniquities of their forefathers (Jer. 11: 10) or when Lamentations cries "our fathers have sinned and are not; and we have borne their iniquities" סָבַל, Lam. 5: 7.

Whether the punishment for sin affects only the doer of the sin or whether it affects his relations and his descendants is the question at issue in Ezekiel 18. The basic principle is simple— the soul that sinneth, it shall die, v. 4, 20. This simple and severe judgment is only reversed by the gracious will of God. Even the soul that sinneth lives if he returns from his way; then—one might say with v. 25 "The way of the Lord is not equal"—"none of his transgressions that he hath committed shall be remembered against him", v. 21-22. On the other hand there is no communal punishment. The son shall not bear the iniquity of the father, neither shall the father bear the iniquity of the son, v. 20. Yet there is the other case where one rises or enters to take the place of the others. Even the complaints that we have to bear the iniquities of our fathers, Lam. 5: 7, can be cited as an example; one can detect here something like the "filling up on my part that which is lacking" of Col. 1: 24. Num. 30: 15 is a case of real vicarious atonement where a man who has failed to fulfil a vow made by his wife bears the blame instead of her if belatedly he makes her vow null and void. Ex. 28: 38 is an even clearer case: Aaron bears the iniquity of the holy things which the children of Israel hallow in all their holy gifts. Ezekiel bears figuratively, or makes amends for, the iniquity of the house of Israel and the house of Judah, 4: 4-6; the servant of the Lord, however, bears vicariously in actual suffering (the punishment for) our iniquities, Isa. 53: 11.

4. "Your iniquities have separated between you and your God": *that is perhaps the clearest statement the Old Testament makes on the nature of sin,* Isa. 59: 2. Is it speaking of sins as the individual ungodly acts and consequences of an otherwise godly or (with reference to God) neutral disposition, or are individual sins for the Old Testament merely the outcome of the sinful depravity of man, of his sinfulness? That is ultimately the key question in any discussion of sin in the Old Testament.

a) It will be helpful therefore to proceed from preliminary observations on the passage concerning the Fall to conclusions. *1.* The purpose of the story is unmistakably aetiological: it seeks to explain why something is as it is. *2.* This aetiology is unmistakably intended to be historical in the sense that where something is explained its present character is explained by telling that at the beginning of history this and that happened. *3.* The difficulties explained are all mentioned in the course of the narrative: why the serpent is different from all cattle and from all beasts of the field: why it goes upon its belly; why it always eats dust; why there is enmity between it and man and between its seed and man's seed; why a woman has pain in pregnancy and childbirth; why a woman desires her husband; why the ground is cursed so that it brings forth thorns and thistles; why a man lives from the plants of the field; why he must eat his bread in the sweat of his face; why men wear clothes and why they no longer dwell in the garden of Eden. All these questions are answered in Gen. 3: 14-24, and if 2: 4-25 be added we find still more questions to which an answer is given. *4.* The narrative in no way suggests, either by particular words or particular emphasis, that any one question or any set of questions is to be considered as of greater importance than the others. *5.* No question is posed or answered in the passage concerning the origin of sin or guilt. *6.* It reckons with the possibility of man snatching at the tree of life. This is not forbidden; it is rendered impossible by the expulsion from the garden. *7.* In the whole of the Old Testament the story of the Fall plays no part: it is nowhere mentioned.

b) The story of the Fall would always have been correctly understood if the serpent in Gen. 3: 1 ff. had not been identified with Satan. The error of this identification is evident from a survey of Old Testament statements about Satan.[142]

i. Satan, Hebrew שָׂטָן from the verb שָׂטַן and שָׂטַם to show enmity, to oppose, is the Old Testament's term for men who lay hold of others in order to do them injury. David could become in the course of the battle the Philistines' Satan— adversary, opponent (ἀντίδικος), 1 Sam. 29: 4. The sons of Zeruiah become David's Satan, tempter, when they ask whether Shimei should not be put to death, 2 Sam. 19: 23. Likewise in politics, 1 Kings 5: 18; 11: 14, 23, 25; or before a judge, Ps. 109: 6; a man can be Satan for another, i.e. antagonist, adversary, Matt. 16: 23. Even an angel, as in the Balaam incident, can undertake to act as adversary, Num. 22: 22, 32. In all these cases what we are dealing with is a temporary expedient; there is no suggestion of a being who is Satan.

ii. In a vision of the year 520 B.C. (Zech. 3: 1-2) the high priest is seen standing before the angel of the Lord and at his right hand stands the Satan (הַשָּׂטָן with the article). The Satan accuses, שָׂטַן, the angel of the Lord defends. In this case Satan is a functionary in the divine economy, whose constant and proper function is to accuse and charge. He is the Slanderer (διάβολος = Teufel, devil) who slanders and misrepresents (διαβάλλε).

iii. A similar instance of the word Satan with the article is found in Job 1: 6—2: 7. He is a בֶּן־אֱלֹהִים, a being who comes like the others from time to time into the presence of the Lord, 1: 6; 2: 7; there is no suggestion that he is intolerable, on the contrary God speaks with him, asks him about his activities; he is invited to share God's joy over his servant Job and when he doubts, and is inclined to believe the worst instead of the best, when he is inclined to assume that personal advantage is the motive of all action, he is permitted by God to tempt Job, to make a bet indeed on his goodness. One should observe these passages closely in order to realize how far this biblical Satan is removed from the Satan of later times.

iv. There remains one passage in the Old Testament where Satan appears—1 Chron. 21: 1. This verse and what follows is a repetition of 2 Sam. 24: 1 ff. 2 Sam. 24: 1 runs: "And again the anger of the Lord was kindled against Israel, and he moved David against them, saying, Go number Israel and Judah." 1 Chron. 21: 1 runs: "And Satan stood up against Israel and moved David to number Israel." Here he is no longer called the Satan, הַשָּׂטָן, but Satan, שָׂטָן. The word has developed from being the term used to describe the temporary condition of someone or other to being the description of a functionary, and then further in this one passage to the name for a being. Satan is complete and appears with full status as God's opposition. It was not Jahweh that moved David to the unfortunate numbering of the people, it was Satan. Now Satan is the epitome of evil and disturbance, almost Anti-god. But Satan is all this only here in this late corner of the Old Testament, and the passage is not merely isolated—it is also the end of a process of which the stages, as we have shown, lie before us in the Old Testament. On the basis of these stages there is no justification for the belief that the serpent represents Satan. Indeed, the punishment meted out to the serpent is eloquent against it.[143]

c) In conclusion, concerning the story of the Fall, this is the opinion to which we are driven: i. The story culminates in a series of explanations of the origin of certain arrangements and phenomena in the contemporary world. ii. The story is intended as history, not *Urgeschichte*[144] (history of the beginnings). iii. The story knows nothing of a Satan, as it belongs to a period long before the Exile and Satan appeared only after the Exile. iv. The story does not say even incidentally, far less as its main contention, anything about man's sinfulness, his depravity, the so-called Fall or the disruption of the order of creation. Note then the silence of the story on these matters, a silence which could not be more marked; note also the completeness of the story in spite of this silence. Adam and Eve are disobedient and are punished for it. In order to avoid further disaster, "lest he put forth his hand, and take also of the tree of life, and eat, and live for ever", Gen. 3: 22, they are driven out of the garden. The result is death, which is, however, in itself natural (3: 19, "for dust thou art") and which would have been prevented by the eating of the tree of life. Just as the so-called story of the Fall says nothing and knows nothing of Fall and its dogmatic significance, so also it says nothing and knows nothing of death as the wages of sin. Death in this passage is natural and the only thing which happens in the passage that has reference to death is that a measure is taken which averts any disturbance of the natural operation of death.

5. Let us pose yet again a question on sinfulness in the Old Testament. To what extent is it taught in the Old Testament? The so-called Jahwist, who represents the older stratum of Genesis narratives, knows nothing of it. Indeed he has considerable difficulty in explaining the cause of the flood. Jahweh sees that the wickedness of man is great in the earth, and that every imagination of the thoughts of his heart is only evil continually, Gen. 6: 5:—the result is the flood, which destroys the wickedness of man. Yet man unaltered continues to live in Noah: the flood does not have the effect of a purification: the inclination of a man's heart is evil from his youth, Gen. 8: 21. Noah however finds grace in the eyes of the Lord, 6: 8; he therefore survives the flood. The Fall does not prevent Noah's virtue nor does the Jahwist anywhere suggest that the wickedness of man's heart is to be traced back to it.

The priestly writer knows nothing of Paradise, Fall, or cursed ground. He tells the story of the flood as a tradition, not in terms of his own interpretation. Noah is able to survive the flood because he is a righteous man and blameless and because he walks with God, Gen. 6: 9. The rest of the earth is filled with violence; all flesh has corrupted His way, Gen. 6: 11-12. The purpose of the flood is not purification; the end of all flesh is come, the purpose is annihilation. Noah, the man who is righteous and blameless, remains alive and with him his three sons, who are married, 7: 7. The four wives also are spared. The question arises as to the moral standards of these eight persons after the flood, since the whole world of men stems from these eight. A parallel utterance to 8: 21 is not found. A reference to the Fall is impossible, for the priestly narrative (1: 1-2: 4a; 5: 1-28, 30-35, 6: 9-22; 7: 5-9, 11, 13-16, 18-21, 24—8: 2a, 3b-5, 13-19; 9: 1-17 is complete in itself) knows nothing of it. If one assumes that the pronouncement "all flesh had corrupted his way upon the earth", 6: 12, holds good for the eight also, then Noah is certainly an exception. If the seven of Noah's family are also righteous and blameless—and otherwise they would inevitably have shared the fate of all flesh, 6: 13—then it appears that the corruption of all flesh even before the flood is not an unconditional dogmatic assertion. Certainly in the priestly writings it is neither explained nor assumed. In short, the priestly writings contain nothing whatsoever about the general sinfulness of man. They contain likewise nothing about a connexion between sin and death.

Other statements in the Old Testament are all incidental, and neither in form nor in purpose are they fundamental or generally valid. They are very much at variance one with another. "I was perfect toward him and kept myself from mine iniquity. Therefore hath the Lord recompensed me according to my righteousness", 2 Sam. 22: 24, Ps. 18: 24; it is scarcely probable that the writer of these words was familiar with a doctrine of total depravity. "I am clean, without transgression; I am innocent, neither is their iniquity in me", cries Job in his anguish (Job 33: 9). Against this there is the other idea that, where a man of God goes in and out, God is bringing to remembrance the woman's sin, 1 Kings 17: 18; and yet another idea that besides our iniquities which God sets before Himself and which are also known to us, there are also secret sins which are seen in the light of His countenance, Ps. 90: 8. It would be wrong, however, to equate these secret sins with unconscious sins. They are the same sins which Ps. 19: 12 calls hidden; one knows very well that one commits them but one does not want them discussed, indeed one does not want it known that they have been committed. God, however, makes His light to shine upon them.

Ps. 51: 5 goes a step further: "Behold I was shapen (born) in iniquity; and in sin did my mother conceive me". It is not the father but only the mother who conceives and then gives birth to a child in labour—only she is here involved; the begetting of children is therefore not considered in itself sinful. Who is speaking? One who can say that he has sinned against God only. Against whom then has he not sinned? Can any individual say that he has sinned only against God and not against men? That is scarcely possible. Then perhaps the people, the community is speaking.[145] They know they have sinned against God only, not against other nations who are blood-guilty, Ps. 51: 14. May God deliver them from that. May He therefore wash them thoroughly from their iniquities, v. 2, 11, for the sinful people is ever sinful right from the beginning. Our passage is confession and in no way claims, except very naïvely, to hold for all men. Rather this is like the rhetorical question in Job 14: 4: "Who can bring a clean thing out of an unclean? —not one!" Here it is roundly stated that all are unclean and no clean thing can come of them. The statement is made roundly and blandly but also, as even Catholics say,[146] quite suddenly and as if inserted. The last passage which has been cited in support of the doctrine of original sin is Ps. 58: 3: "The wicked (godless) are estranged from the womb: they go astray as soon as they be born, speaking lies." What is expressed here is, however, the persistence of those who are sinners; there is no statement that this persistence in sin is general.

Jeremiah is the Old Testament author whose pronouncements on sin surpass all others in profundity. The nation's characteristic is her wickedness or baseness, 1: 16; 2: 19; 4: 18. the baseness of her deeds, 4: 14; the baseness which the people keepeth fresh, as a well keeps fresh her water, 6: 7; no man of the people repented him of his baseness, 8: 6; they have a base heart, 3: 17; 9: 13; 16: 12; they are taught to do base things, 13: 23. It is really quite inadequate to translate the Hebrew רָעָה, רַע, base: it could be translated evil (that would express better the radical nature of the baseness) or malicious (that would rightly indicate that a definite act of will is intended) or corrupt (that would express a complete turning away from what should be); and none of these words would exhaust the content of רַע.

The effects of this wickedness of the Israelites are copiously described by Jeremiah. They forsake God, 1: 16; 2: 13, 17, 19; 5: 19; they are backsliders, 2: 19; 3: 22; 5: 19, they revolt and go, 5: 23; they are all greivous revolters, 6: 28; they have a revolting and rebellious heart, 5: 23; they slide back by a perpetual backsliding, 8: 5; they make their neck stiff, 7: 26; their faces are harder than a rock, 5: 3. The results are clear: they are refuse silver, 6: 30; they are all adulterers, an assembly of treacherous men, 9: 2; wise to do evil, but to do good they have no knowledge, 4: 22. This fearful state of affairs is due to the fact—and this is Jeremiah's last word on sin—that their wickedness is not folly or mood or anything else of a temporary nature but a conscious and determined attitude. My people *love* to have it so, 5: 31; they hold fast deceit, they *refuse* to return, 5: 3; 8: 5; they *refuse* to know me (God), 9: 5; they were good but they changed, 2: 21; they act not merely from a wicked heart but from the stubbornness and hardness of their wicked heart, 3: 17; 7: 24; 11: 8; 16: 12; 18: 12. Thus far Jeremiah goes and the Old Testament with him—they say that the heart and the will of the Israelites is hardened in wickedness. The formulation of a systematic doctrine, however, and the statement that all men are evil, that man is depraved, that this depravity originates in the Fall of his original parents and that through this Fall the whole order of creation was distorted—all this is quite foreign to the Old Testament.

52. MAN'S EXPEDIENT FOR HIS OWN REDEMPTION: THE CULT

1. There is no suggestion anywhere in the Old Testament that sacrifice or any other part of the cult was instituted by God. It knows only the regulation of already existing sacrifice by divine instruction. The cult stands therefore mid-way between anthropology and soteriology, between man's need of salvation and God's arrangements for it. The cult can be considered, and this happens in the New Testament, as a shadow of the things to come; Col. 2: 17. But it is begun and continued and accomplished by man; it is works, not grace; an act of self-help, not a piece of God's salvation.

Indeed, the cult is a bit of ethnic life. Israel takes it over from the heathen. Cain sacrifices without being commanded to do so, and Abel likewise, Gen. 4: 3-4. Sacrifice is the way of the world. Noah does it also, Gen. 8: 20. Moses knows what "holy land" means, without God's having to tell him, Ex. 3: 5. *Religionsgeschichte* is able to account for and explain practically all the component parts, arrangements, rites and ceremonies of the Old Testament cult. Where it cannot do so, it is not the particular character of the Old Testament and of its revelation which prevents it but rather the great antiquity of the practices involved.

Just because the cult is a bit of ethnic life *the prophets* are always setting question marks against it, doubting its propriety, rejecting it. "Did ye bring unto me sacrifices and offerings in the wilderness forty years?" Amos 5: 25. This question expects "no" for an answer, which historically is wrong but which is correct to this extent—that it was not God but men who instituted the cult. We say the cult, for in the Old Testament the cult is almost identical with the sacrifices; there is little more to it than that, above all there is hardly any proclamation of the word. "I spake not unto your fathers, nor commanded them in the day that I brought them out of the land of Egypt concerning burnt offerings or sacrifices", Jer. 7: 22. The statement is unambiguous and unconditional. The sacrificial system does not owe its origin to God. His will is operative only in the regulation of it. "To what purpose is the multitude of your sacrifices unto me? I am full of the burnt offerings of rams.

When ye come to see my face, who hath required this at your hand?" Isa. 1: 11-12. Many more passages of this sort might be quoted, and they are important. What they do, however, is to show that the full presentation of all the individual items of the Old Testament cult belongs to the study of Hebrew archaeology, that comparative *religionsgeschichte* must also set itself the task of explaining the origins and development of the Old Testament cult, and that this cult deserves only very limited discussion within a theology of the Old Testament.

2. We therefore dismiss the question of the origin of sacrifice, for it would take us far into prehistoric times. Also it probably has not one but several answers. Sacrifice arose in various ways which may have intersected one another and superimposed themselves on one another. As far as theology is concerned the only question of importance is that concerning the meaning of sacrifice within the scope of the Old Testament. And here we must distinguish clearly between the meaning sacrifice has in itself and the meaning it has for those practising it.

Failure to make this distinction has caused much confusion. We begin with the clarification of the meanings of the sacrifices themselves. There are really two kinds of sacrifices, however numerous the names of sacrifices may be. There are "communion" sacrifices, and gift sacrifices or gift offerings. Gift offerings can also be called homage offerings.

3. The *communion sacrifice* is always the sacrifice of a slaughtered animal, זֶבַח. But the essential thing about it is not the slaughter of the animal but the effecting of communion. It is achieved when someone wants to eat the flesh of an animal which is sacrificial. For the Hebrews the ox, the sheep and the goat were sacrificial animals. The choice was of course based on ethnology, not on theology. When anyone wants to eat and therefore to sacrifice one of these animals, he cannot do it alone but he needs a number of men to eat it with him, Ex. 12: 3-4.[147] Those who share the meal, by the mere fact that they eat together, become a fellowship. How long such a fellowship lasts and how binding it is is not known, since it is nowhere stipulated nor does it matter here. The important thing is the fact that the sacrifice and the sacrificial meal create communion or fellowship—the members of the company at the meal are called brothers, אַחִים. Since all the members of the people of Israel share the meal at sacrifice they are all brothers, Ex. 2: 11; 4: 18,

Deut. 15: 3 (a foreigner: thy brother). The sacrifice creates "communion" amongst the partakers. Therefore it is a communion sacrifice.

One of the participants in the sacrificial meal is God. Ye shall eat, says Deuteronomy (12: 7) *before* the Lord your God, and rejoice. God shares in the meal. It is therefore possible for a Hebrew to be called not merely Abijah, "Jahweh is my father", but even Achijah, "Jahweh is my brother". The two fellowships, that of the human participants amongst themselves and that of the human participants on the one hand with God on the other hand, are concurrent. This sacrifice creates *communio* therefore but certainly not anything like *unio mystica*. There is no question of mystical fellowship with God any more than with one another. The Old Testament knows nothing of mysticism. The fellowship formed creates not union, otherwise the term brother would not be in place; it creates an offensive and defensive alliance; there is reciprocal acknowledgment ("I will be your God, and ye shall be my people", Jer. 7: 23; "our God", Ps. 95: 7; "thy people", 79: 13) one stands up for the other, those involved live together in a relationship of חֶסֶד וֶאֱמֶת,[148] a mutual obligation that can be trusted. Jacob offered a sacrifice in the mountain, and called his brethren (i.e. Laban and his people) to eat with him, Gen. 31: 54. The Passover lamb which each household must eat, Ex. 12: 3-10, is called a sacrifice of the Lord's Passover, 12: 27. Israel may not enter into any covenant with the inhabitants of the land—they might be invited to eat of their sacrifices, Ex. 34: 15, and that would be entering into fellowship with their gods. The word for communion offering, זֶבַח, occurs 162 times; the commonest word for gift-offering, עֹלָה, occurs 286 times. Even these figures give some indication of the history of the communion sacrifice. As will be explained, its importance waned considerably as time went on.

4. There is a type of offering where a gift is offered to God. The purpose of the gift is to acknowledge the majesty of the recipient and to express the donor's feeling of respect—hence the name *gift offering* or homage offering. The difference from the communion offering is obvious. God receives a part of the communion sacrifice (at most a small part) in order to belong to the fellowship, whereas He receives the whole of the gift offering except the small part which the presiding priest receives as his due or compensation for his trouble. In effect the whole sacrifice belongs to God. The communion offering on the other hand belongs to the entire company of those partaking of the meal.

The oldest word for gift-offering is מִנְחָה. It is equivalent to tribute, present, and occurs also in a non-technical and profane sense. Jacob sends animals to Esau, of whom he is afraid, as a present, Gen. 32: 14-16. Joseph's brothers in a similar situation bring fruits to him as a present, Gen. 43: 11; the children of Israel sent a present to the king of Moab, Judg. 3: 15, etc. Someone gives a gift to another person to show his respect for the other person. It is entirely his own affair and done of his own free will. That is the מִנְחָה. Later this word is transferred to sacrifice and narrowed in meaning to become "meal offering", Lev. 2: 1, 3, 4; 7: 9; I Chron. 23: 29, etc. But מִנְחָה as the grain offering is the result of a long history in the sphere of sacrifice; I Sam. 2: 17 means, as 2: 13-16 shows, a meat offering מִנְחָה.

An equally old and even more explicit term for the gift offering is כָּלִיל, "the whole": Samuel took a sucking lamb and offered it as a burnt offering, a whole offering unto Jahweh, I Sam. 7: 9. Every meal offering of a priest shall be wholly burnt; it shall not be eaten, Lev. 6: 23; this gives incidentally the definition of the word. It was retained till late times but occurs seldom, probably because it designates the thing so superficially and because it is supplanted by better words.

The word עֹלָה, however, is the word which gained ever-increasing currency to designate the gift offering. It is usually translated burnt offering because it was burned. Originally the expression used was הַמִּנְחָה הָעֹלָה, "the present that ascends (in the fire)". Essentially that is correct. Ex. 29: 18 says "thou shalt burn the whole ram upon the altar, it is an עֹלָה for the Lord". Only God enjoys the burnt offering, since, apart from those portions which may not be sacrificed and those that fall to the priest as his due, the whole is burned.

5. The offering of a slaughtered animal and the gift offering can therefore be regarded as two sharply contrasted types of sacrifice. In the gift offering, man disposes of something which belongs to him for one reason or another. He gives. He surrenders his gift completely. He surrenders it by destroying it in

the fire. He surrenders it because he seeks God's face, His forgiveness, His favour, His goodwill. In the gift offering he does not seek God's fellowship. The gift offering does not establish a relationship; it underlines in fact the distance between the two. It is an act of homage, a token of respect, submission, surrender to him who receives the gift. At least this is roughly the line which the gift offering follows.

Another idea may be introduced, however. When Ehud brings the present to the king of Moab, Judg. 3: 15, his intention is to provide a cover for his deed. The gift due is produced, the Moabite can neither expect nor demand more. The gift is payment, duty and limit. The more adequate the gift, the more assured one may rest of protection and favour from him to whom one has paid homage. Man in the Old Testament used his sacrifice in this way also. He accumulates his sacrifice. "In the beginnings of your months ye shall offer two young bullocks, and one ram, seven he-lambs of the first year without blemish" together with a meal offering and drink offering for each animal; all this shall be offered "beside the continual burnt offering and the drink offering thereof", Num. 28 : 11-15. When Hezekiah consecrated the Temple anew by the Levites, seventy bullocks, one hundred rams and two hundred lambs were burned as a burnt offering, 2 Chron. 29: 32, together with other gifts. "I am full of burnt offerings of rams and the fat of fed beasts", Isa. 1: 11.

In the bleeding sacrifice the idea of renunciation is not present. God receives but the tiniest part of the sacrificed animal. The participants, a group of sanctified men (they may of their own free choice give portions to their wives), consume the sacrificed animal. The sacrifice is a feast, a happy meal. It is but proper and reasonable to give God a share, the first share, for the herds come from Him; He is Lord of the earth, Ps. 24: 1; He is, simply, Lord. But the communion feast with God is celebrated with carefree confidence, with head erect, not bowed. They are free men with a free God. Only as men, when they are most truly men, observe a certain restraint in their friendship in order to disclose the full measure of their love for their companions only in their extremity, so in this fellowship proclaimed and renewed in the sacrifice there is a certain coolness and restraint. It is to be remembered also that it is the laity who officiate at this sacrifice. A priest is only necessary in so far as he must establish that the day is an appointed day, that the participants are sanctified, Zeph. 1: 7, and that the animals and the slaughter comply with cult requirements. As the priestly influence in the cult grew, however, the communion sacrifice declined. It was replaced by the secular slaughter, Deut. 12: 15—the hart and the gazelle, the clean and the unclean, that is tantamount to saying without any reference to cult regulations—or it became the concomitant of the burnt offering. In later times one finds both burnt offerings alone and burnt offerings elaborated by the addition of a bleeding sacrifice in its own right.

6. We turn now from the distinction between communion offering and gift offering to observe distinctions of a quite different sort, distinctions among the sacrifices common in the cult, in the later priestly cult, *according to their purpose*. The same offering—say a burnt offering—can serve different ends; it may serve as a token of thanks, as recompense, as atonement, as supplication, homage, ordinary daily worship, etc. Conversely various offerings, a burnt offering, a meal offering, a drink offering may serve the same purpose; thanks, supplication, recompense. While many other details are of interest only to the archaeologist, the question for what purpose individual offerings are made and what meaning the offerer attaches to them is definitely a theological question.

The offering creates for God a רֵיחַ נִיחֹחַ. The expression is commonest in the priestly writings (Lev. 17, Num. 18, and Ezekiel 4 times) but the Jahwist also knows it, Gen. 8: 21; and it is by nature very ancient. "Noah offered burnt offerings on the altar. And the Lord smelled the sweet savour; and the Lord said in his heart, I . . . ." 8: 21. The Septuagint translates it ὀσμὴ εὐωδίας, "fragrance of a sweet smell", the Vulgate *odor suavitatis* and Luther similarly *lieblicher geruch*; but these are foolish twists of the true meaning, which emerges clearly in Ezek. 5: 13 where הֲנִחֹתִי חֲמָתִי בָם can mean only "I soothe my fury toward them". Thus נִיחֹחַ is "soothing" and רֵיחַ נִיחֹחַ "soothing smell". Gen. 8: 21 is not the only passage which speaks of God smelling the offering. David suggests that God should accept an offering to smell if He has anything against David, 1 Sam. 26: 19. The gods, who neither see nor hear, also cannot smell, Deut. 4: 28, although they have a nose, Ps. 115: 6; but Jahweh who can, may not smell the solemn assemblies of Israel, Amos 5: 21.

Again if the people persevere in disobedience and resist God's correction He refuses to smell the savour of Israel's sweet odours, Lev. 26: 31. But if after He has chastised them they turn again to serve Him, then for the sake of the sweet savour He will accept them when He brings them out from the peoples and is sanctified in them in the sight of the nations, Ezek. 20: 41.

One observes that the idea contained in the term "sweet savour", far from being incidental and insignificant, is, from the time of Ezekiel onwards, quite fundamental. God's wrath is active and must be soothed. *The offering appeases God's wrath.* That is its purpose whether it be a burnt offering, Lev. 1: 9; a meal offering, 2: 2; a bleeding sacrifice, 3: 1, 5; or a sin offering, 4: 29, 31. The sweet savour has become the common denominator of all sacrifice.

7. In the above fact we have a bit of the history of Old Testament sacrifice; that bit indeed which is theologically significant. A glance at two other sacrificial concepts will still further clarify this significant bit of history. The one concept is that of the קָרְבָּן. It is astonishing that this word occurs 80 times but only in Ezek. 20: 28; 40: 43 and otherwise in the priestly writings (Lev. 1: 2 to 27: 11—40 times; Num. 5: 15-31: 5—38 times). The word is the noun of the verb הִקְרִיב "to bring near, to offer", and means therefore "oblation". One senses that it is a late word from its very abstractness. Every sacrifice is called an oblation in the priestly writings, for here every sacrifice is an act of consecration and homage and its purpose is that God may receive a gift. This theological systematization was not unknown in earlier times. The bleeding sacrifice itself as communion sacrifice, while it retained its full content, was to a certain extent an oblation for the Lord as it is now called, Lev. 3: 1, "If his oblation be a שְׁלָמִים, bleeding sacrifice. . . ." One sees clearly in this sentence or in 1: 3 how the oblation is the predominant idea; it can be a burnt offering, 1: 3; a meal offering 2: 1; a sin offering, 4: 23, or something else. The characteristics of the individual sacrifices, if not obliterated altogether, are certainly greatly modified to give place to the monotony of the oblation idea.

The history of the word זֶבַח, bleeding sacrifice, slaughtered offering, moves in the same direction. While in earliest times this word occurs only alone, Gen. 31: 54, 1 Sam. 2: 13, and later also retains this usage, Amos 4: 4, Zeph. 1: 7, Neh. 12: 43, it does become more and more linked very definitely and by a significant development with the word שְׁלָמִים,[149] so much. so that it is sometimes displaced by this word. זֶבַח, Num. 15: 8, and זְבָחִים, Josh. 22: 7, stand alongside שְׁלָמִים. The two ideas are therefore not quite the same. שְׁלָמִים is a *schlussopfer* (the idea of being quits). The usual translation *Heilsopfer* has no sufficient justification. The word is added as explanation to זְבָחִים, Ex. 24: 5, 1 Sam. 11: 15—slaughter sacrifices which are שְׁלָמִים. Then comes the stage where they are attached—sacrifices of שְׁלָמִים, Ex. 29: 28 (9 times in all), and: a slaughter sacrifice of שְׁלָמִים, Lev. 3: 1 (35 times in all; 19 times in Lev., 15 in Numbers and once in 1 Kings 8: 63). Finally the stage is reached where זֶבַח disappears altogether from the series of sacrifices and שְׁלָמִים takes its place; e.g. Ezek. 45: 15; 46: 2, Lev. 9: 22, Num. 29: 39 —27 times in all. It appears that זֶבַח, which lost its significance as the communion sacrifice more and more, was neutralized and finally replaced by שְׁלָמִים.

8. Two types of sacrifice, חַטָּאת and אָשָׁם, reveal their meaning and purpose in their name. Their history too, however, reveals traces of the process of theological systematization to which we have referred. The word אָשָׁם occurs with the meaning guiltiness, Gen. 26: 10 (if a Philistine had lain with Isaac's wife, it would have brought guiltiness upon all the Philistines); Jer. 51: 5 (the land is full of guilt against the Holy One of Israel); Ps. 68· 22. In Num. 5: 7, 8 it means a restitution for guilt, in 1 Sam. 6: 3, 4, 8, 17, Isa. 53: 10 it means compensation, expiatory sacrifice, and in 2 Kings 12: 17 and 33 other passages (Ezek. 4, Lev. 27, Num. twice) it is used for guilt offering. If anyone undertakes a certain abstinence and during the period of the abstinence there is a sudden and unforeseen death in his house, that man is unclean and he must make a guilt offering besides other offerings. "If anyone lieth carnally with a woman, that is a bondmaid, betrothed to an husband, he must bring a ram as אָשָׁם, guilt offering", Lev. 19: 21. These and other stipulations are in themselves hard to understand but the greatest difficulty of all is this, that e.g. in Ezek. 40: 39, 2 Kings 12: 17 etc. the word חַטָּאת stands alongside אָשָׁם and the question arises how they are to be distinguished.[150] Originally אָשָׁם must have been compensation and חַטָּאת the consciousness of sin; later the two ideas tended to coincide.

The word חַטָּאת means, roughly 200 times, iniquity, sin. "What is our iniquity that we have committed against the Lord our God?" Jer. 16: 10. The same word also is used some 170 times for purification, sin offering: "It is a purification, חַטָּא'. And the priest shall take of the blood of the sin offering, חַטָּאת . . . and the priest shall make atonement for him as concerning his sin, חַטָּאת", Lev. 4: 24-26; purification . . . sin offering . . . sin, the Hebrew for all three is חַטָּאת. But now if חַטָּאת also means sin offering (as it does 14 times in Ezekiel, 62 times in Leviticus, 35 times in Numbers: cf. the numbers for אָשָׁם above) what is the difference between the two words אָשָׁם and חַטָּאת in passages like Ezek. 40: 39, 2 Kings 12: 17 where they stand side by side? The two words obviously cover the same ground, so that the one could have taken the place of the other and made it superfluous. If this has not happened it is obviously because the two types of sacrifice have lost their essential character, and it has become more important that the guilt offering and the sin offering are offerings than that they are offerings specifically for sin and guilt and not for any other purpose. The sacrifice in itself is the thing which increased in importance.

9. One type of sacrifice of which the purpose is clearly discernible and was not effaced is the תּוֹדָה, the so-called *thank offering*. "Make a sacrifice of thanksgiving of that which is leavened!" Amos 4: 5. This offering comes evidently after the more obligatory slaughter sacrifices and tithes, 4: 4. It contains leaven, which in the sacrifice is strictly forbidden, Ex. 23: 18, Lev. 2: 11. Even where it is mentioned along with burnt offerings and bleeding offerings, meal offerings and frankincense, Jer. 17: 26, there is a distinct caesura between it and the others. It is found where one gives praise to God for favour received, Jer. 33: 11, Jonah 2: 10, Neh. 12: 27, etc. It is also found where a convicted or confessing sinner[151] acknowledges God, Josh. 7: 19, Ezra 10: 11; but in the penitence rites of the organized cult this note of joy is not heard. The priestly material scarcely mentions the תּוֹדָה any more, and when it does it is not always clear what it means, Lev. 7: 13, 15. One is inclined to

think that here and elsewhere תּוֹדָה is no longer an act or the rendering of a gift but merely a formula, Ps. 118: 1.

10. All the Israelites' *offerings by fire* fell to the house of Eli, 1 Sam. 2: 28. The priests shall eat the offerings of the Lord made by fire, Deut. 18: 1. These two passages show that אִשֶּׁה offering by fire[152] is old but apart from them it occurs only in the priestly writings (Exodus 3, Leviticus 41, Numbers 16=60 times). The word is quite insignificant and merely describes the manner of the sacrifice: the sacrifice is consumed by fire. It is, however, for that very reason that the word is popular in the priestly writings—it is sacrifice to God for sacrifice's sake.

11. Since the Old Testament cult was not instituted but tacitly adopted as the natural practice of men who know God we know nothing of the *number and regularity of sacrifices* in earlier times. Sacrifice was always made in accordance with the rules, but whether the rules demanded sacrifice daily or weekly or monthly or at some other intervals we do not know. Only later are we told exactly how many sacrifices of any particular kind are due when they are due. Sacrifice becomes entirely a performance. Even in later times, however, an individual can make a sacrifice by himself, Lev. 1: 2; but one does not know whether in this passage it is a case of a free resolve or a cultic requirement as in Lev. 4: 1 ff. In early times these voluntary sacrifices, not demanded by any regulations, are in the majority. In the case of Cain and Abel it is entirely their own idea to bring an offering, Gen. 4: 3-4. Noah does it out of gratitude for his salvation, Gen. 8: 20; Abraham in order to pay homage to God who appeared to him, Gen. 12: 7; Isaac for the same reason, Gen. 26: 24-25; Jacob because a mutual understanding had been reached, Gen. 31: 54; Jethro in order to praise God for the salvation of Israel from the hands of the Egyptians, Ex. 18: 10-12; Balak and Balaam in order to question Jahweh, Num. 23: 1-5; Gideon in order to secure recognition of Jahweh, Judg. 6: 25-31; Manoah to speak his thanks, Judg. 13: 16, 19 —there are as many sacrifices as there are motives for sacrifice. One makes a sacrifice when one feels inclined to do so, and in addition one makes a sacrifice when the use and wont in the sanctuary requires it. The two coexist. It is only in the systematization to which the Exile gives rise that an aim is adopted which tends to magnify the regulation at the expense of independent and personal motives.

12. Two possibilities do remain open for private individuals
at all periods, two possible additions to the sacrifices of the
official priestly cult which are made entirely at will. One is
the נְדָבָה or *free-will offering*, the other is the נֶדֶר or *vow*. The
two are quite different from one another. The free-will offering
is a gift, e.g. an animal which is burnt as a burnt offering or
consumed as a bleeding offering by the cult-community. In the
case of valuable free-will offerings it seems that in early times
they were publicly proclaimed at festival times, Amos 4: 5,
probably in order to stimulate others to like generosity.
"They brought the free-will offerings of everyone that willingly
offered a free-will offering unto the Lord", Ezra. 3: 5. In this the
will of the donor remains free; he may offer even a crippled
animal as a gift, a thing he may not do in the case of a vow,
Lev. 22: 23. Why is there this difference?

The reason is that the free-will offering is entirely an affair
of the individual's free will and must remain so; the public cult
exerts no influence whatsoever. It can at most withhold its
interest in these free-will offerings, and permit them rather than
require them; and this seems to have been done. We do not
hear very much about the נְדָבָה. That is significant. On the
other hand the vow attracted public attention and received
priestly regulation. It does not become a cult institution, for it
retains its voluntary nature, but it receives cultic status. We
possess several examples of a vow: Jacob vows a vow saying,
"If God will be with me . . . so that I come again to my father's
house in peace, then shall the Lord be my God, and this stone
which I have set up for a pillar shall be God's house: and of all
that thou shalt give me I will surely give the tenth unto thee",
Gen. 28: 20-22; Israel vows that if God delivers the Canaanites
into their hands they will devote their cities to Him, Num. 21: 2;
Jephthah vows that if God delivers the children of Ammon into
his hand he will offer up for a burnt offering whatsoever comes
forth of the doors of his house to meet him, Judg. 11: 30-31;
Hannah vows that if God gives her a son she will give him unto
the Lord all the days of his life, 1 Sam. 1: 11; Absalom vows that
if Jahweh brings him again to Jerusalem he will serve the Lord
in Hebron, 2 Sam. 15: 8. The last two show that vows do not
belong only to heroic antiquity but also to situations where a
woman is childless or a man an exile. The action of the crew of
Jonah 1: 16 shows that thanks as well as wishes may lead to

vows. When a free-will offering is made, usually on the spur of the moment, there is no question of an occasion or a right to make it or a limitation of size or condition or circumstances that would make it null and void, whereas when it is a vow all these things can be involved, Num. 30: 3-15. In this case the priest is consulted; his influence increases, Num. 6: 2-21.

The vow is therefore important, since it can be incorporated in the cult as the free-will offering cannot. A vow can lead to a burnt offering, Num. 15: 8, or a bleeding offering, Lev. 7: 16, Num. 15: 8; but the ox or the sheep used must have no blemish, Lev. 22: 21. Even men can form the content of a vow, for they are evaluated in gold according to a fixed scale, Lev. 27: 2-8. One can almost hear the priests bustling about busily: one sees how important the vow is for the cult.

13. In several passages we come across *lists of cultic activities*: burnt offerings, bleeding sacrifices, tithes, heave offerings, vows, free-will offerings and the firstlings of the herd and the flock, Deut. 12: 6; heave offerings and firstlings possess in this cult context a certain polemical character, indicating as they do that God gives increase, not the gods of the Canaanites; burnt offering, meal offering, drink offering, sin offering, the daily burnt offering and the drink offering thereof, vows, free-will offerings, peace offerings, Num. 29: 36-39; burnt offerings, meal offering, bleeding sacrifice, drink offerings, each on its own day, sabbaths, gifts, מַתָּנָה, vows, free-will offerings, Lev. 23: 37-38. It is significant that introducing and abridging the four types of offering which according to the last passage are to be made daily, is the phrase "by way of making an offering made by fire". It has become a matter of indifference whether it is a burnt offering or a meal offering or a drink offering or a bleeding offering or what it is—each, robbed of its individuality, has become an offering by fire. The history of the cult in the Old Testament could not be more clearly illustrated than it is in this incidental note.

14. Let us try now to outline this *history of the cult.* As already stated, the ethnic elements of the cult were simply taken over by Moses and his contemporaries. The new thing is not a particular sort of cult but the exclusive reference by Moses' Hebrews of the ordinary cult to Jahweh. How far Jahweh's claim to lordship caused elements to be excluded, how far it reformed others to bring them into line with Jahweh's exclusiveness—the priestly rulings about the firstlings of the herd and the flock, the holy gift קָדָשִׁים, etc., are such a reformation of Canaanite cultic practices—we cannot tell. At any rate all accepted cult from the time of Moses is made to refer to Jahweh the one God. When one invokes a god one invokes the name of the Lord, Gen. 4: 26. One swears by the life of Jahweh, 1 Sam. 20: 3; He is named in blessing, Gen. 24: 31, and in cursing, 1 Sam. 26: 19; in vows, Gen. 31: 13; in all situations in which a god can be named. The same confession of Jahweh is also found in nomenclature, though there at an early stage the confessional characteristic is forgotten. Proof of this is the appearance of abbreviated names, where regularly the divine part of the name is dropped, נָתָן "he has given" for נְתַנְיָה, "Jahweh has given". The theological content of the cult in earliest times is altogether small and for the obvious reason that, apart from a few formulae, at this period of Old Testament religion the word in the sense of doctrine or confession is lacking. There is no preaching, and theology is summed up in the phrase "Jahweh and not Baal or other Gods". In other words Old Testament theology of early times shares with heathen "theology" the stock of language available but changes the subject. It says Jahweh where other "theologians" say Baal or some other name. This situation holds until the time of the prophets. Even from their preaching, however, it is clear how difficult it still was for them to speak in theological terms. The terms and the concepts were just not there. Ezekiel is the first to produce any sort of system.

"According to the multitude of his fruit he hath multiplied his altars", Hos. 10: 1. In terms of the traditional fiction that the cult laws of the Old Testament were Mosaic, the idea was formed and long held that while there were many altars and cult stations there was a strong unity of ritual and of theology. This assumption is false; there is nothing to justify it. Indeed it is highly improbable. It is nearer the truth to say "the more cult stations, the greater the variation in cult". "Ephraim multiplied altars, the altars serve them only to sin", Hos. 8: 11. If Amos and Jeremiah can assert that nothing was known about cult in Moses' time, Amos 5: 25, Jer. 7: 22; if Amos and Isaiah can harshly describe the forms of the existing cult as hateful to God, Amos 5: 21-24, Isa. 1: 10-15; if the acceptable alternative to the existing cult is not a purified, reformed or spiritualized cult (Mic. 6: 6-8) but a way of living inspired by thoughts of the kingdom of God, and if no contrast is ever mentioned with the cult revealed through Moses, it is surely because until the time of Jeremiah, i.e. until the time of the Exile, there was no standardization of cult practices. The regulated cult with its inherent theology is a product of the Exile.

Jeremiah's statement that Jahweh when He brought the fathers out of Egypt gave them no commandment about burnt offerings and bleeding sacrifices is striking. It does not say that the fathers who left Egypt did not sacrifice; in fact they did, and Amos attacks in 5: 25 the intention of these sacrifices. The point is, however, that the sacrifices which the fathers made were not made on Jahweh's instructions. They are not revelation, they were adaptations of ethnic practice. It must be carefully noted, however, that Jeremiah—like Amos before him—had no interest in a purely historical fact but considerable interest in a fact that had practical results. What could be for Jeremiah the practical results of the fact that Jahweh did not demand any sacrifice from the Israelites at the Exodus? Surely this: that until the time of Jeremiah and still in the time of Jeremiah himself there was no cult and no cult regulations for which divine institution could be claimed. For Jeremiah all cult is unnecessary human contrivance.

This does not mean that the well-known cult stations like Bethel, Gilgal, Shiloh, and Beersheba did not early take care to make rules for their cult and to have these rules observed by those who frequented them—rules which were regarded as of divine origin. But it was the state sanctuary in Jerusalem that was the first to be provided with widely recognized cult regulations. The prophet Jeremiah, however, does not recognize them, though he never once employs many words to explain his rejection of them. He, with the prophets that came before him, says still less about what the cult should be. All cult is the same to the prophets we know, up to the time of Jeremiah. The cult for them can be indirect opposition to the commandments of God. Never once do they say that there could be cult which God demanded; there is not so much as a hint of any such idea. Nor can one evade the importance of the sentence by saying that the cult and its questionableness were not discussed by the prophets. The passages have been quoted above which disprove that. The tendency of the cult to magnify itself, the importance in the cult of expense, size, show, beauty, quality—these things Amos and Isaiah saw clearly. Nevertheless while the prophets reject the existing cult they do not agitate for an improved or quite different cult. In place of cult they advocate social righteousness. *Until the time of Ezekiel the cult does not belong to the Old Testament revelation.* Nor can one use Deuteronomy to argue against this, for its regulations for the great feasts, 16: 1-17, and its abrogation of the old communion sacrifice (that is what it amounts to in 12: 1-28) do not touch on the essence of the cult. The stipulations about firstlings and tithes, 26: 1-15, come nearest to it where in the old-fashioned way one is bidden rejoice before God in harvest, 26: 11. But then comes Ezekiel.

Ezekiel does not come alone, nor does he come on his own initiative. He comes in the time of the breakdown of the national form of Old Testament religion; he emerges from this breakdown. Not without cause, 14: 23, did Jahweh chastise Jerusalem; He does it for His name's sake, 20: 9, 14, 22, 44. He stakes His life on it that He will show Himself with a mighty hand and an outstretched arm and with fury poured out, king over the house of Israel, 20: 33. Then it shall be recognized—and this underlies the whole course of events that led to the Exile—"that I am Jahweh" (63 times); now Jahweh is no longer a name, it is a concept—the one, true, living and holy God. The cult that had been was corrupt. "I gave them statutes that were not good, and judgments whereby they could not live, and I polluted them in their own gifts", 20: 25-26. God causes everything. Even the corruption of Israel which leads to downfall is His work. Israel's cult before the Exile is—by God's arrangement—impure. The cult is nowhere in the Old Testament more sharply defined as non-revelational.

The same Ezekiel has the task of introducing a new, properly regulated cult, a cult that will therefore be accepted as having divine approval. However much this new cult may differ in technical and archaeological details from the cult enjoined by the priestly writings and from that actually practised in later times, basically it is the same cult. This is proved by the fact, already noted, that the cult terminology used by Ezekiel and by the priestly writers is very similar. The following are the principal features. The cult is the business of the priests. They present the offerings, whether for themselves or for the princes ("the prince shall enter and shall stand by the post of the gate, and the priests shall prepare his burnt offering and his peace offerings, and he shall worship . . . then he shall go forth",

46: 2) or for the people. ("The Levites shall slay the burnt offerings and the sacrifices for the people", 44: 11). The priests are in all cases the מַקְרִיבִים, the bringers of the קָרְבָּן which becomes the general term for all sacrifices (see pp. 18 ff.). They are the men who bring to Jahweh the most holy gifts, the meal offering and the sin offering and the guilt offering, 42: 13. The cult has become entirely a priestly affair. The prince stands afar off, 46: 2; the people stands afar off, 42: 14; 46: 3. The people, 45: 16, and the prince 45: 17, 22-25, may prepare the provisions and the animals used in the cult, but that and their idle presence at the ceremonies is the sum total of their part in it. *The cult is the priests' business.*

The ancient terminology is still current. Ezekiel speaks of burnt offerings; he knows also the bleeding sacrifices, he frequently mentions the מִנְחָה and always in the sense of meal offering, he is constantly speaking about sin offerings and guilt offerings and twice he mentions the comprehensive קָרְבָּן. On the other hand he does not yet know the offering by fire, אִשֶּׁה, and he prefers to say שְׁלָמִים, "peace offering", rather than bleeding offering. All these are, however, like so many elderly pensioners now. They have had their day. Their individuality is gone. Where they are listed, 40: 39; 42: 13; 45: 17, the aim is to give an impression of quantity rather than of variety. Their individual importance is gone. The cult is no longer concerned with the particular significance of each practice but merely with the cult as such. Thus it is possible to call sacrifices most holy gifts or, to translate the Hebrew more accurately, most holy things, 42: 13, for in fact the giving is not mentioned. *The cult has become an end in itself.*

Ezekiel writes quite crudely, "when ye offer fat and blood, my food", 44: 7. God needs food and His food is fat and blood. One must not imagine that this statement would come under the judgment of Ps. 50: 13, where God rejects the idea of His eating the flesh of bulls and drinking the blood of goats. Such a rejection was once necessary. An anthropomorphic conception of God as eating fat and blood may once have existed, but certainly not in Ezekiel's mind. Indeed it is just because Ezekiel is free of all anthropomorphic notions that he can make use of so anthropomorphic a way of speaking. No: his concern is quite different. He uses the phrase "fat and blood, my food" to stress that the cult exists for God's sake. The cult was originally man's attempt to express to God his gratitude, his supplications, his confession, his desire to atone, his excuses, his worship; for Ezekiel it is no longer that. Rather it is now God's great claim on man. It is man's service to God. It is not by accident that in Ezekiel the ancient idea of the sweet savour again comes into prominence. God gave Israel fine flour and oil and honey for food, and the people have set these good things before idols for a sweet savour; Ezek. 16: 19. Now comes the change. The whole house of Israel shall serve Jahweh. "In mine holy mountain . . . will I accept them, and there will I require your heave offerings and your first fruits, with all your holy things. With a sweet savour will I accept you", 20: 40 ff. The whole cult is now an institution which provides what God likes.

15. But what of the people—if by this theologizing of the cult, which reserves it entirely for the specialists, the priests (Lev. 1-7 shows how paltry a part is granted to the laity), they are excluded from the cult, what remains of public worship?

1 Chronicles, which traces the cult not to God's instructions to Moses and Aaron as the priestly writings do but to the arrangements made by David, indicates two new cultic items which neither Ezekiel nor the priestly writings know. The one is song, the other is prayer. *Song* demands technical ability. Therefore those qualified are divided into groups according to their particular talent, 1 Chron. 25. *Prayer* (including the Psalms) is too much a matter for the individual to permit of being systematized completely. In the Old Testament therefore it appears[153] following impressive patterns, but there are no binding directions given concerning either its content or its outward ritual. It is only later that rules are evolved for prayer, times of prayer, preliminary conditions and formulae.

Prayer, song (Pss. 100, 108, 147, 150) and the study of Scripture are three elements of the cult which it is possible to practise even in a foreign land. Israel lives in a foreign land from the beginning of the Exile, even when a number return home, even when the Temple and the city walls are rebuilt, Neh. 6: 15, and the sacrifices are again offered, Neh. 12: 44-47. There in the strange land the ancient portions of the Old Testament are kept together, the new portions are added and the whole is read and learned and taught. In Jerusalem sacrifice;

abroad prayer, song and Scripture; common to both, circum-cision, fasts, Sabbath, abstinence and acts of piety: that is the cult of the Old Testament in its fulness—an obstinate, intricate, self renouncing, desperate human attempt not to extort salvation—the fear of God and the recognition of His holiness preclude that—but to deserve it. And all the time God of His grace makes a gift of salvation, Isa. 55: 1.

Part Three

JUDGMENT AND SALVATION

53. COMMANDMENT AND LAW

1. GOD'S first act of grace towards man was to give him, at his creation, His command. God creates men and says to them "Be fruitful and multiply, and replenish the earth and subdue it; and have dominion over the creatures", Gen. 1: 28. Man's task is earthly civilization. God forms Adam and puts him into the garden of Eden to dress it and to keep it, Gen. 2: 15. Adam's task is work. It is wrong to suggest that work in itself is a curse. According to the Bible a curse, the curse of wearisome toil, is laid on work because of Adam's disobedience, Gen. 3: 17-19,[154] but work itself has already been commanded. The early history of man proceeds step by step with one commandment after another. All men are allowed to eat flesh but they are at the same time forbidden to taste blood and to shed human blood, Gen. 9: 4, 6. All male descendants of Abraham and all who belong to their households are commanded to be circumcised, Gen. 17: 10-14. The law is given to the people of Israel at Sinai; Moses comes and tells them all the words of Jahweh and all the judgments: and all the people declare themselves willing to do all the words which Jahweh hath spoken, and on the basis of these words the covenant is sealed, Ex. 24: 3, 8. One day, however, all peoples will go up to the mountain of the Lord, to be taught His ways and to walk in His paths, for out of Zion shall go forth the law, Isa. 2: 3. Life belongs to the context of the law. Life is under the law. The word for this is מִשְׁמֶרֶת, "service"—a significant word.

The scope of the commandment therefore increases gradually in the period covered by the Old Testament to include the whole of life. Were a modern theologian to write the Old Testament by his own wits he would have to introduce right at the beginning a paragraph in which men are given a thorough grounding in the fundamentals of social morality. The absence of such instruction in the Old Testament is conspicuous. There are countless fundamental imperatives which the Old Testament never gives as commandments. On the contrary it presupposes them, it takes them silently for granted. It is silent about them because they follow inevitably from the great primary, all-inclusive fact of commandment itself; they are a simple deduction from it. The Old Testament does not reveal a sum of laws, so that what is not expressly commanded may not be done and what is not expressly forbidden is permitted. That would be a scribal misunderstanding and an idea that never occurred to any Old Testament man. God's command exists. His law is valid. It is valid even when it is not expressed, for *the law is merely God's claim to lordship*. Even where the King has not said in words what he requires or forbids, his people know his will.

2. Two things followed from this. The first is that all individual commandments and all bodies of laws comprising a number of commandments, of which there are several in the Old Testament, are from the theological point of view never anything other than sets of examples. They are never complete.[155] In respect both of their origin and their reference they have an incidental character. They sometimes bear the marks of their period and of changes they have undergone (compare 2 Sam. 13: 13 and Gen. 20: 12 with Lev. 18: 9, Deut. 27: 22; and Gen. 29: 23, 28 with Lev. 18: 18). Nevertheless all the temporality and incompleteness does not alter the fact that the law, where it exists, reveals the unconditional sovereign will of God. God gives the law that man may obey; and both law and obedience are unconditional.

The second result of the fact that God's people know God's will, even if it is not expressed, is this: that the Old Testament conception of revelation is not confined to what God has made known in words; it goes considerably beyond this. God's will is known even when God does not express it. How is it known? When David had cut off the skirt of Saul's robe "David's heart smote him", 1 Sam. 24: 5, and likewise when he had numbered the people, 2 Sam. 24: 10. If he were to shed blood without cause it would make his heart to stumble, 1 Sam. 25: 31. In these three passages one can say that לֵב, heart, is almost equivalent to conscience. But the idea of conscience was never developed or valued in the Old Testament. When in Job 31 one reads those noble moral obligations to which Job submits himself one cannot fail to be deeply impressed by the loftiness of this moral apperception. Yet the fact of the unexpressed and nevertheless clearly understood revelation of the divine will carries us far beyond these examples of conscience and moral apperception. In the Old Testament God reveals Himself and His moral requirements chiefly in the requisites for a prosperous

community life. The aim of all human life is שָׁלוֹם, i.e.,
when the word appears in this connexion, prosperous life—God
wants men to thrive. It is for that reason that He blesses them,
Gen. 1: 28. And that is why the Aaronic blessing concludes with
the wish that the Lord will lift up His countenance upon thee
and give thee שָׁלוֹם, prosperity, Num. 6: 26. That is why also
the complaints which the prophets raise against their contemporaries are complaints about sins which destroy communal
life. For this reason also Isaiah can say the wicked have no
שָׁלוֹם, prosperity, 48: 22; 57: 21. From the knowledge of
what would make for prosperity man recognizes, even when
there is no specific commandment or prohibition known to him,
what the will of God is and His requirements of man. Therefore
he can borrow laws from other nations or in course of time
replace old commandments with new without being afraid of
infringing the will of God or altering it in any way.[156]

3. The variety of sources of individual commandments is
seen in the number of words there are for commandment, none
of which say quite the same thing but which all emanate from
the same will. Commandment itself, i.e. an order which a
superior gives to his subordinates and expects them to obey,
is מִצְוָה from צִוָּה to order. A king gives to a peasant a
commandment, cf. Solomon to Shimei, 1 Kings 2: 43; likewise
God gives to Samuel through Saul the commandment to wait
seven days, 1 Sam. 10: 8; 13: 8; in both cases something is
commanded which concerns only the individual situation. It
is different in Ex. 20: 6, Ezra 9: 10 and many other passages.
In these it is a question of a number of commandments which
God has given and which are to have permanent validity. There
is no suggestion of this idea with מִצְוָה. It can be positive or
negative. It can mean either commandment or prohibition.
A number or even the whole sum of commandments can also
—and this is theologically significant—be covered by the
singular: "the commandment of our God", Ezra 10: 3; "all
the commandment which I command thee this day shall ye
observe to do", Deut. 8: 1. This usage is not infrequent. Indeed,
when one tries to define the content of that which is denoted
by the word מִצְוָה one finds no distinctive characteristics. All
that God commands or forbids can be called מִצְוָה.

The word instruction or statute, חֹק, and its feminine חֻקָּה
do not occur as frequently as מִצְוָה. By derivation it means

that which is cut in or graven, hence prescribed[157] or appointed;
but in effect it can scarcely be distinguished from מִצְוָה. The
new moon and full moon festivals are a חֹק for Israel, Ps. 81:
5. The fifth which the Egyptians give of their land, Gen. 47: 26;
the striking of the door posts with blood on the day of the
Passover, Ex. 12: 24; the duties and rights concerning the
fulfilment and annulment of vows between husband and wife
and father and unmarried daughter (Moses says Jahweh
commanded them, צִוָּה, they could therefore also be called
מִצְוָה) Num. 30: 16; the instructions concerning festivals,
Deut. 16: 12; the four-day lamentation for Jephthah's daughter,
which the daughters of Israel hold annually, Judg. 11: 39 ff.:
all these and many others are called חֹק. Even the shining of
the sun by day, the moon and the stars by night, and the
violence of the sea, are called חֻקִּים, which brings the word
very near to what we would call a law of nature. No one has
ever managed to determine, however, when one should say
מִצְוָה and when חֹק, and when one or other is inadmissible.
The most one can assert is that חֻקָּה indicates something
concrete more often than חֹק; also in Job 38: 33 it signifies the
laws of the heavens almost in the sense of the laws of nature.

The word מִשְׁפָּט, judgment, instruction, commandment,
which occurs frequently and is well attested in ancient texts is
distinguishable from the two foregoing words for commandment more in respect of derivation than of usage. It means
properly the proposal which is made for the settlement of a
dispute or a suit at law. The proposal for settlement naturally
develops into a ruling. This establishes the claim that is just,
and therefore מִשְׁפָּט comes to mean claim or demand—the
priest's claim on the people, Deut. 18: 3, "when the needy
maketh his just demand", Isa. 32: 7. It is a short step from that
to the meaning "the right which one can demand"—the king,
I Sam. 8: 9; daughters, Ex. 21: 9; the fatherless and the
widows, Deut. 10: 18. When therefore Scripture speaks of the
מִשְׁפָּט of God, as it frequently does, the word has a particular
shade of meaning and that is not so much the just statutes of
God as the *just claims* of God. God, who is the Lord, can demand
and He does demand. The Passover shall be kept according to
His statutes and His demands, Num. 9: 3. God brings forward
demands by which the congregation shall judge between the

smiter and the avenger of blood, Num. 35: 24. "In the land
which Jahweh giveth them the Israelites shall observe to do the
statutes and the demands", Deut. 12: 1. "In the wilderness I
gave to the descendants of the house of Jacob my statutes and
*made them to know my demands which men must obey in order to
live*", Ezek. 20: 11. There is no other Old Testament word
which portrays so clearly the imperative nature of the law, the
divine claim. It is to be regretted that no one has ever tried to
establish whether, when God is the subject, מִשְׁפָּט could not
always be translated "demand"; whether indeed it must not.

The word תּוֹרָה is a contrast to these others in so far as
originally in the case of a תּוֹרָה the initiative lay not with
God but with man. When one does not know whether food is
impure if one touches it with the skirt of one's garment in
which one carries holy flesh, one should ask the priests for a
תּוֹרָה on the question, Hagg. 2: 11 ff. Man puts the question,
God gives (through the priests who give the instructions, Jer.
2: 8; 8: 8) the answer.

When the land is to be divided into seven portions Joshua
casts יָרָה[158] lots, and according to God's arrangement in the
lot, Joshua makes the allocation, 18: 6, 11 ff., תּוֹרָה is therefore really the instruction of the cast. But this instruction comes
from God—He gives many instructions, Hos. 8: 12, they are
His instructions, Ex. 18: 16. But since these are not precepts
whose validity is weakened by time, but are as a rule permanent, one is right to call them law. תּוֹרוֹת means therefore laws,
and there are many such laws. In the passage concerning the
gathering of the manna the translation should be "my commandments and my instructions", Ex. 16: 28, because the
giving of the manna comes to an end, Josh. 5: 12. At Sinai,
however, God gives by Moses statutes and demands and laws
made between Him and the children of Israel, Lev. 26: 46.

Indeed, there are a great many such laws: the law concerning
the burnt offering, Lev. 6: 2; the law concerning a woman with
child, Lev. 12: 7; the law concerning leprosy, Lev. 14: 57; the
law concerning the Temple, Ezek. 43: 12—one could enumerate
about twenty of them which are expressly called by this name;
as one might expect, they are found mostly in the priestly
material. Quite early however we find the term הַתּוֹרָה, the
law, used for a collection of all or many individual precepts:
"Thou hast forgotten the law of thy God", Hos. 4: 6. "Give ear

unto the law of our God", Isa. 1: 10. "They have rejected the law of the Lord of hosts", Isa. 5: 24. "They will not hear the law of the Lord", Isa. 30: 9. One would prefer to use the word teaching or instruction in these passages rather than law, in order not to lend support to the idea of a written law, which certainly would be a gross misunderstanding; for the written law, which is a late phenomenon, is frequently called simply "the law". "Ye have not kept my law", Jer. 16: 11. "Jehu took no heed to walk in the law of the Lord", 2 Kings 10: 31. "I will give thee the tables of stone and the law and the command- ment" (מִצְוָה "the" commandment as collective for the commandments!) "which I have written that thou mayest teach them", Ex. 24: 12. This is the (relevant) statute of the (comprehensive) law, Num. 31: 21. Deuteronomy still speaks freely of "this law", 1: 5; 4: 8; 17: 18, 19; 27: 3, 8, 26; 28: 58, 61; 29: 20, 27; 31: 9, 11, 12, 24; 32: 46;[159] which obviously dis- tinguishes the deuteronomic bodies of the law from other abrogated bodies of law, but one cannot draw the conclusion from this that the fact of the law as a unified whole is questioned and that detached bodies of law, one replacing the other, are to be regarded as independent entities. The very opposite is the case.

The fact that there is "the law" is for the writer of Deuter- onomy and also for his predecessors—certainly as far back as Isaiah and how much farther we do not know—quite certain. And because there is "the" law there must be codes of law, not several at one and the same time but one valid for every period as it comes. The deuteronomist, under the influence of the prophetic preaching and particularly that of Isaiah, is con- cerned with these very codes, for since "the" law does exist— a modern theologian would say "in the mind" but the Bible does not say so—it must be capable of being reduced to one body, one collection of (necessary) laws. *The law codes are the law in words.* If it did not exist, they would not exist. But it is not the laws which make the law, but the law which makes the laws; and the incidental formulation of the (temporal) laws is not one and the same thing as the law, nor is there behind the formulation of the individual law code any idea of a verbal inspiration, so that whole law codes can simply be replaced by quite different ones—e.g. the code of Deuteronomy by the laws of Ezekiel and these again together with the code of Deuteronomy by the laws of the priestly writings—just because through the whole process of being put into words "the" law remains unshaken. It is only when Judaism at the end of the Old Testament revelation becomes torpid and dead that the sense of this spirituality and freedom of inspiration is lost. Conceiving of the law as something fixed, and explaining and forcing its details into some kind of unity, they paid the penalty in slavery to the dead letter. Woe to the scribes!

The laws תּוֹרוֹת unite to express the law הַתּוֹרָה, which is never fully expressed but always fully in operation. That is the law of Jahweh "which should be in thy mouth", Ex. 13: 9. The book of the law of Moses (that is undoubtedly the correct translation, not the lawbook of Moses; cf. Josh. 8: 32, 1 Kings 2: 3), Joshua 8: 31; 23: 6 ("which Jahweh hath commanded", 2 Kings 14: 6, Neh. 8: 1); "the law of Jahweh, the God of Israel", 2 Kings 10: 31; "all the law that my servant Moses commanded them", 2 Kings 21: 8; Deuteronomy, according to the famous identification of De Wette, is called the law of Moses, 2 Kings 23: 25; "the law of thy God", Hos. 4: 6; "they have trespassed against my (God's) law", Hos. 8: 1; "the law of our God", Isa. 1: 10; "they have rejected the law of the Lord of hosts", Isa. 5: 24; "they will not hear the law of the Lord", Isa. 30: 9; "they have forsaken my law", Jer. 9: 13; "they have not kept my law", Jer. 16: 11. One sees from these passages, to which many more could be added, that the law as God's claim that must be obeyed is something which is constantly recurring. According to the Old Testament revelation there is no life without God's law.[160]

It is very characteristic of the nature of the Old Testament revelation that in passages which speak in programme fashion of the whole sum of commandments, statutes, precepts or laws none of the words listed is repeated, but another simpler and at first sight less illuminating word is used. Deuteronomy speaks occasionally of the "words of this law", 17: 19; 27: 3, 8, 26; 28: 58; 29: 28. The introduction to the Decalogue runs: "And God spake all these words", Ex. 20: 1. The law is called quite simply "the word which I command you", Deut. 4: 2. In Jer. 6: 19 "they have not hearkened unto my words and they have rejected the law", God's words and God's law are parallel and synonymous. *The law is the word of God.* "Because thou hast rejected the word of the Lord", 1 Sam. 15: 23; "he sheweth his word unto Jacob, his statutes and his judgments unto Israel", Ps. 147: 19. This sheds a new light on the formula found in the prophets,[161] "the word of the Lord". It is ambiguous and can stand for accusation, rebuke, threat and promise, but it also means from the time of the earliest prophets onwards God's demand, His law—"a famine and a thirst of hearing the word of the Lord", Amos 8: 11; "they shall wander from sea to sea seeking his word", Amos 8: 12. The prophets too are entrusted with the publication of the law; not of course of specific statutes and certainly not of cultic ritual instructions, but of the great comprehensive will of God with its claims on the whole man and the whole of life, and its saving intention.

4. We come now to the purpose and value of the law. What does God intend to achieve by the law? The purpose of the law, whether in detail or as a whole, is pedagogical. God the Lord gives to men, who are His subjects, through the law the opportunity to prove themselves. God proves Abraham. נִפָּה, and commands him to sacrifice his only son, Gen. 22: 1 ff.—an Elohist passage. God gives the children of Israel a statute and an ordinance and proves them thereby, Ex. 15: 25—a Jahwist passage. This idea that the commandments and the law are a pedagogical contrivance is therefore an original element of the Old Testament revelation. Deuteronomy in its homiletic way makes this idea even clearer. God puts the people to the test in order to know (better translated to learn) "what was in thine heart, whether thou wouldest keep his commandments or no", Deut. 8: 2. "Jahweh your God proveth you to know whether ye love the Lord your God with all your heart and with all your soul", Deut. 13: 4. The same idea is found in passages influenced by Deuteronomy. God proves Israel, "whether they will keep the way of Jahweh to walk therein", Judg. 2: 22; to know whether they would hearken unto the commandments of Jahweh, Judg. 3: 4. God leaves Hezekiah to act, in order to try him, "that he might know all that was in his heart", 2 Chron. 32: 31. For this reason the Psalmist prays that God should prove him, Ps. 26: 2, and in the same breath he asks that God will examine him.[162] To prove and to examine show the same thing: *The purpose of the law is the confirmation of the faithful.* The law is παιδαγωγός.[163] It is significant that this idea is dropped in the priestly writings; it is not compatible with the absolute sublimity of God.

Following on from this we can now appreciate the meaning of a term for commandment or law which we have not yet mentioned. It is a word which gains currency only with the

Exile—the word עֵדוּת. The Jahwist tells how Laban and
Jacob made a mutual agreement and as a "witness", עֵד,
thereof they made a heap of stones.[164] The testimony of these
stones consists in their calling to mind the mutual claims and
obligations, Gen. 31: 44-48, עֵדוּת is equivalent therefore to
reminder. One can really render the word, and especially its
plural עֵדֹת, monitions, law, laws. The law is the testimony
of the claims God makes on His people. "They have not hearkened unto thy testimonies, thy laws wherewith thou didst
testify against them", Neh. 9: 34. Because the ten commandments are the basic testimonies of God to His people, the ark of
the covenant in which they are to lie is called the ark of the
testimony, Ex. 25: 22 (and in 11 other passages); the tablets of
the Decalogue the two tablets of the testimony, Ex. 31: 18;
32: 15: 34: 29; the tabernacle even the tent of the testimony,
Num. 9: 15 (and in 4 other passages), or the dwelling of the
testimony, Ex. 38: 21, Num. 1: 50, 53; 10: 11. All of these
reveal the law as a means of divine grace for the purpose of
trial and preservation.

5. The true measure of salvation which the law is meant to
bring is really in having divine favour and in joy. God intends
His law to be a means of salvation in the highest sense. In the
passages quoted earlier which give the reason for God's putting
Israel to the test, the result of the proving, e.g. Abraham's
proving, remains completely open and can consist in the
people's complying with the law. The impossibility of man's
obedience is by no means a part of the Old Testament revelation. Deut. 8: 16 goes a step further in this direction: God puts
Israel to the test to do them good at their latter end (that is,
when they have stood the test). The law is accordingly the joy
of God's faithful people. "I have rejoiced in the way of the
testimonies", Ps. 119: 14; "I cleave unto thy testimonies", Ps.
119: 31; "blessed is the man whose delight is in the law of Jahweh",
Ps. 1: 2. This point of view is seldom expressed, however; indeed
these are practically isolated examples, and they are late.

54. DISOBEDIENCE AND PUNISHMENT

If man does not hearken to God's commandment he is disobedient. Disobedience is the original sin and the epitome of all
sins great and small. Basically it does not matter what their
nature or consequences or form is at all; they are all one in this

—that they are disobedience. God confronts man's disobedience with the question, "What is this thou hast done?" Gen. 3: 13; 4: 10. Whether it is Eve eating the apple or Cain murdering his brother the question remains the same. God by His question summons man to responsibility. The purpose of the question is to establish the truth and make man reflect; it is not asking for defence or discussion. When God has established disobedience He inflicts the punishment right away. Punishment issues naturally and inevitably from the sovereignty of God. Disobedience is violation of the sovereignty of God; punishment is the making good of this violation.

The above is not true of every reference to punishment in the Old Testament. Indeed, quite often the idea of expiation is absent altogether. Adam must leave Paradise not because of his disobedience but rather in order that he may not live for ever, Gen. 3: 22 ff. Adam must die, but again not because of his disobedience: death is described by God Himself as man's appointed lot, Gen. 3: 19b. No; Adam is punished for his disobedience in having toil and sorrow added to his work, Gen. 3: 17-19a. And yet this curse turns out to be a blessing: "thou shalt eat the labour of thine hands: happy shalt thou be, and it shall be well with thee", Ps. 128: 2. Eve for her disobedience will have the pain of childbirth, Gen. 3: 16, but the woman shall be saved through her childbearing, 1 Tim. 2: 15. Cain is cursed from the ground because of the murder of his brother and must be a fugitive and a wanderer, but "whosoever slays Cain, vengeance shall be taken on him sevenfold"; he remains under God's protection, Gen. 4: 11-15. Even God's punishment is blessing and there is no particular expiation attached to the punishment, no sacrifice of any sort; the punishment is expiation in itself. That changes later. David is punished for having numbered the people and the punishment is a pestilence among his people; therefore he makes a sacrifice on account of it, and Jahweh is moved by his entreaties for the land and the disease is removed forthwith, 2 Sam. 24. If anyone commits a trespass in the holy things of the Lord he must make restitution with a fifth part in addition and make atonement with the ram of the guilt offering; then he will be forgiven, Lev. 5: 14-16. When, however, a man sins unwittingly he must make atonement with a ram for a guilt offering, and he will be forgiven, Lev. 5: 17-19. Job goes the length of offering burnt offerings for his children when they feast, according to the number of them, all in case (he didn't know) they had sinned, Job. 1: 4 ff. When Achan has confessed to appropriating forbidden spoil he is stoned, Josh. 7: 1-25. Uzzah dies because he put forward his hand to the ark of God to take hold of it, 2 Sam. 6: 6 ff. Azariah, in whose reign the people still burnt incense in the high places, is smitten with leprosy unto the day of his death, 2 Kings 15: 4 ff. Israel "hath received of the Lord's hand double punishment for all her sins", Isa. 40: 2. These examples could be multiplied but we have already listed enough to indicate at least this: that the Old Testament has no unequivocal teaching to offer on the relation between disobedience and punishment. And can the explanation be other than that the Old Testament's concern is first and last not so much punishment and expiation as grace and salvation?

No one has yet written an account of the development in Scripture and in history of the relation between disobedience and punishment, but this at least can be said: No disobedience escapes God's notice or His punishment. If Adam and Eve must quit Paradise and Cain his field, it is a way of expressing the violent disturbance of the relation between God and sinners. In modern terms, one can speak of a disturbance of the order of creation. One is also entitled to ask whether the Old Testament believes that this situation will always persist. The same question arises from the story of the tower of Babel, Gen. 11: 7. Will men never again speak one language? Is the door of Paradise for ever closed? are Cain and his people for ever outcast and accursed? When this question is asked—a question which the Bible does not contain but which it certainly forces upon us—these stories begin to whisper promises. *Even punishment is grace with God.*

"Thou shalt put away the evil from the midst of thee", says Deut. 13: 6 (and 8 other passages in Deuteronomy) and the priestly writer in Gen. 17: 14 and 23 other passages has it "that soul shall be cut off from his people". These are a proclamation of God's holy severity. There is no remedy for sinfulness; the others had to be freed from the contagion, Josh. 11: 20; for the incorrigible sinner who can only persist in sin his end is grace; but this has nothing to do with forgiving grace. It should be noted that it is Deuteronomy, Ezekiel and the priestly writings which speak like this; for them God's inviolable holiness is more important than His pardoning grace. In the older prophets and again in the Psalms there is no trace of this gloomy outlook.

Alongside these there are punishments which are temporary

and which provide opportunity for repentance, such as that which David suffers for numbering the people and for his sin against Uriah and Bathsheba, 2 Sam. 12: 13 ff. This latter example shows that death is not necessarily punishment; the fact that Bathsheba's newborn child dies is a punishment for David, but not for the child himself, 2 Sam. 12: 15-23; as far as the child is concerned the fact that God permits him to die is a sign of God's inscrutable disposal of life, not of His wrath. God chastises David, but His chastisement is love, Ps. 118: 18.

Again there is the priestly doctrine that sacrifice is needed for punishment as expiation, Lev. 5: 14-16; indeed that sacrifice alone without further punishment is sufficient as expiation, Lev. 5: 17-19. This is but one aspect of the whole intention of the cult (§ 52). The cult puts itself forward as attempt by man, not appointed but only contrived, to effect redemption by himself. Magic takes the place of ethics; sin as that which man must and can expiate seeks to displace guilt as that which God, and only God of His grace, can forgive. Here the Old Testament comes up against questions which only the New can remove.

Finally it should be noted that the solution of the questions raised by disobedience and punishment lies not in forgiveness which God grants to the individual, but in redemption which He prepares for His people and for the whole world.

55. EXPIATION, PROPITIATION AND FORGIVENESS

1. The cultic "technical term"[165] for expiation is כִּפֶּר. Is the term only a "technical" one, and what are the thoughts behind it? The word occurs 91 times, 69 of them (Lev. 48, Num. 15, Ex. 6) in the priestly writings; there it is always "technical". It appears in a further nine passages of post-exilic date. The old prophets, Amos, Hosea, Isaiah, and Micah, do not have it. The two oldest examples are however found in the Elohist writings: one of them is non-theological—Jacob wants to propitiate Esau by means of a present, מִנְחָה, Gen. 32: 21; the other is theological—Moses seeks to make reconciliation with God for his people's offence by means of his intercession (not by a sacrifice), Ex. 32: 30. Both passages have this in common—that they are concerned with making the person propitiated change his mind or, more correctly, forget his anger; and not with an expiation as an act representing compensation for the failure to give due acknowledgment to the offended party. It is a question here of propitiation, not of expiation. The incident takes place in a moral and not in a cultic context.

This is not so in three very ancient passages where the word occurs. Because Saul had left behind a blood-guiltiness against the Gibeonites which had never been removed, there is famine in the land of David for three years. Then David offers to make an expiation, 2 Sam. 21: 3, and delivers to them seven of the children of Saul for execution. That is compensation—the injury to the honour and rights of the offended party is recognized and loss is symbolically made good by means of an action which otherwise was in no way due. Here therefore we must be speaking of expiation.

2. Both usages have maintained their position alongside one another in all ages. A wise man can appease the wrath of a king with his word, says Prov. 16: 14, and there is in 2 Chron. 30: 18 the prayer of Hezekiah that the good Lord should provide the means of reconciliation, should atone for every one who seeks God, though he be not cleansed according to the purification of the sanctuary. Here God is the one who acts. He atones in that He is surety for them, Ps. 65: 4. "When our transgressions are too great for us thou wilt atone them", Ps. 78: 38; "but he being full of compassion atoned their iniquity", Ps. 79: 9; "help us and atone our sins", are to be similarly interpreted. This has nothing to do with sacrifice or other expiatory rite. It is a question of propitiation or atonement by sheer grace. Here therefore one could almost render כִּפֶּר forgive.

Even where God is the agent, however, it can be that כִּפֶּר has to be translated "expiate". Thus Deut. 32: 43 (in a Psalm) reads "God will avenge the blood of his servants and will render vengeance to his adversaries, and will make expiation to this land of his people". There can be no doubt that this is the correct translation since it is a thing, the land, that is to receive the כַּפֵּר. So also in Deut. 21: 8 a man is found slain and no one knows who has smitten him; the dwellers in the nearest city with the assistance of the priests perform a ceremony (not a sacrifice) and then they pray "make expiation for thy people whom thou hast redeemed". Thus they make expiation for themselves.

It is clear that this is a case of expiation, even from the ceremony in which they say "our hands have not shed this blood", 21: 7; a "blood burden", not blood-guiltiness, lies upon them. Sin has been committed; therefore expiation is necessary. But the sinner is not known, there is therefore no one who in confession and remorse could desire to restore a right relation between himself and God; it cannot therefore be a case of propitiation.

3. Expiation is the removal of the objective cause of disturbance between God and man when the honour or privilege of God is offended. Thus expiation can and must be made for the altar, Ezek. 43: 20, 26, and the whole temple, Ezek. 45: 20. For this reason seventy weeks of years are decreed for Israel and for Jerusalem until the measure of their faithlessness be fulfilled and expiation made for iniquity, Dan. 9: 24; the duration of the penal suffering is measured by an objective standard. For this reason also in the priestly writings, כִּפֶּר which there always means "expiate" plays an important rôle. The cult is there objectified; it has become an expiatory institution. Thus we have in Lev. 19: 22 the elaborate but carefully constructed sentence: the priest (the agent) shall make expiation (expiatory act) for him (the beneficiary) with the ram of the guilt offering (means employed in expiation) before the Lord for his sin which he hath sinned (occasion of expiation). It is hard to say what the words "before the Lord" mean. Jahweh is no longer the recipient; He is also not the provider of the expiation. The sentence would lose nothing in content if the words were removed. The cult has become an end in itself, expiation is made for expiation's sake, no longer for God's sake.

4. With propitiation the situation is quite different.[166] Here everything hinges on personal relationship; God is angry with man on account of his guilt. Man has alienated himself from God by his sin. The two have become separated from one another. The purpose of propitiation is to restore to man access to God, Rom. 5: 2. The prophet Jeremiah prays, "atone not thou their iniquity; i.e. grant no propitiation, deal thou with them in the time of thine anger!" Jer. 18: 23. To pray that God should make no expiation would be meaningless. For it is man who makes expiation. Propitiation, however, is not man's action but the free resolution of God. It is this resolution that the prophet seeks to influence. Here he is praying for the continuance of God's wrath. Nehemiah prays similarly "cover not their iniquity!" Neh. 3: 37. These prayers seek to preclude propitiation. For propitiation consists in this: that man returns to God that God may return to man, Zech. 3: 1. "If ye search

for me with all your heart I will be found of you", Jer. 29: 13 ff.
It is a question of a personal attitude, not of the execution of
something positive. Propitiation therefore veers away from
expiation towards forgiveness. There are within its scope
counterparts to the prayers of Jeremiah and Nehemiah—
Abraham prays for Sodom and is heard, Gen. 18: 23-32; Amos
beseeches the Lord for Jacob and "this shall not be", Amos
7: 1-6; Job prays at God's own instigation for his friends and
Jahweh accepts his prayer, Job. 42: 8 ff. In this case Job's
friends offer a burnt offering for themselves; but God's resolve
is influenced not by the act of expiation but by Job's intercession. It will be observed that sacrifice may certainly accom-
pany propitiation and forgiveness without affecting them in the
least. Such sacrifices are not in themselves efficacious actions;
they are merely tokens of recognition of the sovereignty of God,
and as such they are offered.

5. Indeed, prayers for forgiveness also, or rather especially,
have their preliminary conditions. They must be prayers and
they must be spoken from a remorseful heart and with resolutions for improvement. "Whoso confesseth (his transgressions)
and forsaketh them shall obtain mercy", Prov. 28: 13. "Come,
let us return unto the Lord: for he hath torn and he will heal
us", Hos. 6: 1. "He is a God who healeth all shortcomings,
תַּחֲלוּאִים, who forgiveth all guilt", Ps. 103: 3. What does this
mean here? The shortcomings or weaknesses that are mentioned
are obviously the sinful tendencies of the saints which prevent
their being faultless (תָּם or תָּמִים). God is angry because of
them but His anger, for all it is so great and righteous—one
could almost say justified—has its bounds. Because God is
long-suffering and full of love for the saints, He neither lets
His wrath continue nor does He let it work itself out as He
might. God lets a sin pass, הֶעֱבִיר חַטָּאת, He overlooks it,
2 Sam. 12: 13; He does the same with a deliberate sin or crime
(עָוֺן), 2 Sam. 24: 10, Zech. 3: 4, Job 7: 21. God does not
treat the saints with the severity which the number and gravity
of their transgressions deserve. He does not requite them for
their wrongs as they should be requited. Rather His love is like
the love of a good father for his sons: ever and again he forgives.
He puts away the saints' acts of rebellion. Ps. 40: 13 shows what
that means: "mine iniquities have overtaken me, so that I am
not able to look up." If God did not intervene, the consequences

of sin would kill the saint. God prevents this because He knows that man is earthly (Paul would use σάρξ) Ps. 103: 8-14. Here then we have forgiveness in constant action because it is in constant demand. It is grounded in love. It is quite without reference to expiation. It is necessary because God is compassionate and also because man is earthly and full of shortcomings. This forgiveness is wholly individualistic; it has reference only to the saints, not to the condition of mankind, not even to the condition of the whole people. This forgiveness is also quite a-temporal, the same to-day and to-morrow. It knows nothing of a desire for salvation. Such quietistic piety, which is scarcely found in the Old Testament, leads neither to judgment nor to the cross.

6. Forgiveness is expressed in Ps. 103: 3 by the word רָפָא, to heal, and in 103: 12 by הִרְחִיק, to remove. It will be of value to examine these and the other words which the Old Testament uses for forgive. "God heals" is one of the great salvation phrases. "I will heal their backsliding", Hos. 14: 5; we shall have to speak of this passage later. It never occurs again, however, in the sense found in Ps. 103: 3. The nearest is Ps. 107: 17, 20—"they are afflicted[167] because of their faithlessness . . . he sendeth his word and healeth them"; or Lam. 2: 13, "thy breach is great: who can heal thee?" "To remove", Ps. 103: 12, is merely a chance metaphor for forgive. Likewise it is more a chance metaphor than a literal expression when in Isa. 38: 17 (a passage having the character of a psalm) we find, "thou has cast all my sins behind thy back".

On the other hand, where כִּסָּה is used it is not easy to determine whether the metaphorical idea of covering is still present or whether it really has given place to its developed meaning "forgive". "Thou coverest all their sin" (thou forgivest?) Ps. 85: 2; and in Ps. 32: 1 כְּסוּי חֲטָאָה is one whose sin is covered (forgiven?). In both of these passages another expression stands alongside which one certainly can only take metaphorically—"thou has taken away the iniquity of thy people" (put an end to it) Ps. 85: 2; "one whose transgression is taken away" (an end put to it). This usage occurs also in Mic. 7: 18—"who is a God like unto thee who takest away iniquity" (puts . end to)? This passage also is not prophetic but of the nature of a psalm. It has an equally metaphorical elaboration: "that passeth by faithlessness". There are similar instances in Amos 7: 8; 8: 2: "I will not again pass by them any more". That would make two passages where the earliest prophet speaks of forgiveness, but significantly he says that God will not forgive. One can find a forgiveness expressed where God says He wishes to wipe out sins, מָחָה. "I, even I, am he that blotteth out thy transgressions—for mine own sake, and I will not remember thy sins", Isa. 43: 25. "I have blotted out as a thick cloud thy transgressions, and, as a cloud, thy sins: return unto me, for I have redeemed thee", Isa. 44: 22. In view of this invitation "return" can one really speak of forgiveness? Is it not rather the promise that if Israel returns, their sins will not count any longer with God? The worshipper prays in Ps. 51: 9 that God will hide His face from his sins and blot them out. The only other ancient passage, Jer. 18: 23,[168] is, like the Amos passages above, negative: "do not blot out their sin!" so also Neh. 3: 37, Ps. 109: 14.

The true word for forgiveness is סָלַח. It is always used of God (described as good and סַלָּח, Ps. 86: 5) and means to be indulgent, to overlook an offence that has been committed. The earnestness of this overlooking varies from passage to passage. Naaman the Syrian is converted to Jahweh by the healing of his leprosy and will in future worship Jahweh, even in his Aramaean home, on the earth taken from Israel and will no longer sacrifice to other gods; but when he accompanies his king into the temple of Rimmon and then, as a servant, bows himself to Rimmon, may Jahweh overlook it; here סָלַח is forbearance, not real forgiveness, since there is no remorse and no resolution to abandon the thing regretted, 2 Kings 5: 18. Jahweh will show indulgence to the remnant whom He leaves of Israel and Judah so that one shall find no iniquity and no sin any more; here סָלַח is complete pardon which takes away all iniquity, Jer. 50: 20. The word occurs in the same sense in Jer. 31: 34 and 33: 8; in all three places the pardon is a promise for the great conversion at the End. But this promised forgiveness appears only in these three Jeremiah passages and nowhere else. Otherwise the word always means not to inflict a punishment for an offence and not to bear a grudge on account of it; the forgiveness does not extend beyond the concrete instance and does not basically alter the relationship between God and His people. Even the Elohist uses the word: may God show indulgence when Israel has worshipped the golden calf,

Ex. 34: 9, and when Israel lacking faith wanted to stone the spies, Num. 14: 19 ff.; and in both cases one can connect this indulgence with a failure to respond to the test of faith. The word occurs in the priestly writings: Jahweh shows indulgence to the woman who has made a vow which her father or her husband disowns, Num. 30: 6, 9, 13. On the other hand, the word does not appear at all in the old prophets except in Amos 7: 2 where the prophet prays Jahweh to pardon. It has a certain currency which suggests it was in favour at that time, in the deuteronomic age: Deut. 29: 19, 1 Kings 8: 30, 34, 36, 39, 50 (=2 Chron. 6: 21, 25, 27, 30, 39), 2 Kings 24: 4, Jer. 5: 1, 7; 36: 3.[169] But even in Jeremiah it has no really significant meaning.

7. To sum up, then, one can say this: the Old Testament does not teach that God changes His mind in a single event of His *heilsgeschichte* or shall do, so that from that moment forgiveness is there for anyone who is willing to receive it. It speaks only occasionally of forgiveness and certainly does not put it as the centre of its scheme of salvation. Forgiveness plays no part at all in the teaching of the early prophets. Where it does occur, however, it is as a rule a question of forgiveness from case to case, removing the disturbance caused by sin without leading to a new life which makes these disturbances basically impossible. In a few passages, Jer. 31: 34; 33: 8; 50: 20 forgiveness appears to be bound up with thorough-going salvation; but there it is a consequence of salvation, not a starting point or presupposition of it; also it is not brought about by an event of the *heilsgeschichte* but by a free act of God's gracious will.

The entire salvation which the Old Testament revelation proclaims depends much more upon judgment which eradicates the sin that has been committed and upon conversion which saves men from the possibility of future sin.

56. SALVATION BY JUDGMENT

1. The idea that salvation is that event which brings man blessing and prosperity runs entirely contrary to the spirit of the Old Testament. *All salvation is to be related to God alone, not to man.* Therefore judgment is also salvation, for judgment is restoration of the honour and holiness (*heiligkeit*) of God. These are injured and diminished by the sin of man. The end judgment has in view is the full restoration of these two things, so that really the whole earth is full of His glory, Isa. 6: 3, and the name of the great king is terrible among the Gentiles, Mal. 1: 14.

Thus even the flood that is sent on sinful mankind is a divine act of salvation. It establishes away at the beginning of history God's right to destroy corrupt mankind for His honour's sake, and the bow in the clouds is both the token of God's indulgence and also the sign of God's right to judge when the time is fulfilled to which reference is made in the phrase "While the earth remaineth", Gen. 8: 22. One must not miss the point—that this "while" indicates a definite period of time and does not open the door to infinity. So long as one does ignore this point the flood is meaningless, nothing more than an unsuccessful attempt by God to rid Himself of sinful mankind; an attempt of which He repented. On the same grounds it is wrong to describe the great prophets as resolute prophets of doom and to excise with the shears of criticism from their proclamation all intimations of salvation; for the great concern of the prophets (in so far as it is admissible to speak of people who are merely messengers and deliverers of a word they are commissioned to speak, which they have not chosen themselves, as having a concern) is the honour or holiness of God; they are jealous for it, 1 Kings 19: 10. Thus they can and they must announce in the same way God's judgment and the salvation which for His honour's sake He will prepare for His people. How the two parts of their proclamation are integrated is a secondary question, almost a rationalistic question. On the same grounds the book of Job will not really be understood from the theodicy where Job and his friends (in other words man) ask how far God is righteous in His dealings with man. That is human questioning and it ends, whether one looks to the saga, 42: 10 ff., or to the poem, 42: 1-6, in surrender to the unlimited supreme will of God; Mal. 1: 2 ff. There remains nothing for man to do but to submit in faith to that which is good in the sight of Jahweh, 1 Sam. 3: 18. Jahweh waits for the time when He can be gracious. But the way to grace which He prepares lies through judgment: for He is a God of judgment, Isa. 30: 18. He advances His claim for obedience. He sits in judgment. Then He shows grace.

2. The earth and things earthly, human life and activity, have their appointed days, Gen. 8: 22, their set time (pp. 90 ff.). The day will dawn when the time is fulfilled. Then comes the day of Jahweh, the day of the Lord. One realizes at once from the oldest passage in which the day of the Lord occurs, Amos 5: 18, 20, that already in the eighth century this was a familiar

theologoumenon taken over from an earlier time. The fact of the day of the Lord, the fact that it will one day, soon now, break in—these are familiar and current ideas. The question is only what the day of the Lord will be like.

The people long for it to come, for they think it will be light. For the people, God exists for blessing. His mighty breaking in will be the final unfolding of the divine blessing, the bright beginning of which they see already in the general upsurge. They do not think of their sins, of poverty, oppression and shamelessness within their gates. Therefore Amos raises his cry of woe. The day of the Lord is darkness and not light, it is pestilence, affliction and judgment, it is not a thing to long for—so say all the prophets. "It is a day of chastisement, in which Ephraim shall become a desolation", Hos. 5: 9. "The loftiness of man shall be bowed down, and the haughtiness of men shall be brought low, in that day in which Jahweh alone shall be exalted", Isa. 2: 17. "Howl ye; for the day of the Lord is at hand; as destruction from the Almighty" (there is a pun on שַׁדָּי) "shall it come", Isa. 13: 6. "Cruel with wrath and fierce anger" it comes, Isa. 13: 9. These passages as it happens are not genuine and one would have to confess ignorance of Isaiah's point of view were it not that there occurs the phrase "the day of visitation", 10: 3, and there are passages which speak of "that day" as a day of judgment, 3: 7, 18; 7: 17, 18, 20, 21, 23; 9: 13. Micah also does not have the expression "the day of the Lord" but he knows of "that day" when they will lament with a doleful lamentation, and say, "We be utterly spoiled!" Mic. 2: 4. "The day of the Lord is at hand, the day of the Lord's sacrifice", Zeph. 1: 7, 8; it is a great and bitter day, "a day of wrath, a day of trouble and distress, a day of wasteness and desolation, a day of darkness and gloominess, a day of clouds and thick darkness", Zeph. 1: 14, 15, "the day of the Lord's wrath", 1: 18. The slain shall be at that day from one end of the earth even unto the other end of the earth, Jer. 25: 33; it is a day of vengeance, Jer. 46: 10, Isa. 61: 2; 63: 4, in which the false prophets fail, Ezek. 13: 5; the time of (the judgment of) the heathen, Ezek. 30: 3. As the Isaiah and the Micah examples show, the scope of the concept is far in excess of its currency, though it extends to Mal. 3: 23 and Zech. 14: 1, the song of Lam. 2: 1, 22 and to the wisdom literature, Prov. 11: 4.

3. The idea of the judgment which God executes when His great and fearful day comes is the groundwork of the prophetic proclamation. Its forms and scope may vary to include a part of the people, the whole people, all peoples, the whole world. One must not look for revelation concerning God's judgment in the Jahwist or the Elohist. They are concerned with prehistoric time; they end their contributions with the occupation of Canaan, Judg. 2: 9,[170] Josh. 24, and have no interest in what is coming. The books of Judges, Samuel and Kings tell of what has been; 2 Kings 25: 27-30 is a ray of light to brighten up a dreadful end, but nothing more. The four historical books, 1 Chronicles, 2 Chronicles, Ezra and Nehemiah reach their end and aim in the establishment of the true cult. As in the priestly writings, the true cult is sufficient in itself; world events lose their importance completely in the quietism of this cult. The deuteronomic writers have a purely pedagogical concern—to prepare the people for obedience to God; this obedience is a matter of life and death, Deut. 30: 15, 19; life is the people's continuance in the promised land, death is not judgment but utter destruction, 30: 18; Deuteronomy knows of nothing beyond these two possibilities. There remain therefore the prophets, for in the other books of Scripture, with the exception of Daniel who in this respect belongs to the prophets, one finds nothing about the judgment: anything they do contain is merely an echo of the message of the prophets.

4. *Amos* is interested only in Israel and her immediate neighbours. The judgment comes upon the neighbouring peoples; whether it destroys them utterly is not clear, 1: 3—2: 3. For there will "perhaps"—so says the prophet, 5: 15—be an escape, 5: 6. But finally—so says God through His prophets— God's eyes are upon them for evil and not for good, 9: 4; the end is come upon my people Israel, 8: 2; God does not pass them by any more, 7: 8; the evil day breaks upon them, 6: 3; the sanctuaries are laid waste, 7: 9; pestilence carries off everyone, 6: 8-11; the king dies and the people must go into exile, 7: 11, 17; the sinful kingdom will be destroyed from off the face of the earth, 9: 8a. Amos speaks only to Israel and he speaks likewise only of Israel. Cosmic considerations arise only casually, 8: 9. And as for the "remnant of Joseph", 5: 15, how can we tell whether it is a God-given hope or just the prophet's cherished desire?

Hosea also knows the days of visitation and the days of recompense, 9: 7, but note they are "the days", not "the day". Everything here is vague and strange and questionable—from

Hosea indeed one can gather nothing definite about the day of judgment. *Isaiah*, however, speaks clearly. The Lord of hosts is exalted in judgment, 5: 16. He wields the rod of correction, 30: 32. An annihilation, and that determined, is heard from Him, 28: 22. He sifts the nations with the sieve of destruction, 30: 28. The Philistines will be killed by hunger, and the remnant of them shall be slain, 14: 28-32. Damascus, the kingdom of Aramea, will be destroyed, 17: 1-6, 9-14, though gleanings shall be left as a remnant, 17: 6. Samaria falls before a strong one of Jahweh, 28: 1-4. Egyptians and Ethiopians are ruined, 20: 1-6, 31: 1-5, and Assyria too, who carries the people into captivity and for whom God once hissed that it should be the implement of His wrath on Judah—even Assyria must go, 10: 5-11, 13-16; 31: 8a. But it is specified peoples, not all peoples, to whom Isaiah intimates the judgment, and when he speaks of an accompaniment of thunder, flame of devouring fire, storm, tempest and hailstones (30: 30) Isaiah does not mean to include the cosmos —he rarely speaks the language of universal eschatology. He confines himself to politics and pedagogy, and pedagogy for him refers to the judgment into which God will enter with His people. Jerusalem is ruined and Judah is fallen, 3: 8; the men shall fall by the sword, 3: 25; hell swallows up Zion's pomp, 5: 14; all are humbled and brought down, 5: 15; the cities are waste, the houses are empty and the land is utterly waste, 6: 11; 32: 13, 14; the land shall be forsaken, 7: 16, 23, 25. But it is only "many" who stumble, not "all", 8: 15, and the watchword of all Isaiah's judgment preaching is Shearjashub, the name he gives his son—"a remnant shall return", 7: 3.

Isaiah declares trouble only as a prelude to salvation; *Micah* announces the fall of Samaria, 1: 6, he sees misfortune reaching unto Judah, 1: 9, and Zion becomes a field, 3: 12; for Jahweh devises evil, 2: 3, however much the theology of the day may publish salvation, 3: 5; but Micah says nothing of a judgment of the world. *Zephaniah* therefore, in the second half of the seventh century, is the first true prophet of the judgment of the Lord. Here we find the phrases "the day of the Lord", 1: 7; "the day of the Lord's sacrifice" for which He sanctifies His guests, 1: 8; the day on which they will be punished who say in their heart, The Lord will not do good, neither will He do evil, 1: 12. On that day judgment comes on all that oppress Zion, 3: 19; Philistines, 2: 4-6, Moabites and Ammonites, 2: 8 ff., Ethiopians, 2: 12 and Assyrians, 2: 13; the whole earth will be

destroyed by the anger of the Lord and the fire of His jealousy
1: 18; 3: 8; everything, man and beast, bird and fish will be
utterly consumed, 1: 2 ff.; only the remnant of the house of
Judah shall escape, 2: 7, 9; 3: 13. Here the complex pattern of
the judgment is complete. It comes upon the whole world and
its creatures. The prophet has the heathen in mind, especially
those under whom Israel has to suffer. The sinners in Israel
must also perish. But out of the midst of this cataclysm of
judgment a remnant escapes unharmed.

How far *Jeremiah* belongs to this series is hard to determine,
since there is no clear principle by which genuine Jeremiah
material can be distinguished from non-genuine and later
material. Jeremiah is familiar with the idea of the day of
calamity, 18: 17; he knows how pestilence, sword, famine and
captivity will afflict men, 15: 2 ff.; how there will be no pity or
mercy or forbearance, 21: 7; the land will become a waste,
7: 34, the Temple a desolation, 22: 5, the people a reproach and
a proverb, a taunt and a curse in all places, 24: 9; the sword of
the Lord devoureth from the one end of the earth to the other
end of the earth, 12: 12, when the Lord forsakes His house and
casts off His heritage, 12: 7—but nevertheless the true note of
the final judgment is lacking. Jeremiah's message, in spite of all
its intimations of doom, refers to a political and not to an
eschatological epoch and looks ultimately always towards
healing, return and pardon. The most uncompromising un-
coverer of sinfulness is the messenger of the most merciful
new-beginning. God chastises, 2: 19, but He does not make a
full end, 4: 27, 5: 18. Jerusalem is warned, 6: 8, the people are
tried—and refined, 9: 6; Jahweh is a teacher, 18: 1-12; and when
His teaching bears no fruit, 18: 13-17, the prophet speaks not
so much of a remnant, 6: 9; 31: 7; 23: 3, as of the one half of the
people, the good figs in exile whom Jahweh will regard for good,
24: 5. More than any other, Jeremiah, properly evaluated, is a
prophet of instructive grace and not of destructive judgment.

Ezekiel, however, takes up the idea of the judgment in all its
fulness, systematizes it and gives it also that turn which
causes it to stiffen into apocalyptic. Israel's fathers mocked God
and forgot their duty towards Him, therefore He polluted
them in their sacrifices, 20: 26. Jerusalem played the harlot,
therefore Jahweh discovered her offence before all peoples and
satisfied His fury upon her, so that His jealousy could depart
from her and He was quiet and had not to fret Himself any

more, 16: 37, 42. Were Israel the only thing that mattered, then she should have been lost and that would have been that; but when captivity came in judgment she profaned the name of God, for the heathen said, "These are the people of the Lord!" 36: 20. The honour of God is at stake in the downfall of Judah. Not for His people's sake, but for His holy name's sake, Jahweh acts; for He has pity for His holy name, 36: 21. Therefore out of jealousy for His name, 39: 25, He will show Himself to Israel as the Holy One in the sight of all nations in that He gathers her from the lands of her enemies, 39: 27, as also He set His glory among the nations and let all nations see His judgment that He laid upon Israel when the house of Israel went into captivity for her iniquity, 39: 21, 23. Israel would not be purged from her filthiness till Jahweh satisfied His fury upon her. He could not go back, could not spare nor repent, 24: 13 ff. Jahweh himself had to prepare the sanctuary of Jahweh, 24: 21.

That in Ezekiel is the first act of the judgment. Were it given as the prophet's word and not as a revelation of God one might say it was a grandiose, teleological, theological interpretation of the collapse of Judah. Even then, however, in two respects it is more than a mere interpretation. For one thing there is the reference of the event to the nations. The nations in Ezekiel's geography stretch from the mountains of Armenia to the cataracts of the Nile. What do they care about the fall of Jerusalem, a tiny city perched on its remote heights? It is not the individual Jew who is speaking here; this is the thinking of the prophet of God. God is here a God of the nations, therefore His displeasure and His judgment concern the nations. The other thing is the resolutely theocentric outlook in this account of what happens. God acts for His own sake; God's name is at stake; God's honour is impaired; God's holiness must be recovered in wrath, must prove that it has not suffered. Ezekiel is the prophet with God at the heart of his theology. He is a theocentric theologian.

One is therefore not surprised to find in Ezekiel a second act; judgment on the peoples, making possible salvation, follows judgment on Israel. Babylon alone is left out of account. Is the omission intentional, is it political shrewdness? Or is there some other reason which we cannot discover? At all events the silence concerning Babylon shows that even revelation is modified by temporal and other considerations and indeed it is very important for the proper understanding of what in the Old

Testament can be called revelation. The nations then must be brought to judgment, in Ezekiel's view. Ammon will be destroyed and so shall know that "I am the Lord", 25: 7. Judgment makes way for God's revelation of Himself. "I will execute judgment upon Moab and they shall know that I am the Lord", 25: 11. That is to say, the telos of judgment is the recognition of Jahweh. The children of Israel themselves shall take vengeance upon Edom which (at the Exile) failed them miserably. "I will lay my vengeance upon Edom by the hand of my people Israel, and they shall know my vengeance", 25: 14.

This description of Jahweh taking vengeance is no longer an anthropomorphism; this is an actual aspect of the holiness of God. As surely as fire must burn straw, so God's holiness must consume a people that has injured Israel. Thus Jahweh executes great vengeance on the Philistines and "they shall know that I am the Lord when I shall lay my vengeance upon them", 25: 17. Tyre shall be no more, 26: 21; judgment shall come on Sidon and on all Israel's neighbours that do despite to the house of Israel, 28: 20-24; Egypt shall be a desolation and a waste, 29: 9. All nations shall be reduced to a remnant. Ezekiel is the only one who speaks of a remnant of the nations (36: 3, 5) which are round about Israel (36: 4) besides a remnant of Israel, 9: 8. The remnant of Israel is clearly defined by Ezekiel: it will be scattered to all the winds; it consists of the exiles whom the inhabitants of Jerusalem thought were far from the Lord, 11: 15. The Egyptians, however, on whose league (30: 5) Jahweh will execute judgment, including even the Ethiopian (30: 9) by the hand of Nebuchadnezzar in his day, the day of Egypt, will be scattered for forty years, 29: 12 ff., among the nations and then gathered, a base kingdom, to their land again, 29: 13 f. This shall happen when the "time of the heathen" has come, 30: 3.

In this twofold judgment and twofold remnant, one of Israel and one of the nations, we see Ezekiel's systematizing of judgment, and in the actual timing of the events and in having a "time of the heathen" alongside the "day of the Lord" we can see traces of apocalyptic. In this respect Ezekiel is the spiritual ancestor of Daniel. No prophet knows the hour of the day of the Lord. He can only be aware of its approach; but the time of the heathen has its appointed span, it is in the nature of the concept, and because it is appointed it is also calculable. Forty years, 29: 12 ff., is the oldest apocalyptic figure in the Old Testament. Then comes another apocalyptic element; when salvation has followed judgment, when Israel has borne the shame of the heathen, 36: 6, and this shame has recoiled upon the heathen again, 36: 7, so that Israel has to bear it no more 36: 15; when Israel is gathered out of all the countries, 36: 24, purified, 36: 25, filled with God's spirit 36: 26, and made one in God's hand, 37: 19, so that they are in an everlasting covenant, 37: 26, and the nations know that Jahweh sanctifies Israel in that He puts His sanctuary in the midst of Israel—when this whole process has been completed there follows a final assault which calls everything in question, but which nevertheless authenticates God's work of salvation. Then Gog of the land of Magog "in the latter years", 38: 8—again not a prophetic but an apocalyptic expression—will assail Jerusalem like a storm, 38: 9. Then the full force of the judgment breaks loose. Earthquakes shake the land of Israel. The fishes of the sea, and the fowls of the heaven, and the beasts of the field, and all creeping things that creep upon the earth, and all the men that are upon the face of the earth, shake at his presence. The mountains are thrown down and every wall falls to the ground. Jahweh orders every kind of terror. He executes judgment with pestilence, blood, flood, hail, fire and brimstone. He magnifies Himself and reveals Himself, in a fearful cosmic theophany, before the eyes of many nations and gives them to know "that I am the Lord" 38: 19-23. Then the great reckoning is at an end. Gog falls—"Seven months shall the house of Israel be burying of them", 39: 12. Then God makes a great sacrifice for the birds and all wild life, 39: 17. "From that day and forward" the house of Israel knows that Jahweh is their God, 39: 22. The nations understand that the house of Israel went into captivity for their iniquity, 39: 23. Now God can bring again the captivity of Jacob, 39: 25, and pour out His spirit upon the house of Israel, 39: 29. Out of judgment comes salvation.

It is not necessary to set out in full what the prophets that come after Ezekiel say about the day of the Lord and judgment. The basic elements remain the same; only the details change. Israel is disobedient instead of obedient. They do that which is evil in the sight of the Lord, Judg. 2: 11. They heap up sin upon sin, iniquity upon iniquity, they forsake Jahweh, serve other gods, they refuse to receive correction or to return, Jer. 5: 3. Visitation, Amos 4: 6-11, subjection to foreign rule, Judg. 2: 12-17, the great reminders, like those of the book of Judges and the two books of Kings, and the words of the prophets are

of no avail. Israel persists in sin. In view of the later priestly
laws and the expiation cult which they contain it is especially
significant that none of the prophets, not even Ezekiel, ever
advances the opinion that correct cult could take away iniquity.
When the time of salvation has come, then safeguards and
expiations will be able to preserve salvation. But *no prophet
ever says that sacrifice could bring about salvation.* Salvation can
come only from God's free grace. He must bring about the great
change and He will do it: but first He executes judgment.

57. SALVATION BY REDEMPTION

1. The Old Testament does not present a unified doctrine of
redemption any more than it presents a unified doctrine of
judgment. Statements on redemption are multifarious, whether
they concern the form of redemption or its content or its scope.
One might feel oneself bound, therefore, to conduct an enquiry
into the observations on redemption of each of the prophets in
turn and into anything else relevant; and yet when one had
done so the result would be as unsatisfactory as the attempt to
fit all the available sayings into a comprehensive scheme. A
scheme of this sort would do violence to its various parts, and
would not be historically valid for every period of the Old
Testament revelation. An examination of one after another, on
the other hand, would yield a bewildering mass of individual
points which would conceal rather than reveal that which was
common and basic to them. It is true of redemption as it was of
law (p. 206) that the fact is older than the literary usages of the
word, and moreover the usages are always historically conditioned and limited by their very perspicuity. We therefore
compromise. Two examples must suffice to show how at certain
times the gospel of redemption took shape and how it did not.
Thereafter a more systematic enquiry into the details of the redemption events will deal fairly thoroughly with its familiar forms.

2. Zechariah 1-8 gives a compact account of a prophet's idea
of salvation in the years 520-518. The earth sits still and is at
rest, 1: 11; the horns that scattered Judah are destroyed, 1: 19;
God has returned to Jerusalem with mercies, 1: 16, and is
jealous for Jerusalem and for Zion with a great jealousy, 1: 14.
Jerusalem shall be inhabited like villages without walls by
reason of the multitude of men and cattle in her, and God
Himself will be to her a wall of fire round about and the glory
in the midst of her, 2: 4 ff. Everyone that steals shall be purged

out by the curse, and every one that swears, and wickedness herself quits the land, 5: 1-11. The enemy in the north is chastised in order that Jahweh's spirit might be quieted, 6: 8, and the Temple is built, 6: 15. The people of Jahweh return home from all quarters, 8: 7 ff.; 2: 11, 15; God stands to the remnant of this people in a relationship governed by grace, 8: 11, and many nations shall join themselves to the Lord to be His people in the midst of whom He dwells, 2: 15. Then shall old men and old women sit in the streets of Jerusalem, and the streets of the city shall be full of boys and girls playing in the streets thereof, 8: 4 ff.; the ground shall give her increase and the heavens shall give their dew, 8: 12. The fast-days shall be days of joy and gladness, 8: 18; one will speak truth, imagine no evil in one's heart against a neighbour, and execute true judgment, 8: 16 ff. Judah and Israel that once were a curse among the nations shall be a blessing, 8: 13. Yea, many peoples and strong nations shall come to seek the Lord of hosts in Jerusalem, and to entreat the favour of the Lord, 8: 22. For it is Jahweh who helps His people and makes them a blessing, 8: 13. Jahweh is the מוֹשִׁיעַ of His people, 8: 7.

In order to see this picture of salvation in proper perspective several points should be noted.

a) Zechariah is late, a descendant of many prophets. The old prophets are well known to him, yet he does not mention them, does not hesitate not to adopt their point of view or to deviate from it. That is true even of Deutero-Isaiah, the prophet of the Ebed Jahweh, whose writings appeared only twenty years before Zechariah and who was therefore certainly known to him. Zechariah stands quite alone and is completely independent in giving his message of salvation—a significant warning against any attempt to attribute automatically the views of an earlier prophet to those who follow him. That is contrary to the nature of revelation in the Old Testament.

b) A number of important things are missing in Zechariah, and to note these omissions gives a truer picture of Zechariah's salvation preaching. The important word פָּדָה, to redeem, to liberate, is a notable omission. Also we do not find the equally important word גָּאַל, to redeem or ransom. There is no mention of any person entrusted with redemption by God; God Himself without any mediator brings about salvation; He is called מוֹשִׁיעַ, helper.[171]

c) Zechariah's salvation picture is characterized by simplicity and naturalness of line. Old folks in the streets, many children, happy days, good harvests, banishment of the old wickedness, and an urgent pressing forward towards social righteousness (but not to any sort of change of heart or outpouring of the spirit), peace and the protection of God present in glory—these constitute Zechariah's simple and almost natural salvation. The world concern is not entirely lacking. The nations will know of Israel's salvation and will even use Israel's name as a greeting. They will also share in the worship of Jahweh, but in a general way; there is nothing said about world conversion or world mission. Salvation fades out when it gets beyond Judah; not even the leadership of the people is changed, neither the political leadership nor the high priest's cultic—one cannot say spiritual—leadership. Zechariah's picture of salvation has rounded lines and warm and pious colours; but at the same time it is modest, almost timid; at any rate quiet.

3. Let us look now at Isaiah's picture.[172] Salvation consists first of all of a great transformation of nature. As in the beginning beasts fed on plants, Gen. 1: 30,[173] so it will be in the time of salvation: the lion shall eat straw like the ox, 11: 7. In the animal kingdom there will be peace; the wolf and the lamb, the panther and the kid, the calf and the lion, the cow and the bear shall dwell with one another and there will be no harm done. The peace among all creatures has more than its immediate significance in that it means that salvation time is the end when everything becomes again very good, Gen. 1: 31, and well pleasing to God as it was. Wonderful fruitfulness of vegetation, which takes from work the curse of toil, Gen. 3: 17-19, plays no great part in Isaiah's scheme. One has to go to Amos 9: 13 and Ezek. 47: 12, Joel 3: 18 and the priestly writings, Lev. 26: 5, for that. This transformation of nature is inaugurated when the spirit is poured upon men from on high and the wilderness becomes a fruitful field and the fruitful field is counted for a forest; the growth of vegetation—vegetation in the Old Testament always means life—is enriched, 32: 15. It should be carefully noted that this is the only occasion on which Isaiah speaks of the spirit (the manifold spirit of 11: 2 will be discussed later: it is not relevant here). Isaiah does not know of any general spiritual endowment. Nor does Zechariah—he speaks only of the spirit (4: 6; 6: 8; 7: 12) which God has in Himself and by means of which, not by might or by power, 4: 6, He makes peace.

As well as peace in nature there is peace among men in Isaiah's picture. God arbitrates (p. 32) between the nations 2: 4; that simple statement means that God puts aside once and for all the claims of one nation on another and their disputes, and institutes general peace. The fact should not be overlooked that it is not a case of the nations being deprived of their natural identity in the interests of mankind in general. The philosophical Utopia of mankind in general in which there are no longer any national characteristics is as foreign to biblical realism as the other Utopia of an average man. God's arbitration between the nations means the removal of war; the weapons of war become the implements of peaceful labour and of the harvest, 2: 4. From then on, the nations shall go up to learn the law of Zion and shall walk in the paths of the Lord, 2: 3. At this point the universalism and particularism of salvation are united in Isaiah's picture. All nations enjoy God's leadership. But Zion remains the mountain of the Lord, 2: 3; indeed it is now that truly for the first time, for the nations flow unto it, 2: 2.

One may ask whether Isaiah is not thinking also of a change coming over the surface of the earth. As in Ezekiel there is announced a division of the land among the twelve tribes in which the boundaries form straight lines and the tribal divisions geometric right-angles,[174] and a complete reorientation of the coasts and mountains and valleys of Palestine is therefore necessary, so in Isaiah "in the latter days" mount Zion will be higher than all other mountains, 2: 2. It is clear that the prophet is working here with material that has come down to him. That is true elsewhere also, but in seeking to establish the true validity of the prophetic message one must not rationalize concerning these forms which to us seem so grotesque. They are not metaphorical; they are meant literally. In Isaiah's picture the whole of nature with all its animals is at peace. The whole wide world of nations has peace. The laws of God radiate out on all sides from the mountain of the Lord into the far distance like the rays of the sun, and maintain order among the nations, and from all quarters men come up to Jerusalem to learn the law. The people of God live in the middle and there is access to this God for all nations (this is not mentioned in Zechariah).

One should not overlook the limitations of this picture however. Isaiah says nothing about the nations coming to Jerusalem to worship Jahweh in the cult. (In the postscript to

Zechariah it says that every one that is left of all the nations shall "go up from year to year to worship the King, the Lord of hosts, and to keep the feast of tabernacles, and it shall be that whoso of all the families of the earth goeth not up to Jerusalem to worship the King, upon them there shall be no rain", Zech. 14: 16 ff.) Isaiah has no positive word on the cult. Is this whole idea self-evident to him, or is the Temple only the place of Jahweh's revelation of Himself and of His teaching? The second is more probable. Nor does Isaiah speak expressly of a return of all the nations to Jahweh, rather their position remains vague (the "nations", 2: 2, 4, seek instruction). Certainly this does not imply any missionary undertaking for the community of God in Judah. Mankind is within the scope of God's providence, in His power, enjoying His peace and with access to His teaching: but Israel alone has been admitted to the sphere of grace.

Again, it is not the whole historical people that enjoys the grace of God. On the contrary, the judgment comes on the people as it is, 7: 17; 32: 9-16; the judgment under which the Philistines are annihilated, 14: 30; God makes His vineyard a desolation, 5: 6. But there is always "the remnant that returns", 7: 3. Isaiah the lover of plant-pictures expresses it in this way: "If there be yet a tenth in the people, it will serve for a willow of which, as of the terebinth and the oak, a stump remaineth when they are felled; but"—these last three words have been repeatedly misunderstood—"out of the stump (read מִמַּצַּבְתָּה) comes holy aftergrowth", 6: 13. The idea of fresh shoots breaking from the stump of the felled tree appears again in 11: 1. And for Isaiah this is not merely metaphor: it is fact. The whole people must face the judgment and inevitably will not all escape. A small remnant will remain and will become in the new stock the holy people of holy Israel. Since this is Isaiah's conception it is not surprising that he does not speak of a new heart or the outpouring of the spirit upon all, and since the Exile is not yet in sight he also says nothing of the gathering of the scattered tribes.

The new people is freed from every yoke, 9: 4; Jahweh founds Zion anew, and in her the afflicted of His people take refuge, 14: 32. His people dwell in a peaceful habitation and in quiet resting places, 32: 18, a settled peasant community, 32: 20. The poor find security, 14: 30; the heart of the rash understands knowledge and the tongue of the stammerers is ready to speak plainly, 32: 4; no wicked person holds rank any more or commands respect, 32: 5, for the people receives from God *a leader*—he is never called a king,[175] only God Himself is given that name, 6: 5—whose significance consists in this: that he judges with righteousness and reproves with equity for the meek and subdues all violence, 11: 3-5. He sits on the throne of David, 9: 6; he is a descendant of David, 11: 1. He is equipped with God's spirit, but the manner of the spirit's working in him is carefully defined, 11: 2; he is very far from being a pneumatic plenipotentiary. The fact that he belongs to the Davidic line does not indicate only how realistic and how much bound up with history Isaiah's salvation picture is, it indicates also that it is a man of flesh and blood who is involved, though at first sight the predicates in 9: 6 (not yet satisfactorily explained) might suggest something higher. When we are told, however, that under this Davidic lord there will be endless salvation and judgment and righteousness for ever, 9: 6, it is clear that Isaiah is thinking of a Davidic dynasty. Isaiah's salvation picture in all its parts is grounded in historical reality. But this too should be noted: the shoot out of the stock of Jesse who rules is not the bringer of salvation but the administrator of it. The Davidic leader is guarantor and guardian of salvation. *When, however, one looks for a Messiah for this salvation one finds him in none other than God Himself.*

These are the main points of Isaiah's salvation picture; a word is needed about the time when salvation will be inaugurated. In the phrase "unto us a child is born", 9: 6, which may give information on this point, neither the "us" nor the "is born" should be pressed. The prophet could say "us" and mean a later generation of his people, and "is born" could also be future. The word "child" is, however, significant. The idea is not that the child as a child will rule the nation but when this child is grown then righteousness shall be the girdle of his loins, 11: 5. Consequently a childlike disposition is not a mark of the Davidic guardian of salvation. The reference to the child must have another meaning; and this can only be that the Davidic guardian of salvation is now—for Isaiah "now"!—a child and when he becomes a man (in ten or fifteen years) God will grant salvation.

There is one last feature of Isaiah's salvation picture to which reference should be made, and that is, that not one word is said in it about the cult. Nothing is said about priests, about sacrifices, about the Temple; indeed mount Zion, instead of being called the mountain of my sanctuary, as Ezekiel would say, is called the mountain of the Lord, 2: 3; the Temple is called the house of the God of Jacob, 2: 3, and the rest of the verse shows that it is important only as the place from which go forth law and revelation, the word of the Lord.

4. It would serve little purpose to describe now the salvation pictures of all the other prophets, since they are mainly variations on the same theme; and certainly amidst all the analysis of individual contributions the main concern of Old Testament theology, which is to achieve a comprehensive picture of the salvation teaching of the Old Testament revelation, would suffer. Instead of presenting these different salvation pictures, therefore, we will give an outline of *the various elements of redemption and of salvation.*

a) The word for redeem in the Old Testament is פָּדָה.[166] It means to take a thing or a man out of the possession and ownership of another into one's own possession and ownership[176] by giving an equivalent[177] for it; Ex. 13, 13, Job 6: 22 ff. To redeem is the same as to ransom when the Hebrew is פָּדָה. In all 33 Old Testament passages where God is the one who ransoms—the word is not found in Amos, Hosea, Isaiah, Micah and Ezekiel (see b below)—no equivalent is mentioned. Only in Isaiah 43: 3 ff., where however the Hebrew is not פָּדָה, are we told that God paid a ransom—Egypt, Ethiopia and Seba for Israel, and since Israel has been precious in His sight and honourable, and since He has loved Israel, therefore He gives men for it and peoples for its life. It is obvious that this is a rhetorical flourish, however, since no recipient of the ransom can be named. The motive for ransom is given in Ps. 44: 26—lovingkindness (חֶסֶד) and twice, 2 Sam. 7: 23, 1 Chron. 17:21, we are told that Jahweh is the only God who went to ransom a people, גּוֹי, to make them a people עַם. God ransoms always in grace, and since He is the supreme lord of the world He gives no equivalent when He ransoms. There has already been redemption of the whole people of Israel in the past, Deut. 7: 8; 9: 26: 13: 6; 15: 15; 21: 8; 24: 18; Mic. 6: 4, Ps. 78: 42, Neh. 1: 10. God ransomed His people from slavery in Egypt. God is always redeeming the individual saint: David out of all adversity, 2 Sam. 4: 9; Jeremiah out of the hand of the wicked, Jer.

15: 21; the soul of His servants Ps. 34: 22; the godly from the power of Sheol, Ps. 49: 15; from the oppression of man, Ps. 119: 134; Job in famine from death, Job 5: 20. Then there will be the ransom in the day of salvation. God will ransom Israel from all his iniquities, Ps. 130: 8. The ransomed of the Lord shall return and come with singing unto Zion, Isa. 35: 10; 51: 11.

There is therefore a threefold redemption by ransom. The first took place at the Exodus, the second is constantly being wrought by God in His dealings with His saints, the third will take place when the time of salvation comes.

b) Another word for redeem is גָּאַל.[166] This word also, used 40 times of God, does not occur in Amos, Isaiah, Micah and Ezekiel; and in Hosea, like פָּדָה, only in a rhetorical question, 13: 14. The concept of redemption appears for the first time at the Exile; Jeremiah, Deutero-Isaiah and Deuteronomic passages are its spiritual home and in its personal sense it is a favourite word in the Psalms. The fact that Ezekiel does not use it is not accidental but intentional. When God redeems, He redeems in love and pity, Isa. 63: 9. This rather contradicts the idea of the gravity of God's holiness. In Ezekiel God deals with sinful Israel for His name's sake, not in love. The original meaning of גָּאַל, to do one's duty as a kinsman where blood has been shed, or where a name will die out or where land has fallen into strange hands, is no longer present where God is called גֹּאֵל. In this case the word always means that God frees the redeemed person from the power and authority of another. The Israelites are oppressed, and they that took them captives hold them fast; they refuse to let them go. Then comes their strong redeemer Jahweh, Jer. 50: 34; He redeems them from the hand of the strong, Jer. 31: 11. He does so without giving any compensation, for God is the Lord. Micah says the daughter of Zion must go forth out of the city and dwell in the field and come even unto Babylon in order that Jahweh may redeem her from the hand of her enemies, Mic. 4: 10.[178] It can really be said that גָּאַל used of God means not to ransom, but to set free, to liberate.

Again, the examples of the use of this word bear witness to a threefold redemption: at the Exile, "I will set you free with an outstretched arm", Ex. 6: 6; constant redemption of the saints, "Jahweh is the liberator of the fatherless and the widow", Prov. 23: 11; redemption in the day of salvation, "Fear not,

thou worm Jacob, thy liberator is the Holy One of Israel",
Isa. 41: 14, the liberated of the Lord whom He liberates from
the hand of the adversary, Ps. 107: 2.

c) The redemption promise is first fully developed at the
Exile. The Exile and the scattering of the Jews throughout the
world which it occasioned will be followed by the time of
salvation. There will be several stages in the course of its
coming, and if one ignores the separate scriptural sources which
speak of these stages, and ignores also what they say about
them, one may arrange the stages systematically and in order of
sequence more or less as follows.

It is a remnant of the people that is redeemed. This remnant
is mentioned by Amos, it gains in importance in Isaiah, and it
is known by the succeeding prophets (p. 225); it is what is left
after the *sifting* effected by the judgment.

d) In this remnant, the new shoot out of the old felled tree, a
holy aftergrowth, Isa. 6: 13, God fulfils the decisive *turning*,
שׁוּב שְׁבוּת. The expression is usually translated "turn the
fortune of": "I will turn the fortune of my people Israel",
Amos 9: 14; "when I turn the fortune of my people, when I
heal Israel", Hos. 6: 11; "I will bring you home when I turn
your fortune before your eyes", Zeph. 3: 20. After the judgment
and the chastisement God will turn the fortune of His people,
and it is a turning for good, for healing and for homecoming.
The derivation of the word is difficult, however. I believe it
should be translated: "I gather the captive of Israel", Amos
9: 14; "when I gather the captive of my people", Hos. 6: 11 ff.;
see my lexicon on the subject under II שׁוּב.

e) Then after distress and scattering, 1 Kings 14: 15, Ezek.
5: 10, Ps. 44: 12, comes the time of *gathering*. He that scattered
Israel will gather him, Jer. 31: 10. Jahweh will gather the
remnant of Israel, a noisy multitude of men, He Himself as their
king will pass on before them and be at the head of them,
Mic. 2: 12 ff. Israel will be gathered from all nations even if his
outcasts were in the uttermost parts of the heavens, Deut. 30:
3 ff., and in the four corners of the earth, Isa. 11: 12. With great
mercy Jahweh gathers His people, Isa. 54: 7. The wrath of
judgment lasted for a moment, the bond of mercy will last for
ever, Isa. 54: 8. The nations themselves will bring scattered
Israel on their way, Isa. 66: 20. Then in the glory of redemption
to salvation the redemption from the slavery of Egypt will be
forgotten. They shall no more say, As the Lord liveth! which

brought up the children of Israel out of the land of Egypt, but, As the Lord liveth! which hath brought home the young shoot of the house of Israel, Jer. 23: 7 ff.

Even one example, however, will show how far short a scheme like this falls of covering all the utterances of the prophets: Zech. 10: 9 speaks of gathering and redemption and then goes on simply in v. 9, "they shall remember me and shall live with their children and shall return."[179]

f) The gathering of the people is followed by the *inward renewal*. God will give the returned another heart and another way, and He will put the fear of God in their heart so that they no longer turn away from Him, Jer. 32: 37-40. He will give them a heart of flesh instead of a stony heart, and He will put a new spirit within them, Ezek. 11: 19; a new heart and a new spirit, 36: 26; His spirit within them, 36: 27; He will take away all their uncleanness, 36: 29 .

g) The renewal is followed by a complete *unification*. Again, the political past is influencing salvation forms, as we saw it do in Isaiah (p. 231). The people who are saved shall be a single, united people, Ezek. 37: 15-22.

h) Then will be the time for the *covenant of salvation*. It will be a new covenant, Jer. 31: 31; a different covenant from that which Jahweh made with Israel when He led them out of Egypt and which the people broke. The covenant will be characterized by the fact that God puts His law in their inward parts and writes it on their heart. They will not require to teach one another; they will all know God, from the least of them unto the greatest of them, for—nowhere else is it so clearly stated that sin hinders the knowledge of God—God will forgive their iniquity and remember their sins no more. Then God will be Israel's God and Israel will be His people, Jer. 31: 31-34. This will be the covenant of salvation, an everlasting covenant, Ezek. 37: 26.

i) Amos speaks of the fallen tabernacle of David being raised up, 9: 11. Isaiah makes the shoot out of the stock of Jesse rule the kingdom, 11: 1; 9: 6 ff. Micah follows the same line in his prophecy that the ruler of Israel will come out of Bethlehem, 5: 2.[180] Jeremiah puts it this way: that in the time of salvation David shall have a Branch of righteousness growing in him and that he will never want a man to sit upon the throne of the house of Israel, 33: 15, 17.[180] Ezekiel puts a united people under one shepherd—David, i.e. a descendant of David, 37: 22, 24.[181] Haggai and Zechariah make the Davidic Zerubbabel the leader of the people accredited by God, Hagg. 2: 20 ff., Zech. 4: 6 ff. The united people of the salvation time are under the *leader from the house of David*. Nevertheless, as already stated in the paragraph on Isaiah's salvation picture, the leader of Israel in the salvation time is only God's "manager", put in charge after God Himself, "the redeemer of Israel", Isa. 49: 7, has brought salvation and made it a fact. Salvation comes from God alone. The Davidic leader appointed by God is no Messiah in the sense that by his action or by the course of his life he contributes to the coming of salvation. The Davidic leader of the saved people is no prophecy or foreshadowing of Christ. The New Testament understands Micah 5: 2 as a prophecy of Christ the Redeemer, but the Old expressly refrains from so doing.

5. What of *the nations*? What becomes of them in the day of salvation? How far is salvation also salvation for them? The pronouncements one finds in the Old Testament are various and inconsistent. Amos foresees such a complete upheaval of seasons, 9: 13, as cannot affect only the territory of David, 9: 12; but he does not speak of the nations, 9: 11-15.[180] Ezekiel has them in mind but contents himself with the often repeated dictum that through what God does to Israel and with Israel they will know "that I am the Lord". Isaiah sees it possible for the nations to come to the mountain of the Lord to receive His law and to walk in His way, 2: 3. The saved people will be known among the nations; all who see them shall acknowledge that they are the seed which the Lord hath blessed, says Isaiah, 61: 9. In 56: 3-8 he goes a step further: the stranger will not be excluded from Jahweh's people; the eunuch need not imagine he is abandoned; strangers can join themselves to the Lord and bring their sacrifices, for Jahweh's house will be a house of prayer for all nations and Jahweh will gather others to Him beside His own that are gathered. At the end of the book the writer goes further still. God creates new heavens and a new earth, 65: 17. He will gather all nations and tongues that they may see His glory. He will send such as escape out of the nations to distant shores where men have not heard God's fame, and they will declare God's glory among the nations so that they bring all scattered Jews home as an offering, Isa. 66: 18-20. That sounds like world-mission, and there are other similar passages: Mal. 1: 11. But lest we should jump to the conclusion that we may speak of a universalism of salvation let us quote also Mic. 4: 5: "all the peoples will walk every one in the name

of his god, and we will walk in the name of the Lord our God."
That is polyphony, not symphony.

6. What of the *Messiah*? Has the Old Testament no Messiah
through whom salvation and redemption come? The word and
the concept Messiah are infrequent in the Old Testament, and
though infrequent nevertheless also ambiguous. The priestly
writings designate the high priest Messiah, Lev. 4: 3, 5, 1f;
6: 15, and a great number of passages use the word for the
historical king of Israel—the word meaning in these instances
simply God's anointed, 1 Sam. 24: 6, 26: 9. As a term pertaining
to salvation Messiah occurs very seldom. The name is given to
the Persian king, Cyrus, Isa. 45: 1, because he without knowing
it is used by God to bring the salvation of liberation and return
to the Jews. In the days of the last hardships there is a Messiah
and prince—he perishes; but his mission is not to bring about
salvation, Dan. 9: 25 ff.

We do come across one, however, in a difficult passage, Isa.
52: 13—53: 12, who does not bear the name Messiah but who is
known as the servant of the Lord.[182] He has no form nor
comeliness. His name is unknown. The rest of the Old Testament knows nothing more about him. Yet he it is of whom it
is said that he will see his seed and satisfy himself with the
knowledge of the Lord. Of him it is said that *he* hath borne our
griefs and *he* carried our sorrows. The chastisement of our peace
(salvation) was upon him and by *his* stripes *we* are healed. For
our faithlessness he was led to death. As his form is shrouded
in a dim half-light, so the "we" and the "our" which recur are
indeterminate. But everyone who reads these sorrowful,
importunate utterances feels bound to include himself in that
"we" and that "our". Not far from this Isaiah passage, 52: 13-
53: 12, is 61: 1 where we read: "the spirit of the Lord God is
upon me, because the Lord hath anointed me". If 61: 1 is
written with reference to 52: 13 ff., then one can call the
suffering servant of the Lord a Messiah. If he is a Messiah, then
he is a Messiah who brings salvation—for it says "because of
our faithlessness" and "for our salvation" and "by his stripes
we are healed", 53: 5. This Messiah—if one may really call him
that—is a Messiah who suffers. *He is a Messiah who suffers
vicariously.* At this point the theology of the Old Testament
comes to an end.

In the New Testament the question is asked: "Understandest
thou what thou readest?" Acts 8: 30.

NOTES

1. נָבָל means blameworthy both in terms of knowledge and morality.

2. Admittedly sin later tends to lose its connexion with God and become almost independent.

3. On פֶּשַׁע =rebellion, revolt as the essence of sin, see Koehler, *Zeitschrift für die alttestamentliche Wissenschaft (Z.A.W.)*, 46, 213 ff.

4. אִישׁ means a male, אָדָם men, בֶּן־אָדָם an individual man. See Koehler, *Theologische Zeitschrift*, 1, 1945, 77 ff.

5. The fact that Hebrew has no word for goddess is not accidental in spite of what Stade says, *Biblische Theologie des Alten Testaments*, I, 75. Cf. 1 Kings 11: 5, 33, "Astarte, the god of the Zidonians."

6. These divine beings are thought of in sexual terms in Gen. 6: 1-4 (it is impossible to decide whether it is always so). What we have here, however, is a fragment of an ancient myth abbreviated because it was offensive. For the literary peculiarites of אֱלֹהִים see pp. 36 ff.

7. יָלַד = beget is certainly used of God in Ps. 2: 7 but only in the quite justifiable but metaphorical sense of receiving into sonship; cf. 2 Sam. 7: 14, "I will be his father, and he shall be my son", and Ps. 89: 26.

8. Read רַחֲמַי.

9. On the change in the Septuagint see Charles T. Fritsch, *The Anti-Anthropomorphisms of the Greek Pentateuch*, Princeton Univ. Press, 1943.

10. The expression "God of heaven" is rare in the O.T. Gen. 24: 7, "Jahweh the God of heaven", is a doubtful reading; perhaps it is an abbreviated form of the phrase in 24: 3, "Jahweh, the God of heaven and earth", which is something quite different but also infrequent. The common mode of expression is that God is in heaven, Ps. 2: 4; 11: 4; 53: 2; 103: 19; 123: 1; or even more common that heaven belongs to Him. Lam. 3: 41 "God אֵל in the heavens" is significant when compared with Ps. 136: 26 "the God אֵל of heaven." The latter expression is found nowhere else except in 2 Chron. 36: 23 =Ezra 1: 2, Neh. 1: 4, 5; 2: 4, 20 and Jonah 1: 9, all passages of the Persian period—אֱלֹהֵי הַשָּׁמַיִם. It has long been realized that it is the official Persian expression found in the Elephantine papyri (10 times in Cowley's Index, *Aramaic Papyri*, p. 275 b). The Jews in order to be Persians among the Persians called their God the "God of heaven". At the same time by doing so they avoided other possible designations which might have been to the disparagement of their God.

11. Friedrich Schwally, *Semitische Kriegsaltertümer*, Part I "Der heilige Krieg im alten Israel", 1901, is basic here, and especially the sentence p. 3 "die ursprüngliche kriegerische Natur Jahwes . . .". See also G. von Rad, *Der Heilige Krieg im alten Israel*, 1951.

12. On צְבָאוֹת, see § 12.

13. צִרְעָה is not "hornet", but is connected with the Arabic *dara'a* "to be daunted": see *Z.A.W.* 54, 1936, p. 291.

14. פָּדָה, to redeem means to give something as a substitute for the gift one ought to give but does not give.

15. A אָדוֹן is one who rules as Lord over all he has acquired. Ps. 105: 21.

16. Martin Buber, *Das Kommende*, I *Königtum Gottes*, 1932.

17. The idea of a god being king is very ancient. It cannot be proved, however, that the idea was really borrowed from the great neighbouring kingdoms (see H. J. Kraus, *Die Königsherrschaft Gottes im A.T.*, 1951). On the O.T. idea of kingship see Alt, "D. Königtum in den Reichen Israel u. Juda", *Vetus Testamentum*, I, 1951, 2 ff.; on the "Thronbesteigungs" psalms see L. Koehler, *Vetus Testamentum*, III, 1953, "Syntactica".

18. Martin Noth, *Das System der zwölf Stämme Israels*, 1930, p. 158-162.

19. On the form of the message see L. Koehler, *Deuterojesaja stilkritisch untersucht*, 1923, pp. 102-109. The formula "thus saith the Lord", used more than 400 times, is fundamental for the prophets' consciousness of vocation.

20. It is not accidental that מוֹשִׁיעַ and שֹׁפֵט are interchangeable in the book of Judges.

21. שָׁלוֹם is the Greek ἁρμονία τῶν πάντων, but the difference is significant: the dynamic element in the Hebrew phrase—the Hebrew mind sees everything prospering and growing; the static element in the Greek phrase —the Greek mind sees things in a carefully arranged and harmoniously integrated κόσμος. To translate שָׁלוֹם "peace" is a makeshift; prosperity would be better.

22. The judge as witness—this passage is only comprehensible when it is realized that the basic element in O.T. justice is the arbitration.

23. "There is forgiveness with thee that thou mayest be feared" occurs in a song of repentance where the writer is hoping for salvation. It is therefore an expression of the paradoxical faith which sees even in forgiveness the true proportions of the fear of God. Volz (*Das Dämonische in Jahwe*, 1924, p. 39) misses the point when he talks of the fearful majesty of the gracious and forgiving God. Rather it is the forgiving love of God that holds the conscience in obedience.

24. The difference between רָחַם and חָנַן (and their derivatives) is the difference between to love and to wish well. It is not a difference of degree but of motive. One loves a person whom one is naturally inclined to love; one wishes a person well to whom one is intentionally well-disposed. רָחַם and אָהֵב both mean "to love". רָחַם is natural love: a father loves his child because the child is of his own blood: his love is therefore pity as the love of the strong for the weak. אָהֵב is love because of pleasure and is between equals: a man loves a woman and a friend because they attract him. רָחַם can therefore mean pitying love but אָהֵב cannot. God is therefore רַחוּם and חַנּוּן but not אֹהֵב. Hos. 11: 1 "I loved Israel" and Deut. 10: 18 "who loveth the stranger" are not contradictory.

25. Nelson Glueck has shown that חֶסֶד means "fellowship" or "solidarity" in his book *The Word* חֶסֶד *in Old Testament Usage*, 1927.

26. Bernhard Stade, *Biblische Theologie des Alten Testaments*, I, 1905, p. 88. The passage begins: "Die Idee der Gerechtigkeit . . ." "the idea of the righteousness of God, i.e. the faith that God punishes sins and rewards goodness according to a fixed standard and pursues moral ends in all His works, must have been lacking in the Jahweh beliefs of ancient Israel." Two incompatible things are joined in this sentence; one is the Jahweh beliefs of ancient Israel and the other is the idea of the righteousness of God. This will not do.

27. Read מוֹשִׁיעַ.

28. K. Hj. Fahlgren, *"sedaka", nahestehende und entgegengesetzte Begriffe im Alten Testament*, 1932, following Johs. Pedersen, *Israel, Its Life and Culture*, 1926, has done much to bring into prominence the community element in many concepts. Fahlgren on צַדִּיק pp. 78-109, "צְדָקָה as norm of the community relationship is the constructive and preserving force in society", p. 82.

29. A purely statistical but useful review of this material is given by Paul Vetter, in "Die literarkritische Bedeutung der alttestamentlichen Gottesnamen", *Theologische Quartalschrift* 85, 1903, pp. 12 ff.

30. The use or omission of the article in ancient times is entirely arbitrary. Indeed even later there was no complete agreement about it: L. Koehler, *Deuterojesaja*, 1923, p. 57.

31. The God of Israel as a whole is the God of each individual member of this whole. Thus Achan says, "Of a truth I have sinned against the Lord, the God of Israel", Josh. 7: 20. What is implied is "because I too belong to Israel, I should not have done this". "Jahweh, the God of Israel, fought for Israel", Josh. 10: 42, is equivalent to "since Jahweh was the God of Israel He fought for Israel."

32. Gunkel, Procksch and König are rightly agreed that these are two different gods and that אֱלֹהֵי אֲבִיהֶם is a gloss.

33. Albrecht Alt, *Der Gott der Väter. Ein Beitrag zur Vorgeschichte der israelitischen Religion*, 1929, see § 11.

34. The book of Job is peculiar in other respects in this matter of the divine names. While 40 times it says אֱלוֹהַּ, it says 31 times שַׁדַּי (which only occurs 17 times more in all: see § 9) and within the poem proper 55 times it uses אֵל, אֱלֹהִים only once (12: 8) and Jahweh (in chaps. 1, 2, 40, 42 and 38: 1) 31 times.

35. Ps. 114: 7, read אֱלֹהֵי (Nöldeke).

36. R. Kittel gives the relevant material in great detail, "Jahwe, Jehova" 1900 (*Realencyklopädie für protestantische Theologie*, 3.A., 1900, VIII 529-41). G. R. Driver, "The Original Form of the Name Jahweh" (*Z.A.W.* 46, 1928, 7-25) gives a valuable review of what is now familiar material and concerning pronunciation comes (p. 25[2]) to the same conclusion. Hans Bauer, "Die Gottheiten von Ras Schamra" (*Z.A.W.* 51, 1933, 81-101) adds the name YW (pp. 92-94) and K. G. Kuhn, "Ueber die Entstehung des Namens Jahwe" (*Orientalistische Studien*, Enno Littmann, 1935, 25-42) draws from this philological conclusions which however do not quite come off.

37. The formula יַהְוֶה צְבָאוֹת is no difficulty since it is merely an abbreviation of יַהְוֶה אֱלֹהֵי צְבָאוֹת; see § 12.

38. The recent and careful study of Ex. 3: 13-14 (Oscar Grether, *Name und Wort Gottes im Alten Testament*, 1934, 3-17—it has a comprehensive bibliography) changes אֶהְיֶה v. 14b into יְהוֶה (as earlier scholars have done) and believes the meaning is "I show myself as he that I show myself". Certainly it is correct to say that "being" in the O.T. is not an inactive peaceful existence but an activity that shows itself in works, but the sentence "The tetragrammaton describes God as the God who reveals himself, *Deus revelatus*" (p. 7) goes too far. "I am who I am" defies explanations. God does not reveal to Moses the secret of His nature (=His name). Moses will see who God is from His works. Moses only obeyed the Lord who came to him with a lordly claim. Therefore if any dogmatic formula is to be used it should not be *Deus revelatus* but *Deus absconditus* in the strictest sense. Grether has proved conclusively (pp. 9-17) that J. Hehn, *Die biblische und babylonische Gottesidee*, 1913, 215 ff. is mistaken in his claims that this interpretation of the name Jahweh is echoed in other passages of the O.T. Johannes Hänel, "Jahwe", *Neue kirchliche Zeitschrift*, 40, 1929, pp. 608-41, offers little that is new. Concerning an Egyptian counterpart to Ex. 3: 14 see A. Alt, *Z.A.W.* 58, 159 ff.

39. Jochebed, Moses' mother, would be the only exception (Ex. 6: 20, Num, 26: 59—both belong to late priestly writings). Martin Noth, *Die israelitischen Personennamen*, 1928, 111 doubts the equation of Jo and Jahweh. H. Bauer (see note 36) pp. 92 ff. connects the name with the God YW from Ras Schamra. The first name which certainly contains Jahweh is Joshua; from the period of the Judges there are only 5 (Noth, p. 107); they become gradually more frequent in the time of the kings.

40. "Jahwe so der Gott Israels wie Kamos der Gott Moabs um 850 in moabitischem Munde", *Mesainschrift* line 18.—For names compounded with Jahweh outside Israel, Noth, pp. 108-11. It is improbable that there were any independent of Israel.

41. Note that Enoch like Adam is called "man". Enoch and Adam are only later fitted into a genealogy. Originally they are interchangeable names for the first man. O. Procksch, *Die Genesis*, 1924, p. 57.

42. In Gen. 25: 4 and 1 Chron. 1: 33 Ephah is the first son of Midian; in Isa. 60: 6 Ephah is named alongside Midian. This Ephah is identified by J. J. Hess as the Gaipha near Belbeis of ancient Arabian geography (still to-day under the same name on the Cairo railway—Zagazig). That would mean that Midian stretched to the eastern shores of the Delta— a simple but important commentary on the trustworthiness of the accounts that have come down to us.—Wilhelm Vischer, *Jahwe der Gott Kains*, 1929, pp. 23-24.

43. It is not clear whether or not אֵל is connected with (south) Arabic *'il* and means originally "flowing water" (E. V. Stace, *English-Arabic Vocabulary*, 1893, 67a). If it is, it would mean the divinity of the stream, in support of which Gen. 32: 22-32 has been quoted, a meaning which was then generalized. On the whole it is easier to connect it with the phrase, יֶשׁ־לְאֵל יָדִי "it lies in the might of my hand" and understand it in the dynamic sense as "might".

44. The derivation from the Assyrian *schadu*, "mountain", suggested by Friedrich Delitzsch, is possible and probable. The pronunciation שַׁדַּי would then be a massoretic whim. The meaning would be mountain, lofty one. The suggestion made by J. Zolli, *Rivista degli studi orientali*, XIII, 73-75 that *shadu* is connected with a mother's breast and means therefore "fulness, abundance" is far-fetched.

45. Nöldeke's confession (*Elohim, El*, 1882, p. 1192), "it is not the first time that in a study I have finished up more perplexed than when I began", is true to-day with regard to etymology, in spite of the remarks on Note 43.

46. This means the collapse of the concept of an El-religion as a specific phenomenon distinct "from the Jahweh-religion of later Israel" (Gressmann, *Z.A.W.* 30, 1910, p. 28). See also O. Eissfeldt, "Die Verwertbarkeit der Vätergeschichten in der Genesis usw.", *Prot. Monatshefte*, 17. Jahrg., 1917, pp. 328-56.

47. Alt (see following note) p. 17[2] would like to regard "thy father" as an addition. They are not there with Isaac because he is still alive and worshipping God.

48. Albrecht Alt, *Der Gott der Väter. Ein Beitrag zur Vorgeschichte der israelitischen Religion*, 1929.

49. *Ibid.*, p. 72[4].

50. Aug. Klostermann, *Geschichte Israels*, 1896, p. 76, suggests later removal from the Hexateuch.

51. Victor Maag, "Jahwas Heerscharen" (*Festschrift für L. Koehler = Schweizerische Theologische Umschau* 1950), 27-52.

52. Since the living meaning of קָדוֹשׁ can be grasped from the O.T· itself the etymological discussion of the word is unnecessary. On the concept of holiness see Johannes Hänel, *Die Religion der Heiligkeit*, 1931.

53. All three passages are now considered late.

54. See the exegesis of Hans Schmidt, *Die Psalmen*, 1934, pp. 29 f.

55. Duhm, *Psalmen*[2], 1922, p. 442, has been induced by the great significance of the passage (wrongly) to omit it.

56. Ezra 10: 3 translate: "Let us make a covenant (with one another) before God" and likewise 2 Chron. 29: 10, "It is in mine heart to make a covenant before Jahweh, the God of Israel".

57. On the question whether the Decalogue goes back to Moses see L. Koehler, *Theologische Rundschau*, 1929, 161-184.

58. Prayer in ancient times is not of great importance or frequency. There is no regularity about it, though it is done to rule when it is done. The oldest prayer that has been preserved shows clearly the brevity, objectivity and awkwardness of prayer at that time, 1 Kings 17: 20 and 21 (two prayers). But traces of the ancient formulae necessary in polytheistic times are still there—at the beginning of the prayer the God to whom one is praying is called by name, "Jahweh", then follows the confession of the God invoked, "my God!" That is the prayer of an individual. Israel as a community would pray "Jahweh! Our God!" These two original elements of prayer, invocation and confession, have remained unchanged through all the developments of prayer forms to the present day; they are quite indispensable.

59. Albrecht Alt, *Landnahme der Israeliten in Palästina*, 1925, put the expression into circulation.

60. It is significant that Hebrew man אָדָם = earthborn one, sprung from the אֲדָמָה. For the original mythological stratum of this see Mark Lidzbarski, *Neue Götter, Festgabe für Theodor Nöldeke*, Göttingen, 1916, pp. 86-93.

61. Hebrew שָׁלוֹם. But it is not peace, which is a negative, the absence of war and disturbance; it is rather something positive, undisturbed prosperity and increase.

62. L. Lévy-Bruhl, *Les fonctions mentales dans les sociétés inférieures*, 3rd edn. 1918, is fundamental here. Johs. Pedersen, *Israel, Its Life and Culture*, London, 1926, has made a brilliant application of its findings to the O.T.

63. cf. Hermann Gunkel's lucid exposition.

64. The Temple in Jerusalem is not mentioned in Genesis. 2 Chron. 3: 1 tries to make Mount Moriah out of the land of Moriah, Gen. 22: 2, though its history goes back no farther than David. What was that to the priests of Bethel or Gilgal?

65. It was the events of Isaiah's time when Jerusalem was three times saved from its enemies that gave the Temple of Jerusalem its true glory. Isaiah is the prophet of the "mountain of Jahweh", 2: 3. Yet almost a hundred years later Jeremiah, "of the priests that were in Anathoth", i.e. a descendant of Eli, Jer. 1: 1, 1 Kings 2: 26-27, 1 Sam. 22: 20; 2: 31-33 and keeper of the venerable traditions of Shiloh, has no special regard for the Jerusalem Temple, 7: 4; 26: 6.

66. A "king's sanctuary" and a "royal temple" is Amaziah's name for Bethel, Amos 7: 13.

67. For a detailed study of the buildings see the commentaries on 1 Kings and the contributions of archaeologists. The few dates we have used are undisputed, however doubtful other details may be. On the origin of the type of building see Kurt Möhlenbrink, *Der Tempel Salomos*, 1932, and the ensuing discussion on it.

68. The rendering "rear-chamber" for דְּבִיר is undoubtedly correct; it is only later that one finds the term the Holy of Holies. The fact that Israel had no other word than "rear-chamber" for this important part of the building shows that Israel was not familiar with the terminology of architecture on this scale.

69. The small openings are high up from the ground, 1 Kings 6: 4-6.

70. The Hebrews both as compatriots and as fellow-worshippers are called אחים, "brethren".

71. See *Z.A.W.* 1934, p. 160.

72. Gen. 5: 1-32; 11: 10-26; 21: 5; 25: 26; 47: 9, Ex. 12: 40 are our authority. Gerhard von Rad, *Die Priesterschrift im Hexateuch*, 1934, is right in what he says about the structure of the book, but it does not affect our arguments.

73. From the Exodus to the beginning of the building of the Temple is 480 years, 1 Kings 6: 1. 490 years, seventy weeks of years, is the period of exile until atonement is made and, according to the two books of Kings, from the beginning of the building of the Temple till the burning of the Temple is 410 years. 2666+480+410+490=4046, 46 years too many, but our reckoning is not necessarily that of the priestly redactor. Moreover if these figures really belong to the time of Daniel (about 165 B.C.) then what we have is a later application. The system, however, is older than this use of it.

74. It is a misconception to think that the Jahwist and Elohist writings cover the conclusion of the occupation. Both documents, which arose after David, are concerned with the history of early times up to the occupation. They collect all the available traditions and fashion them, each using their particular but their very own vocabulary, into a unified whole which purports to tell the great story of how Israel came to the land of Canaan. Their aim is achieved when they reach the occupation; an aim to which the priestly writer also dedicates himself, using

other material but following their pattern. The bounds are to be reckoned by the subject, not by the modes of expression. They use the literary and stylistic media of their own day.

75. Walter Baumgartner, *Die Klagegedichte des Jeremia und die Klagepsalmen*, 1916.

76. I have shown in my *Deuterojesaja* (1923), pp. 124-127, that the whole of Deutero-Isaiah is one theophany.

77. The expression though it occurs more than 70 times is extremely colourless. It is used of Moses, Deut. 33: 1, Samuel, 1 Sam. 9: 6, David, Neh. 12: 24, Elijah, 1 Kings 17: 18, Elisha, 2 Kings 4: 7, Shemaiah, 1 Kings 12: 22, Hanan, Jer. 35: 4 and three men not named, 1 Sam. 2: 27, 1 Kings 13: 1, 2 Chron. 25: 7; also of the Angel of Jahweh, Judg. 13: 6. How this phrase was selected we do not know. 1 Kings 13: 18, 2 Kings 5: 13; 6: 12 show that "man of God" is the same as *Nabi*.

78. The prophet who misleads the man of God by a lie, 1 Kings 13: 18, into disobedience of God receives neither censure nor punishment.

79. See my study *Deuterojesaja stilkritisch untersucht*, 1923, pp. 102-109. The introductory phrase "Thus saith the Lord" occurs 359 times: 14 times in Amos, 44 in Isaiah, 157 in Jeremiah, 125 in Ezekiel and 19 in Zechariah.

80. Cases where through mishap the formula has been added or lost must receive by process of form-criticism their original form before they can be assigned.

81. The expression "the word of Jahweh (of God)" occurs nearly 400 times. For a series of examples see Jer. 1: 4, 11, 13; 2: 1; the formula does not change until 3: 6. "Jahweh said . . . to me." Why have these matters never been satisfactorily examined? Friedrich Häussermann, *Wortempfang und Symbol in der alttestamentlichen Prophetie*, 1932, and Oscar Grether, *Name und Wort Gottes im AT*, 1934, scarcely mention them.

82. N.B. it does not say "the words of Jahweh".

83. Paul Koschaker: "Keilschriftrecht", *Zeitschrift der deutschen morgenländischen Gesellschaft*, 1935, 1-39, has rightly objected to naïve suggestions that have been made about this.

84. See L. Koehler, "Der Dekalog", *Theologische Rundschau*, 1929, pp. 161-184. The fact that there does not appear in the biblical Decalogue the commandment "thou shalt not lie" raises questions of all kinds. The history of the demand for truthfulness needs to be examined carefully.

85. No assertion is being made about punishment by death.

86. e.g. the commandment to eat no pork. The reason for this was probably that the pig was sacrificed to the gods of the underworld and the Jews were to keep aloof from these cults.

87. "All" does not appear in several passages but it is well attested, it fits the context and the style, and would certainly be intended even if it were not expressed.

88. The Heidelberg Catechism has rightly taken as the essence of its third part the truth that thankfulness is the motive of obedience.

89. The O.T. contains several words which one can translate "to fear"—חָרַד, פָּחַד, יָרֵא. The last is the least psychological in meaning and often amounts to "obey", especially when the infinitive is used as a noun יִרְאָה.

90. See note 107 for N.T. statements about spirit.

91. L. Koehler, "Die Offenbarungsformel 'Fürchte dich nicht!' im AT", *Schweizerische Theologische Zeitschrift*, 1919, pp. 33 ff.

92. Mic. 3: 8, "full of the spirit of Jahweh", is a gloss as is shown by the prosaic style and the construction of the verse. The exegetes (Wellhausen, Nowack, Marti, Sellin) agree.

93. The remaining passages in Isa. 1-35 which would qualify 4: 4; 11: 15; 29: 10; 34: 16 are regarded by most exegetes as not Isaiah's.

94. Duhm and Eichrodt, *Die Hoffnung des ewigen Friedens*, 1920, pp. 58 ff., argue for the authenticity of the messianic passage, but Volz has misgivings which carry considerable weight.

95. Sellin, *Das Zwölfprophetenbuch*, 2.A. 1930, p. 502.

96. See W. Baumgartner, *Archiv für Religionswissenschaft* XXVI, 104 f.

97. Also Sellin, *Das Zwölfprophetenbuch*, 3.A., 1930, p. 573.

98. In Ps. 35: 5, 6 "Jahweh" is to be omitted as Gunkel does. The messenger of Jahweh who brings the pestilence, 2 Sam. 24: 16, is called in 1 Chron. 21: 15 the destroying angel and therefore here also as in v. 12, 16, 18, 30 he is an "ordinary" angel with a particular task to perform. This is true also of 1 Kings 19: 7, 2 Kings 1: 3, 15; 19: 35 = Isa. 37: 36.

99. Note also the following passages: "messengers of Jahweh" Judg. 2: 1, 4, 5; 5: 23; 6: 11, 12, 21-23, Zech. 12: 8, Ps. 34: 7 (in Judg. 2: 5; 6: 12, 23 note the transition to Jahweh alone): "messenger of God" Gen. 21: 17; 31: 11, Ex. 14: 19, Judg. 6: 20 (the interchange of messenger of God and messenger of Jahweh is due to contamination of the sources —so also 13: 9) 13: 6.

100. J. Morgenstern, *The Book of the Covenant* (=Hebrew Union College Annual, Vol. V), 1928, 45 ff., finds the basis of the concept of the glory of Jahweh in the special significance that was attached to the first rays of the sun on the morning of the autumnal equinox (and also vernal).

101. L. Koehler, *Deuterojesaja*, 1923, pp. 124 f.

102. M. Lidzbarski, *Neue Götter, Festgabe für Theodor Nöldeke*, Göttingen, 1916, pp. 90-91 אָדָם, man of the earth, comes from אֲדָמָה earth, ground, like *homo* from *humus*. It is shown that חות, a Phoenician-Punic goddess of the underworld = Eve. Then comes the Punic earth-god אָדָם. Now one can understand how the serpent—a deposed divinity jealous of Jahweh—can speak with Eve. See also note 60 and 143. It is foolish to want to omit the tree of life. The two trees in the middle of the garden bear the qualities which distinguish gods—a higher standard of knowledge and life constantly renewed. As progenitor of men the individual Adam has a rival in Enoch, Gen. 5: 6, who is likewise called "man".

103. עֵזֶר כְּנֶגְדּוֹ, Gen. 2: 18, means literally "a partner who suits him". Luther's translation "a helper to be with him" is too vague in the second half and wrong in the first. For since God created the beasts first, in order to reach His aim, and created woman only when they did not fulfil the desired purpose (*non inveniebatur adjutor similis ejus*), it is clear that the woman was not thought of at first as a helper.

104. Matt. 22: 30.

105. Isaac de la Peyrère: *Systema theologicum ex praeadamitarum hypothesi; pars prior*, 1655. The book was burned in Paris, its author having been unfaithful to Calvinism in Rome.

106. The striking views of the formation of the child in the mother's womb found later in Job 10: 10 may have influenced the ancient account of the origin and therefore the nature of man.

107. The N.T. retains the changeable nature of the expression. In Rom. 8: 9 "to be in the spirit", "the spirit dwelleth in you", "to have the spirit", are all the same. In this changeableness the difficulties of the spirit-body problem show themselves. The O.T. does not know the expression "the spirit makes his dwelling in someone." It does know of strength, Isa. 51: 9, 52: 1; terror, Ezek. 7: 27, shame and disgrace being able to clothe a man or envelop him. The N.T. has the phrase "to put on Christ" (as a garment), Rom. 13: 14, and the slightly different metaphor "to be in Christ", 2 Cor. 5: 17, and also the metaphor reversed, "Christ in you", Rom. 8: 10. The fact that "be in the spirit" ="have the spirit of God dwelling in one" ="have the spirit of Christ" ="have Christ in one" shows that the biblical writers had no adequate expression for the operation and nature of the Spirit. In the passages quoted above it is wrong to look for any differences.

108. For Paul also there are no fixed and exact lines of demarcation between flesh, psyche and spirit and their appendages.

109. Several individuals have either several or only one נֶפֶשׁ as in Hos. 9: 4. The numbers for each are almost equal. Nevertheless, נֶפֶשׁ, when compared with לֵבָב or לֵב does tend towards individualization. A study of the reason for נַפְשֵׁנוּ in one place and נַפְשֹׁתֵינוּ in another would be well worth while. The best examination of the subject is Charles A. Briggs' "The use of נֶפֶשׁ in the O.T.", *Journal of Biblical Literature*, XVI, 1897, pp. 17-30. Lorenz Dürr, *Z.A.W.* 43, 1925, 262-269 is a useful semantic investigation of the problem with references to newer works.

110. Semasiologically נֶפֶשׁ moves from "desire, longing", which is frequent and ancient, to "striving". What we call soul is in the O.T. the living, moving, striving side of man's nature. The meaning has had a development very like that of רוּחַ wind, breath, spirit—from dynamic to static.

111. At least in metaphorical and poetic language.

112. It is significant that most biblical Hebrew uses the word מֹחַ which means in Job 21: 24 marrow (of bones).

113. W. Caspari, *Imago divina* (Reinhold-Seeberg-Festschrift), 1929, translates "in accordance with our plan" (p. 198). On the dogmatics of the question A. H. Cremer, "Ebenbild Gottes" (*Haucks Realencyklopädie* V), 1898, pp. 113-118, is still the best.

114. L. Koehler, "Die Grundstelle der Imago-Dei-Lehre, Genesis 1: 26", *Theologische Zeitschrift*, Basel, 4, 1948, 16-22. P. Humbert has rightly and impressively attacked my exposition given in the first and second editions of this book. Examples from classical literature go far back to Minucius Felix, 17- 2; Ovid, *Metamorphoses* 1: 85 f.; Xenophon, *Memorabilia* I 4: 11; the oldest perhaps belong to a time before the priesthood. They should be collected and examined sometime.

115. Procksch, *Jesaja I*, 1930, p. 339: "the saying is to satisfy Israel's great demand for resurrection of the dead". It is unnecessary to go into all the interpretations of this obscure passage. None of them goes any further than our translation goes.

116. Translation "before death": Kittel, *Psalmen*, 1914, p. 198; "receiving after death": König, *Psalmen*, 1927, p. 602; "rescue": Gunkel, *Psalmen*, 1926, p. 210; "immortality of the sufferer": Schmidt, *Psalmen*, 1934, p. 95.

117. Peters, *Das Buch Job*, 1928, p. 203; there also there is a valuable bibliography.

118. Holl, *Die Geschichte des Worts Beruf*, 1924.

119. The O.T. world picture is a less clear version of the Babylonian; see Zimmern, *Die Keilinschriften und das AT*, 3.A., 1903, pp. 614-643.

120. Gen. 24: 7 is rightly regarded by Procksch as an addition.

121. The word itself is Egyptian; Erman-Grapow, *Wörterbuch der ägyptischen Sprache*, I, p. 47.

122. For the derivation see *Theologische Zeitschrift*, Basel, 1946, 71 ff.: it is also supported by the Arabic (oral information from E. Littmann).

123. Paul Karge, *Rephaim*, 1928.—The psychological explanation of belief in ghosts is that the dead appear in dreams or in visions to those to whom they are bound with ties of affection at some time or other after death. The appearances become less frequent and less clear and finally cease altogether; the ghosts die. It is therefore not contradictory to know that someone is dead and to believe and "experience" that the shadow soul (for a time) lives.

124. נֶגֶד is literally that which is over against, counterpart, הִגִּיד means to place over against someone, therefore to make something known, make visible.

125. Josephus, *Antiquities* I, § 50, says that the serpent originally had legs.—The Genesis passage is called the "Protevangelium". Luther wrote in the margin of his Bible, 1534, "this is the first promise of Christ; Adam with his descendants believed the promise, therefore he became Christian and 'selig von seinem Fall'." In order to find here a prophecy of Christ four things are necessary: *1*. One must understand v. 14 literally, actual serpents being meant, v. 15 on the other hand christologically; *2*. One must understand the serpent not as the serpent but as Satan and the seed, the descendants of Satan also as Satan; *3*. One must construe the seed of Eve and that of the serpent (Satan) as two individuals, Christ and Satan; *4*. One has to imagine in addition to what is there (viz. that one treads on the head of the other and the other bruises the heel of the first) the most important part, namely that the sting in the heel = the death of Christ, a single event, and the treading on the head = crushing of Satan as a continuing action. Each of these four is impossible.

126. Ps. 104: 4, "who maketh winds his messengers" is reversed in Hebr. 1: 7, "who maketh his messengers winds".

127. In English there is a far sharper distinction between messenger and angel than there is in Hebrew or in Greek (*angelos*).

128. An example of how changeable are these great ones is found in Gen. 32: 22-31 which originally, as Gunkel has shown in a masterly fashion, is the story of the *demon* of a river assaulting a traveller by night. In the story we have, the demon has been elevated to the position of a *god*. In the allusion to the story in Hos. 12: 5 the god is again degraded and is now an angel. Demon—god—angel; the order could be different but the changeability is a constant factor.

129. Hebrew שְׂדִים is certainly connected with Arabic *sawida* "to be black", therefore "the black ones". This does not affect the connexion with Accadian *schedu*, a "little black one", who comes once a year and does not leave the people when he comes until they are dead. For a general discussion of spirits and demons in the O.T. see W. Baudissin, "Feldgeister" (*Haucks Realencyklopädie* VI, 1-23) 1899 and Hans Duhm, *Die bösen Geister im AT*, 1904. In Dalman, *Palästina-Jahrbuch* IV, 1908, pp. 49 ff. one learns that still to-day a "sacrifice" is made at the time of building "for the dwelling" with the words "with your permission, O lord of the place". Probably the goat demon and black ones of the O.T. were just as vaguely known as these lords of the place.

130. On psychological questions Johannes Pedersen, *Israel, Its Life and Culture*, 1926, is excellent.

131. Luther and many others both before and since wrongly translate "showing mercy unto many thousands of them that love me". God's acts of mercy to those who love and obey Him need no boosting from the quotation of numbers, and, besides, these clauses are neither a contradiction nor an elucidation of the sentence "God visits the iniquity of the fathers upon the children if they (the fathers) hate Him." It is clear that it cannot be the children who hate Him, otherwise there would be no question of the iniquity of the fathers. The iniquity of the fathers can be visited upon the children and descendants, however, and often is.—In O.T. narrative grace is also operative through the bond which binds the generations. Under Hezekiah God still preserves Jerusalem "for mine own sake and for my servant David's sake", 2 Kings 19: 34; and the seed of David "shall be established for ever as the moon", Ps. 89: 37 ff.

132. Max Löhr, *Sozialismus und Individualismus im AT.*, 1906; the content is more valuable than the title might suggest.

133. Wolf Baudissin, *Die Geschichte des alttestamentlichen Priestertums*, 1889. The first sentence of this careful and admirable study, "The history of the O.T. priesthood or of the priestly family of Levi", contains an inadmissible restriction; the priesthood and the family of Levi are not interchangeable quantities. The statements that only Levites, Judg. 17: 7-10, only descendants of the four (Ex. 28: 1) or of the two remaining sons (Lev. 10: 12) of Aaron or the Levite priests who are sons of Zadok, Ezek. 44: 13-15, may be priests, represent different stages of a long and varied process of regulation. Only the fact of the regulation that not anyone might be a priest remained steadfast; the manner of its observation suffered many modifications.

134. On charismatic kingship see A. Alt in the article mentioned in note 17.

135. The N.T. under the influence of the Septuagint speaks plainly of a royal priesthood, 1 Pet. 2: 9.

136. The view of Hans Schmidt, *Die Erzählung von Paradies und Sündenfall*, 1931. The opposite view is supported by Karl Budde, *Die biblische Paradiesesgeschichte*, 1932. Both expressed their opinions again later without reaching any kind of agreement.

137. J. Coppens, "La Connaissance de Bien et du Mal et le Péché du Paradis" (*Analecta Lovaniensa Biblica*), 1948, and "Miscellanées bibliques" XVIII and XIX (*ibid.*), 1948.

138. On פֶּשַׁע see *Z.A.W.* 46, 1928, pp. 213-218.

139. Arnold B. Ehrlich, *Randglossen*, II, 1909, p. 18 is surely correct in his protest against the usual translation "defraud" and in his assertion that the word means "to forget one's duty". Dionys Schötz, *Schuld- und Sündopfer im AT*, 1930, p. 42 narrows down Ehrlich's statement in an unwarranted fashion and makes it refer to a sacrilegious act against God.

140. The Septuagint renders it 142 times ἀσεβής, 72 times ἁμαρτωλός and 31 times ἄνομος.

141. See L. Koehler, "Der Dekalog", *Theologische Rundschau*, 1929, 161-184.

142. R. Schärf, *Die Gestalt des Satans im Alten Testament*, 1948.

143. It is important to note that נָחָשׁ is masculine, not *die Schlange* but *der Schlang, le serpent*. Adam the earth god and Eve the earth serpent his companion are undergods of the polytheistic period of myth who are employed by the overgod who created them as gardeners and caretakers. The reason for the serpent's (*der Schlang*) leading them astray is his jealousy of God who owns the garden. The serpent's conversation with Eve belongs not to a time when animals still spoke, it is a conversation between non-human beings. When the myth was given its present monotheistic garb, much of it became meaningless. What motive had the serpent for tempting Adam and Eve? There is no answer. How could the serpent speak?—no answer. The whole story hangs in mid air in its monotheistic context. See also note 102.

144. The so-called theological concept *Urgeschichte* conceals only the one simple fact that something is regarded no longer as historical event but, contrary to the intention of the Bible, as merely psychological truth.

145. Rightly stressed again by C. Steuernagel, "Zum Verständnis von Ps. 51", *Sellin-Festschrift*, 1927, pp. 151-156.

146. "A later comment", Norbert Peters, *Das Buch Job*, 1928, p. 146.

147. In this respect and in others the form of the sacrifice is rooted in circumstances pertaining to the history of civilization, and we can sometimes still see the way it worked. Only because man in the Mediterranean world doesn't eat meat often can the eating of meat be bound up with a sacrificial rite. Were meat eaten daily the sacrifice would soon disappear.

148. Nelson Glueck, *The Word "hesed" in Old Testament Usage*, 1927, has shown that חֶסֶד also means "solidarity" and חֶסֶד וֶאֱמֶת therefore "reliable solidarity", and W. F. Lofthouse, *Z.A.W.* 1933 (51) pp. 31-35 has confirmed it. The words occur very frequently (234 times) and form a basic concept which shows that in the O.T., even outside the covenant, community is a concern.

149. The word is *plurale tantum* and even in Amos 5: 22, the only passage where it is singular, the plural שְׁלָמֵי should be read. V. Maag, *Text, Wortschatz u. Begriffswelt des Buches Amos*, 1951, agrees with my exegesis "conclusion offering" but replaces it on p. 254 by "soothing offering" because he understands the ugaritic *slmm* (Krt. 130, 275) as "soothing gift"; this does not appear altogether convincing, since ugaritic texts are always hard to interpret and here a "gift in salutation" or a "present" is a perfectly possible rendering; so that the connexion with our Hebrew term is in no way certain.

150. Dionys Schötz, *Schuld- und Sündopfer im AT*, 1930, gives a useful bibliography.

151. See F. Horst, *Z.A.W.* (47), 1929, pp. 5off.

152. Hans Bauer, *Islamisa* II, 1926, p. 6, explains אִשֶּׁה as *nomen unitatis* of אֵשׁ, the ending—ä having been chosen deliberately to avoid confusion with אִשָּׁה woman.

153. If one does not apply too strict a standard one can count about 85 original prayers in the O.T. In addition there are about 60 whole Psalms and 14 parts of Psalms which may be called prayers, though it is often very hard to determine whether they are or not. The most striking thing is, however, that the form of prayer in the O.T. is not by any means fixed. Not even the many prayers which are literary products rather than real prayers—not even they follow any fixed pattern.

154. Really the curse is that Adam henceforth may not live without trouble on the self-ripening fruits of the trees in the garden, but must win his bread with sweat and toil from the plants of the field—an aetiological myth to explain why man lives by agriculture rather than by horticulture.

155. The commandment not to lie does not appear in the Decalogue. Indeed, there is no clear and simple statement of it anywhere else (Ps. 15: 2 comes nearest to it) and occasionally it is startlingly violated (1 Kings 22: 20ff., Jer. 38: 24-27).

156. Here too that freedom originates with which later ages formulate laws in such a way that they suggest that God gave these laws (though often the marks of their later date are abundantly evident) to Moses at Sinai. This form is neither a *pia fraus* nor a literary cloak, but a result of the certainty that God's revelation even when not expressed is clearly discernible, and that what is only now put into words has the same intention as had the law at Sinai.

157. From חָקַק to scratch or inscribe on (a book, leather) Isa. 30: 8, here set alongside כָּתַב to write on (a tablet). Dussaud, *Les origines cauanéennes du sacrifice israélite*, 1921, p. 10, speaks of "pratiques rituelles ou coutumes populaires depuis longtemps établies qu'on observe sans les discuter". Johs. Pedersen, *Der Eid bei den Semiten*, 1914, p. 17 recalls the Arabic *chaqq*, "what one can demand and what he should do—right and duty".

158. One can see that יָרָה is becoming obsolete—in v. 10 it is replaced by הִשְׁלִיךְ.

159. "The book of this law", Deut. 28: 61, "this law book" 31: 26.

160. This finds its most paradoxical expression when Paul speaks of the law of Christ, Gal. 6: 2.

161. For statistics and comments see Oscar Grether, *Name und Wort Gottes im AT*, 1934, pp. 62 ff.

162. Also in Ps. 95: 9 נִסָּה to put to the test and בָּחַן to examine are placed side by side.

163. Gal. 3: 24; of course the aim "to bring us unto Christ" is not stated in the O.T.

164. Gen. 31: 44, add נַעֲשָׂה לֹ after וְאַתָּה.

165. Schötz (see note 150), p. 102. The prepositional force which כִּפֶּר has is complicated but unequivocal.

166. J. J. Stamm, *Erlösen und Vergeben im Alten Testament*, 1940.

167. Read חֹלִים.

168. Read תָּמַח.

169. נִסְלַח is found 13 times in the priestly writings—indulgence is guaranteed for an individual or for the cult community. Also סְלִיחָה pardon, Ps. 130: 4, Neh. 9: 17, Dan 9: 9.

170. Gerhard von Rad, *Theologische Blätter*, 14, 1935, 250.

171. מוֹשִׁיעַ occurs 32 times in all (Zech. 9: 9—a conjecture); 11 times it is used of someone who helps (or does not help), as the title of the so-called judge, Judg. 3: 9, 15; 17 times it is used of God (and Zech. 9: 9). One must be even more exact: God is the helper of the individual in his distress, 2 Sam. 22: 3; God was the helper of Israel in the past, I Sam. 10: 19; 14: 39, Ps. 106: 21, Hos. 13: 4; God is the helper in the day of salvation, Isa. 43: 3; 45: 15; 49: 26; 60: 16; 63: 8, Jer. 14: 8; 30: 10; 46: 27 (probably none of the three passages is the prophet's own words); Zech. 8: 7 (and possibly 9: 9)—9 (10) times; there is no other God that helps, Isa. 45: 21. Obad. 21 is the only example of the word in the plural: helpers (saviours) shall come up on mount Zion to judge the mount of Esau, and the kingdom shall be the Lord's—this too is a salvation text.

172. We regard Isa. 2: 1-5; 7: 1-4a; 5: 25; 9: 1-8; 11: 1-8; 14: 28-32, 32: 1-5, 9-20 as true Isaianic salvation teaching in spite of the prevailing opinion. The Immanuel text 7: 14, however, plays no part here since we regard it with Edv. Lehmann, "Immanuel-Profetien" (*Studier tilegnede Frantz Buhl*, pp. 98-111, 1925), as a threat; the young mothers, in fear, call their sons "God is with us".

173. This idea is of course very ancient and it is quite by accident that it is only found in the priestly material.

174. Bertholet, *Das Buch Hesekiel*, 1897, p. 250.

175. Note that his Lordship is called מִשְׂרָה not מַמְלָכָה, Isa. 9: 6 ff.

176. There is a real point in putting the two concepts—really different ideas—possession (*Besitz*) and ownership (*Eigentum*), in juxtaposition. (Possession means having something belonging to yourself or to some one else at your disposal. Ownership means you have a right to the thing whether it is at the time at your own or at someone else's disposal.)

177. This ransom, as in Ps. 49: 8 כֹּפֶר, is the λύτρον of Mk. 10: 45.

178. This sense of the word certainly does not originate in Micah.

179. Were the O.T. a textbook of systematic theology the items in our summary would be established terms. Such terms, however, are never found in the O.T.

180. The arguments against the genuineness of this passage are almost unassailable.

181. I regard with many others his title "king" as spurious on account of 37: 25, and on general grounds.

182. H. H. Rowley, *The Servant of the Lord*, lecture 1, London, 1952.

INDEX OF HEBREW WORDS

SELECT INDEX OF BIBLICAL REFERENCES

GENERAL INDEX